MEDIA, LEARNING, AND SITES OF POSSIBILITY

D1566375

Edited by Marc Lamont Hill
& Lalitha Vasudevan

Foreword by Katherine Schultz

PETER LANG
New York • Washington, D.C./Baltimore • Bern
Frankfurt am Main • Berlin • Brussels • Vienna • Oxford

Library of Congress Cataloging-in-Publication Data

Media, learning, and sites of possibility / edited by Marc Lamont Hill, Lalitha Vasudevan.
p. cm. — (New literacies and digital epistemologies; v. 22)
Includes bibliographical references and index.
1. Urban youth—Education—Social aspects—United States. 2. Mass media and education—
Social aspects—United States. 3. Critical pedagogy—United States.
4. Digital communications—Social aspects—United States.
I. Hill, Marc Lamont. II. Vasudevan, Lalitha.
LC5131.M43   373.133′5—dc22   2007004833
ISBN 978-1-4331-0042-0 (hardcover)
ISBN 978-0-8204-8656-7 (paperback)
ISSN 1523-9543

Bibliographic information published by **Die Deutsche Bibliothek**.
Die Deutsche Bibliothek lists this publication in the "Deutsche
Nationalbibliografie"; detailed bibliographic data is available
on the Internet at http://dnb.ddb.de/.

Cover design by Joni Holst

The paper in this book meets the guidelines for permanence and durability
of the Committee on Production Guidelines for Book Longevity
of the Council of Library Resources.

© 2008 Peter Lang Publishing, Inc., New York
29 Broadway, 18th floor, New York, NY 10006
www.peterlang.com

Printed in the United States of America

This book is dedicated to the young men and women whose lives are reflected in the pages that follow. In their words, explorations, images, and stories we continue to find new possibilities for what teaching and learning might be…

Table of Contents

Figures and Tables

Foreword

Katherine Schultz

As I write this foreword, citizens in the United States, and indeed people from around the world, are reeling from the news of the murder of thirty-two students and professors on the campus of a Virginia university. It is too soon to know the full story. It is likely that there will always be multiple versions and interpretations of the event. The facts of the case and the motivations for the shooting may never be revealed as the perpetrator of this violence took his own life. In the midst of the shootings, the young man responsible for the deaths sent a package of media to a major television network. The package contained photographs and a video. How do we read and understand this decision to craft a statement through visual media packaged for what became, as was hoped for, a major media event itself? In the subsequent days, the pictures and a short segment of the videotape were played repeatedly as the public wondered about the ethics and responsibility of the media's decision to broadcast them.

The act of constructing a representation of oneself across multiple modalities for a specified audience is one taken up by the chapters in this fine collection, although their tone is certainly more hopeful and forward thinking. The six provocative chapters, together with the introduction and commentaries, offer guidelines for interpreting this distressing event and the decision made by the shooter to portray himself through visual media.

A central theme in this volume, highlighted in several chapters, is how images and other media are nearly always socially produced. Kelly Wissman describes in exquisite detail how the photographs as well as their accompanying stories are products of social interactions. The social nature of everyday practices, as Leif Gustavson highlights, suggests that the composition of the photographs and videotape sent to the network were produced in dialogue with others, even if this dialogue is silent. They were made for an audience in response to a particular context and version of reality. This does not excuse the horrific actions of the individual, but it leads us to examine the media productions through a different lens, reminding us of our complicity as consumers of the media.

In the midst of this tragedy, many people understandably turn first to blame, searching for culprits and negligence in the university and among the administrators and the social and psychological support system. The media is inevitably blamed as well, criticized for publishing the pictures and video so soon after the event. People suggest that this, and similar events that followed, are copycat crimes and reflect the pervasiveness of violent videogames and unchecked violence on TV. Here again the chapters in this volume are instructive as they remind us that media itself is not good or evil; rather, the meaning is made in the transaction (Rosenblatt, 1988). As authors such as Jeanine Staples instruct us, youth can be taught to critically produce and consume responses to such representations; however, teachers and other adults need to provide opportunities for learning this stance.

The volume addresses several other themes that suggest what is possible and offer lessons learned in spaces located outside formal schooling. They provide images of schooling and education that should be available for all youth, opportunities that might address the hopelessness, isolation, and lack of outlets for communication that seem to characterize the life of the youth involved in the murders. Each chapter in this book raises issues that illuminate the horrible events at Virginia Tech.

Several chapters describe the importance of creating a particular kind of space for the production of media texts. Rachel Nichols, for instance, identifies the particular location she studied as a hybrid space shaped by feminist and liberatory sensibilities. These spaces are often neither solely in or out of school but represent a kind of liminal space that is constantly shifting and shaped by literate practices in schools, homes, and communities. Heather Pleasants describes the presence of school literacies in after-school community-based programs as ghosts of school discourse, suggesting the traces of school discourse and practices in these out-of-school settings. As youth bring photographs to their school or after-school spaces and transport stories crafted in school to their home and community settings, they demonstrate the permeability of these boundaries. I call these circulating literacy practices (Schultz, 2006), or "the identities and socially situated ways of using texts that students carry with them as they move across the boundaries of home, community and school" (Vasudevan, Schultz, & Bateman, forthcoming). The construct of circulation literacy practices helps both to define and to break down boundaries for media productions, as discussed in these chapters.

A final theme is the emphasis in these chapters on relationships: relationships between and among students and teachers, youth and adults. Each chapter explores the particular relationship of the

Route Item

ROUTE ITEM Item Barcode:

3 2 7 1 1 0 0 1 5 7 2 7 2 0

all Number: 373.133 M489h
opy Info: c.1
TO:
Library:
Chicago State Univeraity Library

Location: .CSU CIRCULATION DESK
Address: ILDS: CSU
Chicago State University/LIB 133
9501 S King Drive
Chicago, IL 60628-1598
USA
Patron Category: UBLong
Patron Barcode:

2 0 4 1 1 9 0 0 0 0 1 8 3 4 0 2

4/23/2009 3:12:58 PM

researcher to the youth in the project and at the site. In many cases, as in the chapters written by Wissman and Gustavson, youth are invited to participate in the project as co-researchers. As Dimitriadis asserts, much of this work is relational research. This stance toward youth conveys respect and acknowledges the value of learning from youth what and how to teach. In her detailed description of her own practice as a poet, Korina Jocson reminds us that the best teachers are always learners themselves. Each of these chapters takes seriously the work of youth and the work of teachers, inviting us to learn from both.

This important volume provides us with six case studies of youths' engagement with media production. A key feature of the volume is that each case study is followed by two thoughtful responses. Scholars bring their own backgrounds and research to these responses, making the book both theoretically strong and connected to practice.

These are hopeful essays written in dangerous times. Yet, they are not naïve. Many of the chapters explore the notion of literacy learning as taking risks. Each chapter calls for change, including the transformation of educational settings, pedagogies, and practices. The authors describe what happens when youth work with multiple modalities is taken seriously and allowed to develop. As a collection, this volume points us toward a more socially just world that provides equitable chances for all children to be educated and opportunities for them to bring their lives into the classroom. The anger and isolation that characterize the discussion of the events in Virginia will not disappear if more children are given the opportunities described in this volume. These feelings of despair will not vanish if more students are given opportunities to write poetry, make digital stories, or learn to be a turntablist. By opening up classrooms and educational spaces to the lives and considerable talents of youth, we are taking the first step.

References

Rosenblatt, L. (1988). Writing and reading: The transactional theory. Technical report. Berkeley: University of California, Center for the Study of Writing.

Schultz, K. (2006). Qualitative research on writing. In C. A. MacArthur, S. Graham, & J. Fitzgerald (Eds.), *Handbook of writing research*. New York: Guilford Press.

Vasudevan, L., Schultz, K., & Bateman, J. (Forthcoming). Beyond the printed page: Multimodal storytelling with urban students.

Acknowledgments

We want to acknowledge the following people who gave generously to this volume, and without whom this project would have remained an unrealized nugget of inspiration. The authors of each chapter have been on this journey with us from the beginning. Each brings a passion for understanding the learning lives of young people, and a commitment to rethinking teaching and learning as we know it.

When we conceived of this volume, we sought a way to make the reading experience a dynamic one. We are thankful for the participation of our twelve respondents who have done so by starting the conversation; they made time in their already busy lives to respond thoughtfully to the words and insights of the authors they read.

We are grateful for the efforts of our graduate students whose energy and efforts were instrumental to the book's completion. Decoteau Irby spent many hours attending to various details and tracking down necessary permissions. Stavroula Kontovourki offered critical feedback on early versions of the book, and lent her insights and considerable time to design and compile the index. And Brian Gregory helped with formatting and editing, and offered aesthetic assistance on the overall design of the book.

We are grateful to Katherine Schultz for her generous foreword and, more importantly, for nurturing many of the ideas contained in this volume. Without her intellectual and personal support, this volume quite literally would not have come into existence.

We would like to thank our series editors, Michele Knobel and Colin Lankshear, for their support in making our idea a reality. Finally, we want to thank Sophie Appel and her colleagues at Peter Lang for their help with the completion of this book. Sophie, in particular, provided much needed guidance and encouragement throughout the process and we are grateful for her unending patience.

Chapter One

Moving Beyond Dichotomies of Media Engagement in Education: An Introduction

Lalitha Vasudevan and Marc Lamont Hill

What is media? What is learning? What spaces, relationships, and pedagogies emerge when media and technologies are engaged in teaching and learning? These are among the questions that we raise in *Media, Learning, and Sites of Possibility,* a collection of essays based on empirical research studies that explore the challenges and possibilities for teaching, learning, literacies, and identities that emerge in media- and technology-related work with youth. For today's youth, whose lives echo the growing centrality of popular music, film, and digital technologies, media culture—including media technologies and media texts—provides the landscape upon which they perform various forms of meaning making and identity work. We use the term "media culture" to refer to the broad spectrum of media technologies, media texts, and spaces of media engagement that currently exist and that are emerging daily. For educators who are interested in transforming schools into more democratic and productive spaces, media texts provide an important point of entry into the lived experiences of their students. At the same time, this changing media culture raises concern among many educators who presume a unidirectional relationship between students and media, in which students are seen as the passive and unwitting recipients of an endless series of problematic messages. It is from this stance that artifacts of media culture are either banished from or marginalized within classrooms, and it is this stance that we hope to interrupt with this volume.

The same media culture artifacts that cause concern in schools are repositioned as the object of critical analysis in many media education and critical media literacy projects (e.g., Alvermann, Moon, & Hagood, 1999; Buckingham, 2003). The primary purpose of these approaches has been to engage students as critical readers of media messages hidden beneath the gloss and packaging of advertisements, television programs, and music videos by asking them to consider questions such as *Who produced this text?* and *What voices are heard/are* not *heard?* and *What messages are conveyed through the visual and audio layers of this scene/commercial/video?* This work has moved forward the integration of media and other popular culture texts into curricular discourses. Nevertheless, there remains a tendency in schools to obscure the redemptive possibilities of media texts. That is, media in education is positioned as a curricular tool to educate young people *about* media, thus leaving little room to investigate or engage the critical capabilities students already bring to their study of, play with, and response to media culture (Staples, 2005).

A more celebratory approach to the artifacts associated with media culture emphasizes the transformative and emancipatory potential of media texts and is theoretically grounded in the work of cultural populists (e.g., Fiske, 1987, 1989). Proponents of this approach argue that there are sectors of media culture that provide a resistant space from which to ward off the negative effects of the mainstream culture industry. This is an alternative focus that has influenced some progressive educators to transport media texts into the classroom. However, unlike critical media literacy approaches, a celebratory approach risks overly de-emphasizing the effect of media on youth. Somewhere between these varying approaches to engaging media within educational discourses lies the potential for media texts to be taken up and understood not only as sites in need of critical analysis or performances of productive resistance.

To move beyond these and other dichotomies, we draw on frameworks that afford complex and nuanced examinations of how media are negotiated within formal and informal learning spaces. Through the diverse interpretive lenses the authors in this book use— e.g., sociocultural, black feminist, figured worlds, practitioner inquiry—we are better equipped to recognize the multiple forms taken by media and the varied situated meanings media culture takes on in the learning lives of youth. This collection of research invites us to consider new modes of learning, new media spaces in which to learn, and new media texts from which to learn.

Youth, Media, and Pedagogy

Given the increased salience of media culture in the lives of youth, interest has grown within the educational community in the relationship between youth, media, and pedagogy. Many scholars and practitioners have attempted to craft formal and informal pedagogical spaces that acknowledge the critical role that the sights, sounds, and spectacles of media play in the lives of youth. Much of this work fits within three categories: pedagogy *of* media, pedagogy *about* media, and pedagogy *with* media.

Drawing from McLaren's definition of pedagogy as the "introduction to, preparation for, and legitimation of particular forms of social life" (1998, p. 160), the pedagogy of media speaks to the various ways that media texts function as sites of public pedagogy that authorize particular values, beliefs, and identities while contesting or obscuring others. Many scholars have analyzed media texts to highlight their corrosive effects on youth (e.g., hooks, 1994; Kellner, 1995); others have examined how youth themselves have been problematically constituted through media texts (e.g., Giroux, 1996). Media texts such as billboards, music, films, podcasts, and photographs educate through their content, through what can be seen and heard as well as what is left out. Despite the usefulness of such insights, research on the pedagogy of media has been largely textual and highly pessimistic, focusing primarily on the negative things that media texts "do" to those who consume them.

More recently, the turn to cultural studies within critical education discourse has created new theoretical space for understanding the contours and contradictions of media texts. Rather than viewing media texts as purely helpful or harmful, the cultural studies tradition allows us to see them as sites of struggle between reproduction and resistance (Dimitriadis & Carlson, 2003; Giroux, 1992). Through ethnographic investigations, researchers such as Dimitriadis (2001) and Maira (2002) have demonstrated the complex and dynamic interplay between reproduction and resistance that exists with regard to youth and various aspects of media culture. Such insights are critical for developing a more nuanced and thorough view of youth engagement with media culture.

While many scholars have examined the pedagogical role of media texts within the lives of youth, others have focused on the development of pedagogies about media. For more than twenty years, the rapidly expanding field of media education has focused on students' *media literacy*, or the ability to access, interpret, communicate, and create print, video, audio, and digital media texts (Buckingham, 2003; Hobbs, 1998). In addition, critical media educators have buttressed traditional media education work by encouraging the development of literacies that enable students to analyze structures of power—particularly with regard to race, class, gender, and sexual identity—and develop commitments to social transformation. Educators attending a 1993 media literacy conference identified the following five concepts they felt should be included in the analysis of media messages:

(1) media messages are constructed;
(2) media messages are produced within economic, social, political, historical, and aesthetic contexts;
(3) the interpretive meaning-making processes involved in message reception consists of an interaction between the reader, the text, and the culture;
(4) media have unique "languages," characteristics which typify various forms, genres, and symbol systems of communication;
(5) media representations play a role in people's understanding of social reality. (Aufderheide, 1993, p. 2, cited in Hobbs, 1998)

Although media education literature has made significant theoretical and practical interventions into the relationships between youth and media, there remains a need to examine the complex nexus between media pedagogies, youth identities, and the larger cultural landscape upon which they are situated. In particular, scholars must continue to examine how media education projects are enabled and challenged by the complex relationships and identity performances that emerge from youth interactions with media. We must also examine how such projects are affected, as discussed later in this chapter, by the changing nature and level of access that youth have to media and technology.

In addition to teaching youth about media texts, many educators have attempted to use media texts to facilitate more traditional learning aims. These efforts, which have been particularly popular within literacy classrooms (Hill, 2006; Mahiri, 1998; Morrell & Duncan-Andrade, 2002), have demonstrated the effectiveness of pedagogy with media texts for scaffolding student engagement with curricular knowledge. Unfortunately, the instrumentalist concerns of many scholars and practitioners, no doubt intensified by the technocratic mandates of the No Child Left Behind Act, have emphasized student outcomes over more nuanced understandings of how the use of media texts reconfigures the relationships between teachers, students, and media texts. Thus, while we have gained considerable knowledge about strategies that "work" to engage students' media lives in classroom spaces, we have much to learn about the rapidly changing nature of transmedial meaning making, particularly in the lives of youth (Ito, 2007; Lemke, 2007).

This volume adds to these conversations by paying careful ethnographic attention to the relationships between youth, media, and pedagogy. In doing so, the authors eschew prefigured interpretations in favor of more complex and local readings of the relationships between students and media texts, as well as the broader context in which such relationships are forged. Such insights are essential for fully recognizing the possibilities of pedagogies of, with, and about media culture.

Digital Youth, Multimodal Texts, and New Literacies

The ways in which adolescents are engaging with media and emerging technologies are being documented across various fields of study, including media studies, youth culture, and literacies research. A salient theme present in much of this work is the focus on youth as producers of new media texts, new mediated spaces, and new media-influenced practices. In these discussions, as in the chapters in this book, media is conceived of broadly.

Over the past few years, several studies have been published that describe youth as actors who are simultaneously traversing and creating an increasingly digital communicative landscape (Gee, 2003; Knobel & Lankshear, 2007; Leander & McKim, 2003; Prensky, 2006). Similar to the ways in which studies of literacies beyond the school walls extend our notions of literacy practices and where they occur (Hull & Schultz, 2002; Moje, 2000; Moje et al., 2004), studies of cyberspaces are beginning to extend our understandings of how youth mediate their online selves while engaged in technoliteracy practices (Leander & McKim, 2003).

As young people continue to create and disseminate their media, the media landscape changes. As young people develop their facility with new technologies, geographies, and communicative modes, so, too, must their spaces of education grow and expand to accommodate this evolution. Yet, formalized educational spaces such as schools remain largely tethered to archaic notions of teaching, learning, and inquiry. When new media and technologies are integrated into curricula, they are integrated within existing pedagogical frames that maintain uneven dynamics of power and authority. Thus, the gulf widens between the in and out of school lives of youth (Hull & Schultz, 2002), and what is learned is less about the possibilities of education and more about disciplining of bodies. Such a docile view of education is challenged by the authors in this volume, who present nuanced portraits of teaching and learning with, through, and about media and technologies, and the expressive possibilities they hold. In doing so, they simultaneously complicate the myth that the integration of new media technologies can act as a panacea for the real issues that schools face: under-resourcing, large class sizes, and ongoing surveillance that ranges from the looming presence of metal detectors to yearly high-stakes testing cloaked in the language of accountability.

The salience of media in youths' lives further broadens the scope of inquiry into literacies in this age of increased digitization (Dimitriadis, 2001; Fisherkeller, 2000). All of these emergent discussions about "new literacies" and "new texts" emphasize the importance of media and technologies for discursive meaning making, particularly with regard to the lives of youth. This marks a shift in literacy theorizing, from which youth, and the insights to be gained from exploring their literacy practices, have historically been missing (Moje, 2002).

This emerging body of research is also reflective of an increasingly multimodal communicative landscape (Thomas, 2005; Vasudevan, in press). The media that youth produce and the range of modes with which they are composing are the focus of much recent research across literacy studies, cultural geographies, and youth culture. With the advent of new digital spaces for publication, youth are drawing on documentary technologies—such as the video camera, still camera, voice recorder, and cell phone camera—to produce new kinds of texts. These new texts (digital stories, podcasts, video montages) are reflective of the changes in literacy "as new technologies require new literacies to effectively exploit their potentials" (Leu, Kinzer, Coiro, & Cammack, 2004, p. 1570). Furthermore, these texts reflect the new geographic trajectories of adolescents' literacies (Alvermann, 2002).

As young people navigate cybergeographies such as Myspace.com and Youtube.com and develop their identities as producers of new texts and new spaces, they are also performing new communicative, social, and pedagogical practices. For example, to create an account on the social networking website Myspace.com, users must have the requisite information about how to navigate the web and how to communicate linguistically as well as visually and aurally. They are also engaging in new forms of "reading" and "writing" that involve composing and responding to messages posted on public comment areas and creating slideshows and movies that serve to mold the identities they are cultivating.

To participate in this particular space, young people are finding opportunities within school contexts, at friends' houses, at home, and in community sites where they can use computers to update their personal web spaces and stay up to date on the latest Myspace.com happenings. These are not only new and multimodal communicative practices but also new understandings of socializing, building and maintaining community, and identity work. Similarly, other spaces such as SecondLife.com, a virtual world environment, Youtube.com, a video-sharing site whose motto is "Broadcast Yourself," as well as youth media organizations, such as the Educational Video Center in New York City and Youth Radio in Berkeley, California, provide new communicative spaces in which youth are engaging with media technologies for a variety of purposes and bring to these engagements a diverse set of histories, ideologies, social networks, and knowledges. Within these spaces are found new meanings about the role media plays in the lives of young people, where media lives, how new media technologies are being taken up, and what new texts, practices, relationships, and identities they afford (Goodman, 2003; Soep & Chavez, 2005).

In this book, we have brought together a collection of studies that not only engage media explicitly but show the range and variation of what media is, how media technologies and media texts can be engaged in teaching/learning spaces, and the challenges raised amidst the possibilities that new media and the emerging multimodal landscape hold for education.

Sites of Possibility

The chapters in this book, while explicitly and implicitly exploring the significance of diverse media in shaping the world in which youth live and participate, move us beyond questions of whether or how much media engagement in adolescents' learning is sufficient or beneficial. They do so by offering six descriptions of rich sites wherein the space of learning transformed and was transformed by the use of varied expressive modes. Collectively, they recognize that learning is a multisensory experience, dominated in recent years by multimodal texts such as television programs, magazines, films, and the vast expanse of the Internet. As the chapters in this volume will show, learning occurs across contexts and through engagement with varied texts, resources, and roles. Beyond merely addressing learning as it is defined through statewide standards or other performance measures, these chapters raise questions about what is learned, for what purposes, and through what means. The authors consider the new relationships, identities, texts, and discourses that emerge as teaching/learning sites themselves. They recognize that "[t]he burden is on us, adults, to carve out 'spaces,' to inspire a sense of the 'not yet,' to reinvent schools and communities that are engaging for young people" (Fine, 1997, pp.214—215), and that are reflective of who young people are.

In her chapter about young women in a photography and literacy elective course, Kelly Wissman shares the group's experiences as they develop facility with cameras and assume the role of photographers and authors. She talks of learning as occurring within the community that evolved over time and across new texts and encourages us to think of "learning spaces as profoundly social spaces and nurturing the development of new kinds of relational practices within those spaces."

Heather Pleasants describes in detail the unscripted and unexpected digital storytelling practices that emerged when two girls she worked with at an after-school community center played with the conventions of this growing form of expression (Hull & Zacher, 2004). Pleasants shares her experiences as a researcher and facilitator of this space who had to learn the emerging communicative codes that the two girls were developing as they played with this genre. In her chapter, the moments of literacy learning made possible through the girls' playful explorations of various technologies and media are especially resonant and contribute to how we rethink the salience of play in critical media engagement.

Similarly, Korina Jocson echoes these moments of reflection as she explores digital video poetry as an author and as an educator. She discusses this expressive form as a site for transforming pedagogy and, relatedly, the learning that is embedded throughout. Through her analysis of one of her own poems, a tribute to the late June Jordan, we see Jocson's evolution as a digital video poet in tandem with the new narratives that emerge with the careful multimodal orchestration of new communicative modes.

The importance of multimodality in developing the ethos of a learning space is explored deeply by Rachel Nichols in her chapter about the literacies, teaching, and learning that emerge within the space of a girls' high school literary magazine. Nichols builds on recent discussions about multimodality and multiliteracies as she describes the young women involved in the magazine as multiliteracy pedagogues. Through their dialogue, reflection, and the magazine-related decisions, we see the young women assume a range of roles and responsibilities connected to the production of new literacy space where learning is embedded in the teaching that is ongoing.

In discussing her work with adolescents in an after-school program at an urban high school, Jeanine Staples gives us a description of the urban adolescent as a cultural critic. Through reading, viewing, reflecting on, and raising questions about a range of media and media texts, Staples and the youth who were a part of this program engage teaching and learning as a communal process grounded in the dynamic reading of the world around us. The way we introduce and engage media in classrooms, Staples argues, needs to consider the ways in which young people are *already* critical readers.

Leif Gustavson presents us with a portrayal of a young man for whom turntablism is a creative practice, a communicative mode, and a space for reflection and critique. Learning in this young man's world exists in the intersection between his art and his "reading" of the worlds and words of prominent figures across history, hip-hop, and popular culture. By sharing the experiences of Gil, the artist in this chapter, Gustavson invites us to take seriously the creative practices of youth as rigorous, thoughtful, and systematic and concludes his chapter with framing pedagogical ideas that build on the insights from his study of Gil.

Through the work and words of these authors and twelve critical respondents, this volume provides new insights into the complex, contradictory, yet promising relationships between youth, pedagogy, and media. In this book, we present possibilities for teaching, learning, and research that emerge when media technologies and media texts become a central feature of the learning spaces that youth occupy. Given this goal, this book is not solely about media literacy or media education, nor is it a book that falls squarely within the debates surrounding both of these areas of scholarship and practice. Rather, the spirit in which this book was conceived and the contents that follow challenge us to think beyond existing demarcations and consider the possibilities for teaching and learning that arise when youth and adults engage together in education *with* media.

References

Alvermann, D. (Ed.). (2002). *Adolescents and literacies in a digital world*. New York: Peter Lang.

Alvermann, D., Moon, J. S., & Hagood, M. C. (1999). *Popular culture in the classroom: Teaching and researching critical media literacy*. Chicago: International Reading Association.

Buckingham, D. (2003). *Media education: Literacy, learning, and contemporary culture*. Malden, MA: Blackwell.

Dimitriadis, G. (2001). "In the clique": Popular culture, constructions of place, and the everyday lives of urban youth. *Anthropology and Education Quarterly, 32*(1), 29–51.

Dimitriadis, G., & Carlson, D. (2003). *Promises to keep: Cultural studies, democratic education, and public life*. New York: Routledge.

Fine, M. (1997). Greener pastures. In W. Ayers & J. Miller (Eds.), *A light in dark times: Maxine Greene and the unfinished conversation* (pp. 209–218). New York: Teachers College Press.

Fisherkeller, J. (2000). "The writers are getting kind of desperate": Young adolescents, television, and literacy. *Journal of Adolescent and Adult Literacy, 43*(7), 596–606.

Fiske, J. (1987). *Television culture*. London: Routledge.

Fiske, J. (1989). *Understanding popular culture*. London: Unwin Hyman.

Gee, J. P. (2003). *What video games have to teach us about learning and literacy*. New York: Palgrave.

Giroux, H. A. (1992). *Border crossings: Cultural workers and the politics of education*. New York: Routledge.

Giroux, H. A. (1996). *Fugitive cultures: Race, violence, and youth*. New York: Routledge.

Goodman, S. (2003). *Teaching youth media: A critical guide to literacy, video production, & social change*. The Series on School Reform. New York: Teachers College Press.

Hill, M. (2006). Using Jay-Z to reflect on post-9/11 race relations. English Journal. 96(5), 25-29.

Hobbs, R. (1998). The seven great debates in the media literacy movement. *Journal of Communication, 48*(2), 9–29.

hooks, b. (1994). *Outlaw culture: Resisting representations*. London: Routledge.

Hull, G., & Schultz, K. (2002). *School's out! Bridging out-of-school literacies with classroom practice*. New York: Teachers College Press.

Hull, G., & Zacher, J. (2004). What is an after-school worth? Developing literacy and identity in school. *Voices in Urban Education, 3*, 36–44.

Ito, M. (2007, February 24). Amateur, mashed up, and derivative: New media literacies and otaku culture. Paper presented at the annual meeting of the National Council of Teachers of English Assembly for Research, Nashville, TN.

Kellner, D. (1995). Cultural studies, multiculturalism, and media culture. In G. Dines & J. Humez (Eds.), *Gender, race, and class in media* (pp. 5–17). Thousand Oaks, CA: Sage.

Knobel, M., & Lankshear, C. (2007). *A new literacies sampler*. New York: Peter Lang.

Leander, K. M. (2003). Writing travelers' tales on new literacyscapes. *Reading Research Quarterly, 38*(3), 392–397.

Leander, K. M., & McKim, K. K. (2003). Tracing the everyday "sitings" of adolescents on the Internet: A strategic adaptation of ethnography across online and offline spaces. *Education, Communication & Information 3*(2), 211–240.

Lemke, J. (2007, February 25). New media & new learning communities: Critical, creative, and independent. Paper presented at the annual meeting of the National Council of Teachers of English Assembly for Research, Nashville, TN.

Leu, D., Kinzer, C. K., Coiro, J., & Cammack, D. (2004). Toward a theory of new literacies emerging from the Internet and other information and communication technologies. In R. B. Ruddell & N. J. Unrau (Eds.), *Theoretical models and processes of reading* (5 ed.). Newark, DE: International Reading Association.

Mahiri, J. (1998). Streets to schools: African American youth culture and the classroom. *Clearing House, 71*(6), 335–338.

Maira, S. (2002). *Desis in the House: Indian American youth culture in New York City*. Philadelphia: Temple University Press.

McLaren, P. (1998). *Life in schools: An introduction to critical pedagogy in the foundations of education*. New York: Longman.

Moje, E. B. (2000). *"All the stories that we have": Adolescents' insights about literacy and learning in secondary schools. Kids InSight, K–12*. Newark, DE: International Reading Association.

Moje, E. B. (2002). But where are the youth? On the value of integrating youth culture into literacy theory. *Educational Theory, 52*(1), 97–120.

Moje, E. B., Ciechanowski, K. M., Kramer, K., Ellis, L., Carrillo, R., & Collazo, T. (2004). Working toward third space in content area literacy: An examination of everyday funds of knowledge and discourse. *Reading Research Quarterly, 39*(1), 38–70.

Morrell, E., & Duncan-Andrade, J. M. R. (2002). Promoting academic literacy with urban youth through engaging hip-hop culture. *English Journal, 91*(6), 88–92.

Prensky, M. (2006). *"Don't bother me Mom, I'm learning!": How computer and video games are preparing your kids for twenty-first century success and how you can help!* St. Paul, MN: Paragon House.

Soep, E., & Chavez, V. (2005). Youth radio and the pedagogy of collegiality. *Harvard Educational Review, 75*(4), 409–434.

Staples, J. (2005). Reading the world & the word after school: African American urban adolescents' reading experiences and literacy practices in relationship to media texts. Doctoral dissertation, University of Pennsylvania.

Thomas, A. (2005). Children online: Learning in a virtual community of practice. *E-Learning, 2*(1), 27–38.

Vasudevan, L. (In Press). "A picture can do things words can't": Transformative representations in literacy research. In J. Flood, S. B. Heath, & D. Lapp (Eds.), *Handbook on teaching literacy through the communicative and visual arts.* New York: Routledge.

Chapter Two

"This Is What I See": (Re)envisioning Photography as a Social Practice

Kelly K. Wissman

In the introduction to her book *Secret Games: Collaborative Works with Children, 1969–1999,* photographer and educator Wendy Ewald (2000) reflects on her photographic work with children, providing a meditation on the powerful teaching capacity of children's creative works:

> I embarked on a series of teaching sojourns to various parts of the world which would take up the next thirty years of my life. I knew, of course, that there were risks in guiding children toward genuine artistic expression. There was the risk of challenging a hierarchical and exclusively adult vision of our common humanity. There was the risk of buttoning up in the abstract all uncertainties about innocence, art, and personal integrity.
>
> Yet the children quickly taught me that art is not a realm where only the trained and formally accredited may dwell. The truly unsettling thing about the children's imagery was that, despite their inexperience with what adults might call rational thinking, their images tapped into certain universal feelings with undeniable force and subtlety. (pp. 17–18)

The images produced by Ewald's students in response to open invitations to photograph their families, communities, and dreams do indeed challenge an "exclusively adult vision" of the world. The risk in this endeavor, as Ewald rightly notes, is that young people's own meaning-making processes, understandings, and perspectives can not only replace clichéd and derivative images with fresh and arresting points of view but can also challenge fixed notions about who can be named an artist and what can be considered art. It is in the embrace of this risk, and in the promise of this risk, that I located my own photographic work with young women. It is a risk deeply connected to inquiry, to being open to discovery, to creating venues for this expression to occur, to looking closely and listening even more closely to the stories told in the photographs.

For a little over one academic year, I explored the arts, literacies, and social change within an alternative in-school space created with and for young women of color.[1] This chapter draws from a ten-month qualitative inquiry into the development and enactment of this autobiographical writing and photography elective course that I facilitated and that the students named "Sistahs." In the context of an urban public charter high school, sixteen students and I engaged with socially conscious writers and image makers; used reflective processes to discuss issues of gender, race, and social injustice; took photographs and wrote poetry to create visual autobiographies; and shared this work with each other and with others through conference presentations, exhibitions, and a website. Methodologically situated within the traditions of practitioner inquiry (Cochran-Smith & Lytle, 1993) and feminist research (Fine, 1992), my "praxis-oriented inquiry" (Lather, 1991) involved systematic documentation and analysis of this context and the writing and photography produced by the young women within it.

In this chapter, I explore the kinds of pedagogical practices and relationships that can emerge when photography is viewed as a social practice within an in-school teaching and learning context. Unlike dominant models of photography instruction that conceive of photography as a set of discrete, technical skills to be mastered, I consider photography as a *medium of seeing* that is shaped by the social context, by identity, and by experience. Envisioning photography as a social practice recognizes that the images produced are not simply a transparent recording of reality; rather, the images encapsulate a particular framing of that reality that is highly intentional and unique to the individual photographer. Envisioning photography as a social practice also entails considering the social context in which images are produced and received and considering the shaping influence of those contexts on the images and interpretations of those images. To envision photography as a social practice also means to envision photographers as social beings with historical legacies, emergent identities, and social commitments, all of which can inform the production of the images. Within this framework, photographers approach the process of image making with a sense of intentionality and in the service of a wide range of meaning making. As a medium of seeing, photography therefore suggests multiple kinds of vision on multiple levels.

In many ways, I take my cue in envisioning photography in this way from literacy scholars, who have long promoted the conceptualization of literacy as a social practice. Within the field of New Literacy Studies, researchers have identified and theorized the social nature of literacy to move beyond a focus on skill acquisition and the ability to decode print to an exploration of the meaning and purposes of literacy within people's everyday lives (e.g., Barton & Hamilton, 1998; Street, 1993, 1995). The emphasis on the social nature of literacy marks a significant shift from what Street (1993) calls the "autonomous" model of literacy development. Street (1993) argues that the autonomous model functions to "conceptualise literacy in technical terms, treating it as independent of social context, an autonomous variable whose consequences can be derived from its intrinsic character" (p. 5). In contrast to the autonomous model, Street's (1993) conceptualization of an "ideological" model of literacy does not divorce the social context from literacy, reduce literacy to a "neutral technology" (p. 9), or obscure the sites of power and contestation in which literacy is embedded. By emphasizing and exploring the social nature of literacy practices, the research and theory emerging from New Literacy Studies highlights not only the range and variation of those literacy practices but also the multiple contexts in which they occur. By responding to the call for "closely detailed accounts of the whole cultural context in which [literacy] practices have meaning" (Street, 1995, p. 2), researchers have explored literacy practices in communities (Barton & Hamilton, 1998; Cushman, 1998), homes (Hicks, 2002; Skilton-Sylvester, 2002), community centers (Heller, 1997), and arts programs (Heath, 1993; Heath & Smyth, 1999).

A small number of studies have illustrated how photography can serve as a powerful resource in bridging students' in- and out-of-school lives in ways that challenge misconceptions, enhance literacy learning, and create connections between students, teachers, parents, and community members (Allen et al., 2002; Landay et al., 2001; Orellana & Hernández, 1999). Despite the ways in which these studies suggest the great potential of photography as an educational resource, few studies have taken a sustained look at the affordances of this medium for young people outside the bounded identity of "student" and outside the purpose of enhancing in-school achievement, relationships, and motivation. In other words, we know little about how students appropriate the medium for their own purposes, for their own learning, for their own personal, social, and political intentions. We know even less about how their own gendered and cultural identities shape their creative works. By exploring the students' photographic work from a social practice perspective, we may be able to gain a richer insight into not only the meanings and purposes that students assign to photography but also the kinds of teaching and learning spaces that can support them in these endeavors. Within this place of "risk," as Ewald might say, we might be able to challenge conventional understandings not only of art and artists but also of teachers and learners and of learning spaces.

In this chapter, I use the framework of photography as a social practice to read the students' photographic work and to analyze the multiple ways in which this work was produced, discussed, written about, and reflected upon within the course. I explore the variety of ways that the students utilized the medium of photography as a social practice and specifically examine how they drew upon the medium to fulfill their own personal, social, and political purposes for building relationships, pursuing self-definition, and advocating for social change. I begin, however, with a more elaborated discussion of the pedagogical and relational features of this classroom context.

Pedagogy and Photography as Social Practice

When I began my work in Sistahs, I brought to the course a set of research experiences and emergent understandings about literacies, photography, and cross-cultural research that shaped how I conceptualized my teaching practice and designed the study. Drawing upon my work in community centers and after-school programs, I brought a deeply felt belief in the transformative nature of poetry to cultivate the assertion of subjectivity, transgress silences, and provoke new knowledge. From participating in Wendy Ewald's "Literacy Through Photography" workshop and from working with high school students to complete photography projects in an after-school program, I also brought to the Sistahs course a deeply felt hope that photography could cultivate community and connection. Finally, from work in multiracial educational and research settings, I brought a recognition of the ethical and epistemological complexities of producing knowledge cross-culturally. These understandings informed how I co-constructed this teaching and learning space with the students, how I attempted to pursue the research in a socially responsible way, and how I pursued my pedagogy.

Origins and background of the study

Sistahs began at the request of two students who approached school administrators asking for more opportunities to write in school and more gender-specific programming. As a result, I was asked to facilitate an after-school program. Four students and I met twice a week for four weeks or so after school during the final month of the 2001–2002 school year. We formed an informal, sometimes unpredictable, and often generative writing and photography community. We discussed and analyzed family and documentary photographs; read poetry; learned how to use digital cameras; and talked and wrote about each other's photographs through descriptive review processes, collaborative and individual poems, and reflective narrative writing. When we were asked to put together an exhibition of the students' writing and photography for the school's end-of-the-year celebration, we decided the group needed a name reflective of its nature and purpose. After an unstructured conversation, the students decided on the name Sistahs, which they argued was suggestive of a female space. The designation "Sistahs" rather than "Sisters" conveyed the significance of race and ethnicity in the artistic works engaged with and created within the group.

My initial work with the students during that spring suggested how the site could be a rich context for exploring young women's experiences within a setting created purposefully for them and within which the use of technology (digital cameras) and the practice of writing were configured as means for self-expression and social analysis. The following school year I returned to conduct this work within the space of the school day as an instructor of a credit-bearing course. Sixteen students participated in Sistahs over the three trimesters of the academic year, some for only one trimester and others for two. One student participated in all three trimesters. The majority of the students self-identified as African American. Three students identified respectively as Puerto Rican, multiracial, and Black/Grenadian. One white student participated in two classes before needing to withdraw for academic reasons. The students ranged in age from fourteen to sixteen.

My Racial Identity

In recognizing the complexities of my subject positioning as a white woman within this teaching and research context, I drew on four main approaches to help me reflect upon my subjectivity as well as to work toward the development of responsible "codes of cross-cultural conduct" (Royster, 1996) and responsible cross-cultural knowledge production: reflexivity, self-representation, collaboration, and culturally attuned analytical lenses. Even while I tried to infuse this study with these feminist and critical principles, I nonetheless recognize the limitations of the methods given the entrenched nature of race and racism and my own limitations in terms of perspective and experience.

Young (2000) defines reflexivity as "self-reflection on one's research process and findings, self-awareness of one's social positionality, values, and perspectives, and self-critique of the effects of one's words and actions upon the individuals and groups being studied" (p. 642). Throughout the study I wrote about the tensions and complexities of pursuing this work as a white woman in my field notes. Supported by the prerogatives of both practitioner inquiry and feminist research, writings specifically about race emerged directly from the context of the classroom and from my intertwined perspectives as a teacher and researcher. I often wrote about moments of discomfort or tension in the classroom, as well as moments of open exploration and trust. In writing about these moments, I became engaged in a process of reflexivity in which I not only documented what occurred but also tried to locate my own frameworks for understanding what was occurring, to help me shape and reshape my pedagogy, research processes, and social relationships in the space.

The desires I brought to cultivate an antiracist and feminist context, to craft the course on a daily basis attendant to the students enrolled in it, and to sustain and strengthen this learning community in ways that would support the students' own personal, political, and artistic growth positioned me in this work in a highly invested manner. From a stance of reflexivity, however, I recognized that while these desires were located in liberatory and socially progressive aims, it is also the case, as Ursula Kelly (1997) argues, that no discourse, theoretical framework, or educative work is without homogenizing and myopic tendencies. Working from the premise and condition of the partiality of my understanding supports the cultivation of humility in this work. It also necessitates the pursuit of knowledge claims within it through openness, diligence, and ongoing reflexivity to account for and explore the gaps and fissures and to locate the socially situated nature of the knowledge produced in the context and in this writing.

Infusing this study with opportunities for self-representation reflected another component of my search for responsible "codes of conduct" in this cross-cultural teaching and research endeavor. As a teacher–researcher in the unusual position of being able to design and enact a curriculum almost entirely of my own making, I chose to provide as many opportunities as possible for the students to pursue autobiographical work. While inviting autobiographical engagements was a pedagogical choice, it was also a methodological one in that the poetry, photography, and discussion that resulted became the data of the study. I focused on self-representation in response to the practices of silencing in schools and the politics of erasure of the literacies and lives of African American girls in the educational research literature. My inclusion and analysis of the students' self-representations provide opportunities for their own visions and perspectives to be highlighted and suggest possibilities for their work to contribute knowledge to the field.

Feminist research has long valued collaboration as a method to reduce power imbalances and to promote reciprocity in the research setting (Fine, 1992; Wolf, 1996; Young, 2000). Within this multiracial context, I tried to promote many opportunities for co-construction and collaboration. I endeavored to position the students as agents within this setting to influence the work of the course, to shape the pedagogical practices, and to contribute to communal methods of knowledge construction. I also tried to create a classroom environment open to student voices and direction. While I retained primary responsibility for planning the classes, the readings, and in-class writing, we worked together each trimester to determine the literacy and photography projects. In addition, I opened every class with an invitation for the students to share writing.

Finally, I also drew upon the epistemologies and scholarship of African American women to assist me in working toward the development of responsible cross-cultural knowledge. In addition to the scholarship of Jacqueline Jones Royster (2000), I drew upon the work of Collins (2000) and Dillard (2000). The epistemologies of the poets (e.g., Brand, 1995; Jordan, 1995; Morrison, 1994) and artists (e.g., Trinh, 1991; Wright, 1992) who made up the curriculum also shaped the analysis. In the teaching, design, and analysis, I sought to develop a set of pedagogical and research practices that fostered mutual knowledge generation within and across multiple spaces of difference and commonality.

Pedagogy

Over the span of three trimesters in one academic year, the Sistahs course involved ongoing inquiries into the social nature of artistic creation, literary expression, and knowledge construction. While the students and I considered and analyzed the artistic and literary work of African American women poets and artists, the course also provided numerous opportunities for the students to pursue their own creative work. Recalling the sense of community and inquiry I tried to cultivate in the context and the kinds of knowledge I hoped we could produce together, my use of the term "pedagogy" in relation to the course resonates with Wendy Hesford's (1999) understanding that

> pedagogy . . . refers not solely to teaching methods and curricular content and design but also to the processes by which teachers, students, administrators, staff, and others negotiate and produce knowledge, identities and social relations. (p. xxviii)

My pedagogy was characterized by the creation of intentional and ongoing opportunities for the sharing and interrogating of personal experience, for the consideration of the ways social identities shape literary and artistic production, and for the validation of knowledge claims made by course members in community. The social relationships and recurrent pedagogical practices in Sistahs—sharing family photographs, reading poetry aloud, discussing the significance of race and gender in creating art and knowledge, and incorporating student work as texts of the class—reflected principles of Black feminist epistemology (Collins, 2000). Black feminist pedagogy recognizes the role of experience and cultural ways of knowing that influence how Black women teachers and students shape knowledge construction and classroom practices (Henry, 1993; hooks, 1994; Omolade, 1987). According to Barbara Omolade (1987), Black feminist pedagogy "sets forth learning strategies informed by Black women's historical experience with race/gender and class bias and the consequences of marginality and isolation" (p. 32). As a white woman, clearly I did not share the experiences and perspectives of Black women; however, I did choose to draw upon the scholarship of Black women to inform my choice of texts and to inform the social practices in the setting. I did so as a partial response to Annette Henry's (1993) assertion that the valuation of Black women's epistemologies should be expressed across locations in the educational research community to reinvigorate knowledge production, research, and classroom practice. I also embraced her perspective, along with Collins's (2000), that Black women scholars should be the primary knowledge producers in these areas.

In wishing to acknowledge how Black feminist epistemology informed the development and enactment of the space, I nonetheless recognize my own racial identity as a white woman. At best, this identity limits the fuller realization of this pedagogy; at worst, it renders this invocation of Black feminist pedagogy an act of gross appropriation. Therefore, my intent is to suggest how the students themselves crafted the space in ways that one can see as reflective of the principles of Black feminist pedagogy and to provide context for and analysis of those student acts. For example, the sharing of student poetry and photography became a venue for the realization of the "ethic of caring" (Collins, 2000) as students approached reading and responding to each other's work as significant and often emotional opportunities to affirm, support, and respond to each other and each other's literate and artistic identities, rather than as opportunities to provide criticism through more formal text-centered or image-based responses. This teaching and learning space therefore valued mutual knowledge generation around complex issues of race, gender, and social injustice. In name and by design, through both pedagogy and praxis, Sistahs was designed to support collective arts-based, literacy-rich inquiry into the social practices of literacies and the arts and to facilitate the production of knowledge emergent from and contributive to all course members.

Practices and Processes

In each trimester, students brought in, wrote about, and discussed personal and family photographs. As a daily ritual in the class, the sharing and discussing of these photographs helped to create a context in which images served as conduits for sharing and as the basis for storytelling. This sharing and storytelling often revolved around family members, social events, and childhood memories. To complement and add to this practice, I brought in the early documentary photography work of Carrie Mae Weems (Kirsh & Sterling, 1993). Books such as *The Family of Black America* (Cottman & Willis, 1996) and the Silence Speaks website (http:// www.silencespeaks.org) contributed to our exploration of the cultural meaning and social significance of family photos.

We also looked at and discussed a range of photographs from an assortment of photography books that explored adolescent girls' and women's lives and identities. I approached the discussion of these photographs in ways that embedded a discussion of their technical attributes (composition, tonal qualities, gesture, etc.) within a discussion of the meaning and feelings evoked by the image. For example, for one class I brought in a book entitled *Things I Have to Tell You* (Franco, 2001), which includes photographs of adolescent girls as well as poetry written by young women from across the country. We looked at the photographs in the book and discussed what we could tell about the interests, emotions, and lives of the young women through their photographs. We also considered how the technical aspects of the photographs, such as light, contrast, perspective, and gesture affected our interpretations.

Later in that trimester, I brought in three photography books centered on women's lives. *The Face of Our Past* (Thompson & Mac Austin, 1999) includes a historical survey of images of Black women organized under various themes such as "Family," "Play," "Hair," and "Resistance." *Voices of Our Own* (Deutsch, 2001) includes portraits and self-portraits of ethnically diverse women and girls in the Tenderloin district of San Francisco. The final book, *Eye to Eye* (Baird, 1997), takes a more global perspective and includes photographs and poems by women and girls from Africa, Asia, and Central America. The students worked in groups to discuss the photographs. They marked photos and themes that stood out to them and then shared them with the group. I also asked them to reflect on and share how the photos and themes they selected might inform our own photographic projects. The students were drawn to a variety of images and expressed an interest in exploring a diversity of themes, including women's identity, relationships, family, community, dreams, friendships, and play.

Drawing from Wendy Ewald's (2001) work with children and photography detailed in her book *I Wanna Take Me a Picture*, from Linda Christensen's (2000) work with "Where I'm From" poems with high school students, and from the collective input of the students themselves, I provided invitations for students to photograph their lives and identities centered loosely around exploring women's identity in two broad areas: "Where I'm From" and "Self-Portraits." In the first trimester, the students used point-and-shoot cameras with film to complete their assignments; in the second and third they signed out digital cameras provided by the school and downloaded the photographs onto school computers. We often engaged in individual and group writing about the photographs. At times, I asked the students to write "the story behind the photograph" or to write from the perspective of one of the subjects in the photographs. The students also wrote collaborative poems about each other's photographs. In our work together, mastery of the technology of the cameras was therefore not an end in itself but an entryway into fostering a wide range of artistic expression. While I provided instruction related to the mechanical and technical aspects of cameras and photo taking and while we discussed principles of photographic composition, this kind of knowledge was intended to be used in the service of the students' own personal, social, and creative goals.[2]

Production/reception in the social context: Exhibitions, publications, and presentation

Given the ways in which dominant media outlets bombard us with grossly distorted images of women, given the ways schools tend to marginalize explorations of students' lives outside of school doors, and given how necessary images of love, beauty, and connection seem to be in this time of social, psychic, and imaginative malnourishment, I saw a great deal of promise in taking the students' creative work outside the boundaries of our classroom. In the first trimester, we produced two in-class publications showcasing the students' writing and photography. In the second trimester, three students and I presented photographs, poems, and reflections on the Sistahs learning community at a local educational research conference. In the third trimester, we made an additional presentation to a graduate course at my school of education, submitted our work to an online journal of education (Wissman, 2003), participated in the schoolwide Poetry Jam, and hung an exhibition of the entire year's poetry and photography in the central gathering space at the school. This exhibition was organized around the themes of sisterhood, "Where I'm From," self-portraits, and "I Want to Write" and was included as a part of the school's end-of-the-year celebration for students, parents, and community members.

Maya and Jasmyn, two of the most prolific writers and artists in the course, wrote the following introduction to a public presentation of their writing and photography:

We think this work is a reflection of the things that are left unsaid because of
the scarcity of opportunities that are placed in schools for young, strong sistahs to make a way. . . . Our individual poems emerged from our past and present experiences, the problems we face as young females trying to make a way,
and the way we are being represented in society.

The students position themselves here as artists and writers who
create from experience, struggle, and resistance to dominant regimes
of representation. Maya and Jasmyn directed the audience to consider
the "scarcity of opportunities" for expression in schools, the ways
schools can fail students in their attempts to "make a way," and the
ways young women of color are "represented in society." They drew
attention to these conditions—the contexts from which their work
emerged and through which their identities as writers and artists
surfaced—to inform their audience and perhaps move them toward
action. By then presenting their own and other students' poetry and
photography, Jasmyn and Maya also "said" what has been "left
unsaid" and "showed" what has been "left unshown" to a public
audience. Clearly, the writing and photography produced by the
students were situated within and reached out toward the broader
social context.

Maya's and Jasmyn's sense making and analysis of their own
work provide a framework for considering how the students took up
invitations to consider photography as a social practice within a
classroom environment that was grounded in this perspective and
how they took up these opportunities to work toward a range of their
own personal, social, and political aspirations. These aspirations can
be further considered within the three broad categories of honoring
and building relationships, pursuing self-definition, and advocating
social change.

Honoring and Building Relationships

Throughout the students' photography work, images of family members and friendship predominated. When I invited students to bring in
photographs to share with the group, our room became filled with
baby pictures of nephews, cousins, and little sisters. We entered the
worlds of formal and informal family get-togethers in celebration of
birthdays, reunions, or simply an evening together. We laughed with
the young women in photographs posing together in celebration of
middle school graduations, dressing up together for a party, and
pausing to make silly faces for the camera on the way home from

school. In these cases, the photographs served to bring us together as a group, to provide us glimpses into each other's worlds, to allow us to see where our experiences touched and did not touch. The process of choosing photographs to bring in was also an act filled with meaning and significance about who and what was important to us, affected us, and shaped us.

Within this multiracial group, the photographs provided opportunities for informal sharing about our diverse cultural backgrounds through the use of images and the stories told about them. Renee's images were filled with representation of the many sides of her multiracial family, and her discussion of the photographs illuminated her movements across cultural boundaries, movements that were at times fraught with tensions and at other times fluid. Maria's photos suggested not only her family's continued close ties to Puerto Rico but also her own identification as Puerto Rican and her role as a mentor to other Puerto Rican children in her neighborhood. Geneva's images of her membership in a cultural organization celebrating African American women's connections to Africa provided us the opportunity to hear about her exploration of her African heritage alongside her mother, who also attended the group. My own photographs of my childhood provided moments of levity and seriousness as both my white racial identity and age contrasted with the students' in ways that marked both contrasts and commonalities across locations of difference.

Within this seemingly straightforward and uncomplicated request to bring in and share photographs, the medium of photography coupled with the act of storytelling opened up a range of possibilities for meaning making, relationship building, and learning in the classroom. The choice of photographs became a way to mark significant relationships as well as to build them. At the same time, this practice also opened up opportunities to raise complex issues of gender and racial identity. In presenting our own reflections, as well as listening to the diversity of stories in the group, we had opportunities to consider in an informal way, yet almost paradoxically in a deep way, how these locations shape navigation of our social worlds. "Personal" and "family" photographs therefore opened up decidedly social themes.

I would argue that the very attributes of photographic images— their small size, their capturing of specific moments in time, their ubiquitous presence in our everyday lives—facilitated the emergence and continued discussion of these large and often charged topics within multiracial groups. It seems more manageable to discuss, explore, and complicate these topics when they are brought up in the context of one particular image and in the context of one person's story. Photographs also often generate feelings of great pleasure and great interest. The students' excitement and desire not only to see each other's photographs but also to hear about their particular significance created an unusually receptive and engaged group of listeners. Hearing multiple stories that connected to and contrasted with others opened up a space for the existence of multiple view-points and experiences. Because of the democratic nature of photog-raphy, there was much to connect with and learn from even within experiences that may seem drastically different at first glance.

Many of these same impulses to honor and build relationships, many of these same themes of family and friendship, and many of these same insights surrounding social identities carried over into the students' creation of images in their creative projects. Maria's narra-tive of the photo essay she produced in response to the invitation to document the "people, places, and objects" that shape her is particu-larly illuminating. Although Maria's images are striking in their compositional qualities, I choose to focus here on the meaning making and analysis she provides in her spoken commentary to me about the photographs. Entitled "My People, My Culture," Maria's photo essay and narrative reflect her intentionality as an artist and as a young woman using photography for a range of personal and social aspira-tions. In addition, a portrait of Maria emerges here that suggests the complexities and subtleties of her life, which often become obscured in typical allusions to or descriptions of urban young people. The following is excerpted from an audiotaped discussion in which Maria and I discuss her photographs:

> So, this photo, this picture of the little girl. Her name's J. and, she looks up to me, 'cause she's only seven years old. And she comes to my house and she likes make-up and stuff like that. So she looks up to me, and, because, you know, I get my nails done, I put make-up on, so she looks up to me. And she tells me a lot and I try to help her out.

> And this is her brother, J. And, he likes me. He has a crush on me. But, he's athletic so he asks me to play with him so I play like baseball and whatever. Because I love kids. So that's why I got a lot of little kids in here.

And, let's see. Let's go to my friend. This is my friend K. I knew her for a long time, since I moved on my block. And, we went through a lot and she's still my friend. We talk a lot about boys and stuff that's going on now. And we go over to each other's house.

And, my father, he's one of the best people in my life. He helps me through everything, he understands me, and my sister and my family. And he goes through everything with us—to boys, to money, to love, to everything. And I'm thankful I have him 'cause him and my mom's always there for me, and my sister, no matter what.

My dog! My dog Gizmo. I got him, like, in November. And, the first time, like, he wasn't used to me, like, he would try to bite me and stuff. He wasn't used to the house. But then he keeps me and my dad company.

The Puerto Rican flag. This represents our culture and, like, Hispanic, like, the food, the music, what this stands for, the island, everything about Puerto Rico. And, it represents us because we always get together like on Puerto Rican Day, the parade and stuff.

My teddy bears. My teddy bears, I picked this 'cause each one of them, my family members gave them to me. And my mom gave me this. I had this when I was a little kid, so I'm pretty tight with it. And my teddy bear, my dad got me. He won it. And this one, my sister bought me for Easter. They're all special because each family member got it for me.

And, the last person, my god-sister K. Um, pretty much what I said before, she looks up to me as well. And she's grown up fast so she likes to be on the street a lot so I try to get her off the street 'cause everything is not about the street these days. So, I try to help her as much as I can. And, I knew her since she was 4 years old . . . that's when she got baptized by my dad.

The clarity of Maria's photographic vision is clearly matched by the clarity of her reflections on her sense of self in relation to her family, neighborhood children, and culture. Both her images and her words suggest the prominence of family, friends, and culture in her life and a clear and strong sense of connection and love permeating her life. In her photographs, much like her spoken commentary, Maria foregrounds the uniqueness of subjects. She places them against simple and nondistracting backgrounds and suggests something meaningful about each of them by paying close attention to gestures, poses, point of view, and perspective. As an artist uniquely knowledgeable about her subjects, she captures a range of expressions, from the children's delight, to her father's contemplative look, to her god-sister's slightly mischievous stare and proud tilt of the head. Her father looks directly into the camera, resting his chin on his hand in a manner that suggests both genuine interest and the capacity to listen. In another image, the Puerto Rican flag fills the entire frame, suggesting its prominence to her and her family.

Maria's creative and analytical work can be seen to function as an intervention in and challenge to the dominant cultural scripts that frame teenage girls of color, namely what Niobe Way (1998) calls the "feared and seemingly ineradicable stereotype, the urban teen—pregnant, drug-addicted, violent, fatherless, welfare dependent, poor, Black, and uneducated" (p. 1). Maria's images and words challenge, I believe, these deficit and deviancy discourses circulating in the educational field that reinforce images of all urban young women of color as living in the midst of crisis and despair. In contrast, Maria's photographs and reflections are full of images of family, connection, an abundance of love, and cultural pride. She presents herself as a daughter very connected to her father and as a young woman very influential to the young children in her neighborhood and to another young woman whom she helps "get off the street." In contrast to the materialistic sensibilities that many attribute to urban youth, the material items Maria most treasures are stuffed animals from her family and the Puerto Rican flag.

Joy's photo essay, in which she explored the theme of "Where I'm From," also provides insight into her relationships with family and friends. Her reflections on her parents are particularly striking in their sincerity and their searching quality, as well as in their resonance with Maria's:

> That's my dad. Well, this is, this is actually in Camden, New Jersey . . . We were just coming back from church and my dad went to go change clothes. I took a picture of him because I love my dad so much. I love my mom a lot, too, but I just favor my dad because my dad spoils me. I can talk to my dad about anything, you know? And it's not, and you know, most of the times it's like, you would talk to your mom about everything because you just tell your mom. I talk to my dad about everything—about boys, about everything. My dad is there for me. So is my mom, but she, she, can't handle everything. Like how I say it. My dad make everything, he makes everything blunt, he says it out in the open. He don't hide anything back; he doesn't hide anything from me. So that's why I took that picture.

> This is my mom. This is on Mother's Day. Um, I took this picture of her because this is the outfit I bought her for Mother's Day. And my dad bought her this tennis bracelet and she looked, I thought she looked so nice, and it was a

special day for her so I told my mom that I would take a picture of her after she got dressed with the outfit that I bought her for her day.

Throughout her essay, Joy reveals how she uses photography in multiple and varied ways: to mark special occasions, such as Mother's Day; to express the significance of family members in her life, both to them and later to me; and to describe her sense of self in relation to her neighborhood, best friend, and family. Joy uses photography here as a flexible and dynamic meaning-making medium; photography serves as a kind of entryway to illuminate, render significant, and document aspects of her life. She also seems to use photography to build closer relationships with her family members; she expresses her love for her mom not only by buying her a gift for Mother's Day but also by taking her picture. The diversity of images, the diversity of loves and connections, attest to her multifaceted identity. In addition, her words reflect a rich interior life and a maturing sense of love and appreciation for her parents. In a similar way to Maria's essay, it is this richness, this complexity, that is indeed a counter to the "ineradicable stereotype."

Joy's photo essay, like Maria's, provides a compelling look into photography as a medium capable of provoking a wide range of inquiries, prompting reflection, supporting the development of narrative alternatives to the dominant ones in circulation, and assisting in the discovery and articulation of personal and social issues to express as an artist. Maria and Joy approached this work with a great deal of intentionality, both within the active selection of subjects and compositional choices and in the reflective meaning-making processes evident in the commentary provided on them.

Pursuing Self-Definition

Throughout all three trimesters, photography gave the young women in Sistahs opportunities to frame their own realities through their camera viewfinders. Their photographs of family, school, neighborhood, friends, and self provide a tangible record of what they saw and how. I would argue, however, that this process of becoming image makers was in fact made more complicated and its effects made more insurgent because of the students' social identities as young women of color. Considering the young women's photographic work from feminist (Neumaier, 1995; Trinh, 1991) and Black feminist (hooks, 1995; Wright & Hartman, 1992) approaches to the visual can help highlight what I see as a movement from definition to self-definition.

While rejecting "controlling images" (Collins, 2000)—the derogatory images of women of color in highest circulation—the students actively created alternative images. They therefore moved from critiquing controlling images to controlling the process of image making. This movement is especially evident in their self-portrait work.

Feminist photographers, as Diane Neumaier (1995) contends, "share the recognition that images embody, are indivisible from politics . . . [and] share a consciousness that historically, women have been 'framed' through the process of representation and can be 'reframed' through the same process" (p. 1). Filmmaker and cultural theorist Trinh T. Minh-ha (1991) expresses this complex pursuit of women working both within and against a system of representation in which they are "framed" yet in which their visual creations suggest radically different kinds of "reframing." Trinh's identity as an Asian woman artist also suggests the ways in which the visual projects of women of color originate out of and reflect their often perilous existence in Western systems of oppression and representation—and, most notably, their challenges to these systems. She writes:

> The place from which the woman artist works is always fragile, because empowerment of the self can only be achieved by emptying, reversing, and displacing power relations. . . . She takes the plunge. She risks all or she risks nothing, because she has nothing to save. Seeing differently and hearing differently, she is bound always to challenge the "look" in the cinematic apparatus—of the system of looks that distinguishes cinema from other art forms. (p. 114)

For African American photographers Lorna Simpson and Carrie Mae Weems, the "challenge" Trinh speaks of is paramount to their artistic vision. Both artists in unique ways claim a radical space for themselves as creators of new forms of representation in a tradition informed by prevailing racial and sexual politics of erasure and exploitation. Beryl Wright (1992) highlights the counter-hegemonic nature of the work of these photographers who "operate at the intersection of feminist and African American oppositional strategies to disclose, critique, and resist dominant representations of gender and race constructed by those who have historically assumed the position of primary spectator" (p. 11). Both Simpson and Weems create images that deftly suggest and then go on to deftly critique African American women's historical, economic, and sexual oppression. These desires for social transformation locate Simpson and Weems as cultural workers in the tradition of African American liberation struggles. As Weems herself describes her artistic and social project: "to describe simply and directly those aspects of American culture in need of deeper illumination" (quoted in Piché & Golden, 1998, p. 9).

In considering the self-portrait work of the students in Sistahs who claimed the "position of primary spectator," what is particularly compelling is the craft aspect of this process and what it reveals about their process of self-definition. For example, to take a self-portrait the young women either needed the assistance of others or needed to use a mirror. When working with others, they first had to imagine in their own minds what kind of message they wanted to convey and then determine how they were going to pose themselves for that message to come across. They then had to articulate that vision to their "assistant." As a result, even though they did not technically take the self-portrait, they had significant control of the image-making process and a significant opportunity to make their vision known to their assistant. For example, before class on the day the first trimester's self-portraits assignment was due, I watched as Lynn placed herself in a chair, arranged her journal and papers in front of her, and located her pen. She then told Maya exactly where to stand in relation to her and when to take the picture. She tried two different expressions and directed Maya to take one photo when she was looking away from the camera with a contemplative look and one where she was looking directly into the camera. In an assignment that was ostensibly about the "self," the process was indeed social, both in the coproduction of the images and in the eventual reception of the images by viewers also situated in a social context.

Another compelling component of the self-portraits photography project related to how the writing that occurred in response to the photographs contributed to the process of self-definition. Because of recurring logistical issues that delayed access to cameras until at least midway through each trimester, the ethos of the group had already been developed as a writing community. By the time photography was introduced into the course each trimester, writing was a natural and expected occurrence. Photography was welcomed as another mode of expression by the young women; yet, true to the ethos that had been formed, the photographs gained more significance as springboards for writing. Writing about photographs thus became an essential extension of the self-definition work undertaken in the composition of the photographs. Writing added another, more direct, level of meaning to the photographs, providing an opportunity for the young women to assert their own interpretation of their own photographs. Two important locuses of control were therefore afforded: not only did the self-portrait assignment give the students considerable control over the process of image making, but writing about the self-portrait also gave them considerable control over how the image would be interpreted.

Here, first, is Geneva's self-portrait and poem, from which this chapter gains its title.

Figure 1. Geneva's Self Portrait

What Do You See When You Look at Me?
  This Is What I See

I see a young African American girl wearing long
braids like my African ancestors did.
Eyes that I use to see if someone is good or not so good.
A nose that I use to smell my mom's great cooking.
A smile to tell people that I am happy or wondering and thinking of
all the great things
that are going on in my life.
All these things and more make me and that is what I see.

(What do you think of me?)

In the photograph, Geneva positions herself in front of her home. In the far right corner, her little sister peeks out from the doorway. Geneva begins her poem with an invitation to the viewer/reader to self-reflect and then immediately asserts her own vision, implicitly suggesting that what she sees may not be what "you" see at first glance. In this way, she is calling attention to "self-representation as a field of struggle" (Hesford, 1999, p. xiii) between those who look and those who are being looked at. She claims a confident stance that she is the one who should have the primary voice in this struggle by asserting, "This is what I see." She first calls attention to features that suggest her racial identity, and does so in a way that puts her on a continuum with her "African ancestors." In addition, her self-description of her other physical features highlights her close familial relationships and her self-reflective nature. Throughout, she uses poetry not only to document factually the photographic image of herself with her sister and her home in the background but also to enrich both the external elements the image captures and to draw attention to the internal ones not obviously apparent. In this way, her writing and photography work in tandem to create a multilayered self-portrait, recognizing the limitations and possibilities inherent in both mediums. Most notably, Geneva highlights the limitations of the routinized ways we engage in the process of sense making through visual means. In the title of her poem and throughout, she calls attention to the gaps and misperceptions that accompany both sight and photographic representation. She constructs an image and uses language to address these gaps and misperceptions and to represent herself on her own terms, through her own visual and poetic language.

Lynn's self-portrait also calls into question the assumption of transparent and objective truth in photographic representation and implicates the viewer/reader even more directly in her poem. In fact, in representing herself poetically she employs very little description of herself and instead uses the poem as a forum to question the viewer/reader.

Figure 2. Lynn's Self Portrait

Who Am I?

If you could look at me and tell me who I am what
is it that you would say?
Would you judge me by the color of my skin or
push it all away?
Would you think of me as just another teen that's
confused and lost trying to find her way?
Or would you try to look deep within?
Before you go through the steps of looking before
you think why don't you try to get to know the
person who I really am.

Lynn chose to represent herself visually here as a writer and a
thinker. In the image, she strategically places her journal in front of
her, clasps her pen, and gazes thoughtfully away from the camera. By
refusing to meet the gaze of the viewfinder, she creates a resistant
ethos to the images of exploitation circulating in dominant fields of
representation. By also refusing to write about herself as a young
woman within the dominant tropes she assumes the reader/viewer

brings to the image and her poem, she also creates a resistant ethos to the ways in which visual images both reflect and perpetuate dominant cultural messages. Provocatively, she rewrites the old adage of "thinking before you speak" with the admonition of "looking before/you think." She is calling for her audience to first "look" at her portrait without preconceived notions and *then* to determine what they "think" about her. Lynn's artistic vision here as a photographer and a writer are shaped by the social context in terms of both what prevailing images she is aware of and what alternative images she wishes to create. Like Weems, Lynn seems intent to "to describe simply and directly those aspects of American culture in need of deeper illumination." For Lynn, "those aspects" in need of "illumination" are her own internal resources and her writerly identity—that which is "deep within" and often obfuscated by external judgments related to race, youth, and gender.

In their self-portraits, both Geneva and Lynn name their social locations as African American women. By presenting their photographs and writing, they both also claim their identities as artists. And, as both young women of color and artists, Lynn and Geneva directly address the viewer/reader in their poems. They implicate their audience by disrupting the normalizing gazes that we may bring to the work and by exposing gazes of social repression. They insist that we see them differently and see them, perhaps for the first time, on their own terms. They insist that we see them as subjects who are very much aware of the complex nature of representation and the ways they have been positioned within systems of representation. Through the inquiry questions serving as prominent rhetorical devices in both of their poems, Geneva and Lynn insist that we as viewers assume responsibility for the disruptive visions they promote in their artistic creations.

The young women in Sistahs consistently used writing and photography to express themselves in ways that drew attention to the inaccurate ways in which they believed they were being characterized and consistently asserted their own power to name, represent, and define their own identities and realities. In doing so, they not only critiqued and expressed resistance to controlling images but also engaged in counter-hegemonic expressive practices that supported a movement from definition to self-definition. Therefore, in ways that may at first appear to be counterintuitive, self-portrait work was a profoundly social endeavor. Within a framework of photography as a social practice, the photographs emerged from and reached out toward the social context.

Advocating Social Change

Figure 3. Maya's Self Portrait

As a small group of students and I gathered around a table to pre-pare for our first public presentation of their writing and photography at an educational research conference, Jasmyn located one of Maya's self-portraits underneath a pile of photographs and proclaimed, "This one. We have to use this one." As she held up the photograph (Figure 3) we all seemed to recognize instantaneously the powerful framing potential of this image. Within moments, we decided this image would play a prominent role in our presentation. This image clearly and arrestingly suggests the motifs of women's strength and solidarity present throughout the art and poetry we had been study-ing and throughout the students' own creative works. On an even deeper and more provocative level, however, I believe we were drawn to the photograph because of the unique forms of artistry involved in producing this image and the intentionality with which it was created: Maya took this photograph of herself, by herself. She was solely in control of crafting the image and its message. By framing our presentation with this image, we would be honoring this impulse toward embracing the arts and literacy as venues for the intertwined purposes of both self-definition and social change.

Because this image suggests these intertwined purposes, it has in many ways become what Wendy Hesford (1999) might call an "image metaphor" for my inquiry into photography as a social practice and for the themes of social change often embedded in the students' photography. Here, a young woman physically asserts her strength *and* artistically expresses herself at the same time. These intertwined movements—of one arm raised in a sign of strength while the other arm takes the photograph—encapsulate desires for self-possession and self-representation, for agency and for art, for self-determination and social change. At a later point when Maya described the image to me, she explained, "That's me trying to be a strong Black woman." As in much of the literary and photographic work we presented at the conference, Maya's self-portrait and her description suggest a complex engagement with the creative process to imagine new possibilities for the self and the world through the use of gesture, light, and words and to assert a textured subjectivity to herself and to those who would view her creative works. Artists, as Maxine Greene (2000) writes, hold in productive tension lived realities and imagined possibilities and "know about spaces opening in imagination, even as they understand what it means to be situated in the world and to speak (or paint or dance) from the vantage point of their situations" (p. 293). Making art from and about the self and in recognition of the complex ways in which ideologies of race and gender materially construct the self, Maya creates a self-portrait where she both envisions and enacts herself as strong and powerful, as an artist and a creator.

In many ways, Maya's image shares a resonance with the images produced by Geneva and Lynn, who also claim this medium as a tool for self-definition and who take on identities as artists to use photography for personal and social ends. For Geneva and Lynn, and for Maya, these impulses became enacted throughout the processes involved in creating a self-portrait: determining the message of the image, considering a variety of options for composing the image, and working out the logistical challenges of taking a self-portrait. In writing about the photograph, Geneva and Lynn both purposely addressed an audience through the use of inquiry questions and the

second-person voice in a way that positioned them as artists working
in the service of not only self-definition but also intervention into
dominant ideologies and visual regimes. When we took the students'
work public through exhibitions and publications, these intervention-
ist impulses became even further evident and even sharper because of
the presence of actual audiences ranging from members of the school
community to the broader educational research community. In these
cases, the students were claiming identities not only as artists and
poets communicating to themselves and to each other but also as
public artists and poets communicating to others in multiple social
contexts.

Because of Maya's own political commitments, expressed in both
her poetry and her photography, she agreed to have this image play a
prominent role in the presentation. In conjunction with the image being
shown, Maya chose to read one of her poems in which she speaks
about claiming one's power for personal and collective change:

> Wake up! Get up rise up from your dark sleep
> This world is about to crumble, it's about to fall
> Come on sisters we can't sit still while our
> Life is being fondled with, shake my brothers
> We're losing you by the hundreds and thousands
> And millions we need your manliness to
> Rearrange the deteriorating remains that they left us
> My sisters speak up! I can't hear you!
> What? Say it louder; they muted you for centuries!
> Come on speak up! We are not going to sit in the
> Back ground while the sand in the hour glass that represents the
> Meager lifespan they gifted us with slip away
> Sisters, why are you trembling now release that cannon
> The cannon that you feel in the pit of our belly, yesss
> It's been there for too long release it
> My brothers, stand up wait I can't see you I said stand up
> And crush the barriers that corner you,
> Stand up and stomp on the floating echoes that kill your dreams
> And scatter your sources of education,
> Ignite a flame on the black and white that has labeled you
> Ignorant
> My sisters, I am, I mean we are, I mean they are, I mean us are
> I mean we are all in this fight together

My brothers let this be the push you need to redeem yourself,
To regain your strength, dignity and identity
Wake up!
Rise up and take your stance

Maya's words here suggest these interconnections between personal and social change, between personal awareness and group
solidarity, between internal revelations and public declarations. Her
self-portrait and her poem suggest the socially transformative impulses of the students' work, impulses that often reflected what bell
hooks (1995) calls an "awareness of the radical place that art occu-
pies within freedom struggle" (p. 9). In the poem, with her powerful
image of herself as a backdrop, not only does Maya claim the transformative power of writing, she also calls on her audience to rise up
to fight injustice. She voices both an urgent articulation of social
oppression and a hopeful vision of social transformation. She extends
her own considerable rhetorical and poetic resources to inspire
others—not only our group, but also those she names her brothers, her
sisters—toward solidarity.

Discussion: "Spaces Opening in Imagination"

As an artistic medium so fundamentally concerned with issues of
representation, and as a medium so well-suited for the self-reflexive
pursuit of image making, photography holds great potential for
engaging students in exploring complex issues of identity and for
supporting creative projects focused on the autobiographical. However, consideration of photography as a social practice and as a
medium with the potential to serve a range of personal, social, and
political purposes is rare within prevalent models of photography
instruction, which often reflect exclusive emphasis on skill acquisition.
Correspondingly, as Ursula Kelly (1997) argues, even the most radical
literacy pedagogies have neglected to assist students in paying
attention to the "nature of the gaze," despite the very visual culture
we live in and despite the intertwining of psychic, physical, and
sexual violence within dominant forms of image making. As she
writes:

> Questions of the nature of the gaze and sexual objectification, victimization
> and violence point to the need for literacy practices or ways of reading the

cultural representations through which ways of looking are constructed and deployed. (p. 102)

Within the community of Sistahs, the students envisioned auto-biographical engagements as creative sites for the interrogation of these gazes of social repression and for the foregrounding of their own gazes. What emerges in the students' writing and photography are therefore clearly not only alternatives to what Ewald (2000) termed an "exclusively adult vision" of reality but also alternatives to notions that the uses of technologies within classrooms can be sepa-rated from the social context. By pursuing autobiographical work where race and gender were central components of their inquiry, the students suggest the continuing need for an enlargement of our under-standing of the autobiographical to reflect the socially situated and mediated nature of identities and experience (Hesford, 1999), rather than reflecting a unified, "pure," and authentic self.

The students' work in this context also highlights the primacy of relationships in fostering knowledge production. Within this inten-tional community, the students valued mutual knowledge construc-tion around complex issues and especially around their own emerging sense of themselves. At no time was the students' desire to see and hear each other's photography and writing higher than when they were pursuing autobiographical work. In fact, this work fostered the most engagement, ethos formation, and group solidarity. From a Black feminist epistemological point of view, what occurred in the Sistahs setting suggests the meaning-making processes of young women drawing upon gendered and cultured ways of knowing both individually and collectively to produce knowledge and art.

The students' images emerged from lived experiences and re-flected an awareness of how social identities matter in taking photo-graphs and in constructing knowledge about experience. As artists inspired by the "spaces opening in imagination" (Greene, 2000, p. 293), the students held in productive tension lived realities and imagined possibilities within their creative works and also crafted alternative forms of social relationships within this in-school space. There is great potential in infusing these understandings and these orientations within our literacy pedagogies as well as in visual arts education. With these students as our inspiration, we could ask, How can we create more classroom environments responsive to the insis-tent desires for self-definition of students such as Maya, Maria, Geneva, and Lynn? How can we create more fluid boundaries between schools and communities, between students and teachers, between arts and literacies? How might we work with students in the service of nurturing their own social imaginations?

To envision photography as a social practice requires considering learning spaces as profoundly social spaces and nurturing the development of new kinds of relational practices within those spaces. There is value, I believe, in gathering around a table in a classroom and finding nodding heads after the sharing of a family photograph. There is value in co-constructing a student-centered space where the texts of students' lives become the texts of the class and where the illustrious literary and artistic traditions of socially marginalized groups serve as both backdrop and inspiration. There is a value to this work, I believe, that crosses a variety of interrelated purposes related to students' academic, personal, and artistic growth. Finally, there is value in working toward the creation of spaces for young women that welcome a shared sense of outrage and nurture a shared sense of hope. Here is where I see not only the potential of literacy, photography, and the arts to open up alternative educational spaces within schools for young women of color but also how their literary and artistic works and processes can encourage all of us, in Maya's words, to "take our stance," and in bell hooks's (1995) words, to "enhance our understanding of what it means to live as free subjects in an unfree world" (p. 9).

Notes

[1] While recognizing the limitations and concerns associated with the terminology "of color," I use it to capture the multiple racial and ethnic identities of the students involved in the study, including African American, Latina, multiracial, and Caribbean.

[2] While I had hoped to devote significant time to the discussion, analysis, and possible emulation of the counter-hegemonic work of African American artists Carrie Mae Weems, Clarissa Sligh, and Lorna Simpson, in each trimester I found both that time did not permit and that the students were more eager to use our in-class time for literacy work and to pursue their own photography projects outside of the context. While I often wished for more sustained in-class opportunities to engage with these artists, my choices reflected an interest in fostering a creative arena large and generative enough

for the students to follow their own artistic visions and to craft the course in ways that fit their desires.

References

Allen, J., Fabregas, V., Hankins, K. H., Hull, G., Labbo, L., Lawson, H. S., et al. (2002). PHOLKS Lore: Learning from photographs, families, and children. *Language Arts*, 79 (4), 312–322.

Baird, V. (Ed.). (1997). *Eye to eye: Women*. London: Serpent's Tail.

Barton, D., & Hamilton, M. (1998). *Local literacies: Reading and writing in one community*. New York: Routledge.

Brand, D. (1995). *Bread out of stone*. Toronto: Coach House Press.

Christensen, L. (2000). *Reading writing, and rising up: Teaching about social justice and the power of the written word*. Milwaukee, WI: Rethinking Schools.

Cochran-Smith, M., & Lytle, S. L. (1993). *Inside/outside: Teacher research and knowledge*. New York: Teachers College Press.

Collins, P. H. (2000). *Black feminist thought: Knowledge, consciousness, and the politics of empowerment* (2nd ed.). New York: Routledge.

Cottman, M. H., & Willis, D. (1996). *The family of black America*. New York: Crown.

Cushman, E. (1998). *The struggle and the tools: Oral and literate strategies in an inner city community*. Albany: State University of New York Press.

Deutsch, N. (2001). *Voices of our own: Mothers, daughters, and elders of the Tenderloin tell their stories*. San Francisco: My Window Books.

Dillard, C. B. (2000). The substance of things hoped for, the evidence of things not seen: Examining an endarkened feminist epistemology in educational research and leadership. *The International Journal of Qualitative Studies in Education*, 13(6), 661–681.

Ewald, W. (2000). *Secret games: Collaborative works with children, 1969–1999*. New York: Scalo.

Ewald, W. (2001). *I wanna take me a picture: Teaching photography and writing to children*. Boston: Beacon Press.

Fine, M. (1992). *Disruptive voices: The possibilities of feminist research*. Ann Arbor: University of Michigan Press.

Franco, B. (Ed.). (2001). *Things I have to tell you: Poems and writing by teenage girls*. Cambridge, MA: Candlewick Press.

Greene, M. (2000). Lived spaces, shared spaces, public spaces. In L. Weis & M. Fine (Eds.), *Construction sites: Excavating race, class, and gender among urban youth* (pp. 293–303). New York: Teachers College Press.

Heath, S. B. (1993). Inner city life through drama: Imagining the language classroom. *TESOL Quarterly*, 27 (2), 177–192.

Heath, S. B., & Smyth, L. (1999). *ArtShow: Youth and community development*. Washington, DC: Partnership for Livable Communities.

Heller, C. E. (1997). *Until we are strong together: Women writers in the Tenderloin*. New York: Teachers College Press.

Henry, A. (1993). Missing: Black self-representations in Canadian educational research. *Canadian Journal of Education, 18*(3), 206–222.

Hesford, W. (1999). *Framing identities: Autobiography and the politics of pedagogy*. Minneapolis: University of Minnesota Press.

Hicks, D. (2002). *Reading lives: Working-class children and literacy learning*. New York: Teachers College Press.

hooks, b. (1994). *Teaching to transgress: Education as the practice of freedom*. New York: Routledge.

hooks, b. (1995). *Art on my mind: Visual politics*. New York: The New Press.

Jordan, J. (1995). Introduction. In L. Muller (Ed.), *June Jordan's poetry for the people: A revolutionary blueprint* (pp. 1-9) New York: Routledge.

Kelly, U. A. (1997). *Schooling desire: Literacy, cultural politics, and pedagogy*. New York: Routledge.

Kirsh, A., & Sterling, S. F. (1993). *Carrie Mae Weems*. Washington, DC: National Museum of Women in the Arts.

Landay, E., Meehan, M., Newman, A. L., Wooton, K., & King, D. W. (2001). "Postcards from America": Linking classroom and community in an ESL class. *English Journal*, 90 (5), 66–74.

Lather, P. (1991). *Getting smart: Feminist research and pedagogy with/in the postmodern*. New York: Routledge.

Morrison, T. (1994). The Nobel lecture in literature 1993. New York: Knopf.

Neumaier, D. (1995). Introduction. In D. Neumaier (Ed.), *Reframings: New American feminist photographies* (pp. 1–12). Philadelphia: Temple University Press.

Omolade, B. (1987). A Black feminist pedagogy. *Women's Studies Quarterly, 15*, 32–39.

Orellana, M. F., & Hernández, A. (1999). Taking the walk: Children reading urban environmental print. *The Reading Teacher, 52* (6), 612–619.

Piché, T., & Golden, T. (1998). *Carrie Mae Weems: Recent work, 1992–1998*. New York: George Braziller.

Royster, J. J. (1996). When the first voice you hear is not your own. *College Composition and Communication, 47* (1), 29–40.

Royster, J. J. (2000). *Traces of a stream: Literacy and social chance among African American women.* Pittsburgh: University of Pittsburgh Press.

Silence Speaks. (n.d.). Silence speaks: Digital storytelling in support of healing and violence prevention. Retrieved June 17, 2004, from http://www.silencespeaks.org.

Skilton-Sylvester, E. (2002). Literate at home but not at school: A Cambodian girl's journey from playwright to struggling writer. In G. Hull & K. Schultz (Eds.), *School's out! Bridging out-of-school literacies with classroom practice* (pp. 61–90). New York: Teachers College Press.

Street, B. (Ed.). (1993). *Cross-cultural approaches to literacy.* Cambridge, UK: Cambridge University Press.

Street, B. (1995). *Social literacies.* New York: Longman.

Thompson, K., & Mac Austin, H. (Eds.). (1999). *The face of our past: Images of Black women from colonial America to the present.* Bloomington: Indiana University Press.

Trinh, T. M. (1991). *When the moon waxes red: Representation, gender and cultural politics.* New York: Routledge.

Way, N. (1998). *Everyday courage: The lives and stories of urban teenagers.* New York: New York University Press.

Wissman, K. (2003). "Can't let it all go unsaid": Sistahs reading, writing, and photographing their lives. *Penn GSE Perspectives on Urban Education, 2*(1). Retrieved September 17, 2004, from http://www.urbanedjournal.org/archive/Issue3/notes/notes0006.html.

Wolf, D. (1996). *Feminist dilemmas in fieldwork.* Boulder, CO: Westview Press.

Wright, B. J. (1992). Back talk: Recoding the body. In B. J. Wright & S. V. Hartman (Eds.), *Lorna Simpson: For the sake of the viewer* (pp. 12–24). New York: Universe.

Wright, B. J., & Hartman, S. V. (Eds.). (1992). *Lorna Simpson: For the sake of the viewer.* New York: Universe.

Young, M. D. (2000). Considering (irreconcilable?) contradictions in cross-group feminist research. *Qualitative Studies in Education*, 13 (6), 629–660.

Response to Wissman

Katie Hyde

Wissman's participatory research looks at how young women of color (a student group who called themselves "Sistahs") create and connect with photographs through discussion and writing. She emphasizes the intentionality of the Sistahs' photographic process, which she found achieved three personal and social purposes: building relationships, pursuing self-definition, and advocating social change. In Wissman's analysis, and worth repeating, I found a broader commentary on knowledge—specifically, the benefits of knowledge development beginning with the self, the question of what counts as knowledge, and the stakes at hand for educators who invite an exchange of knowledge between students and themselves.

Starting with the Self

Drawing upon Wendy Ewald's "Literacy Through Photography" (LTP) model, Wissman designed her course so that the learning process would begin with the self. Wissman's chapter provides a testimony to the value of student-centered pedagogy. We see that a crucial component of this approach is allowing students to be the experts. Asking students to investigate and tell their own stories through photography and writing can transform their level of interest and engagement and even their potential as students. Focusing on what is familiar guarantees students will have something, often plenty to say; likewise, it reassures students that their personal stories and experiences represent valuable knowledge.

Like Wissman, the LTP teachers with whom I have worked in Durham, North Carolina, have witnessed their students' evolution as writers, critical thinkers, and collaborators. An example comes from a photography project my former colleague Dwayne Dixon designed utilizing the architectural concept of desire lines—the paths we create to get from one place to another, variations on the routes designated by sidewalks and roads. His fifth-grade students photographed the desire lines they had taken for granted until then. One student, Shawn, focused on the meandering route he had fashioned to get from home to his grandmother's church. To accompany his photographs, Shawn wrote a detailed and elaborate story—a remarkable accomplishment since he usually wrote little to nothing in school. Unlike other classroom assignments and activities, this project brought to light Shawn's autonomy, creativity, and, more intimately, his love for his grandmother. Furthermore, it revealed that his writing "problem" was not about skill but about the style and content of instruction. In addition, with his photographs, Shawn shared a part of his life where he possessed knowledge and power. Belonging to him alone, this path was secret and inaccessible to adult neighbors more accustomed to traveling by car and even to other children, especially white children, who would find themselves lost in his racially segregated neighborhood.

It is clear from this and Wissman's examples that photography focused on the self can easily segue into an investigation of social issues, relationships, and identities. The concrete, nuanced details of Shawn's work provided the starting point for a conversation about how race and age influence the way people move through and negotiate space—an otherwise abstract concept. As Wissman points out, self-portraits also provide an avenue for commentary on and critique of cultural patterns and stereotypes. Wissman's discussion of the social purposes of the Sistahs' photography recalls hooks's (1994) discussion of the importance to black families of both making and displaying family photographs that challenge racist images. She describes walls of purposefully and lovingly placed images within black homes as "sites of resistance" (p. 47).

The exploration of self and social identities through photography has value for all students, including members of dominant groups. I recently worked with multiracial classrooms on a project called "Black Self/White Self," developed by Ewald to explore racial identity. Students first developed a written and visual self-portrait and then created another portrait in which they imagined themselves having a different racial/ethnic identity. One of the challenges for the white students involved recognizing that race is important in their own experiences not only in the lives of students of color. Unlike the Sistahs, they were unaccustomed to examining their identities through a racial lens. When asked to reflect upon the first time race meant something to them, several students of color quickly named specific instances of being singled out or discriminated against on the basis of race; in contrast, one white student confessed, "I truly don't know." Whereas for some students, explorations of identity meant crafting self-representations in conversation with and in opposition to stereotypes, the process helped other students discover that representation is a powerful tool and a contentious topic.

Re-Envisioning Knowledge

Wissman's practice and analysis addresses such epistemological questions as what counts as knowledge, what purposes are served in pursuing knowledge, and who can produce knowledge. She validates the knowledge that her young students naturally possess; furthermore, Wissman considers the pictures the Sistahs produce as knowledge. As with the lyrics sung and stories shared by black women in Collins's (2000) articulation of an alternative, black feminist epistemology, in making photographs, the Sistahs are making knowledge claims. To name the Sistahs' photographs as knowledge reminds us of the underestimated value and complexity of visual information. Moreover, it requires that we recognize students as the producers, not only consumers, of knowledge.

Recall Lynn's poem, which reminds us to "look before we think." Lynn addresses both our way of seeing and our way of representing. She warns against embellishing what we see with preconceptions and advocates for the making of counter-hegemonic images. Even more fundamentally, Lynn asks us to look and look carefully. Her words remind us that photography is a language, a way of communicating. For some, especially nonliterate people or students who lack the Sistahs' skill and passion for writing, photography offers an *alternative* way to say something.

Photography is a complex language, and Wissman's concern about the common misinterpretation of photographs is reasonable. We see in her students' work a skillful interweaving of writing and photography. However, I would caution against relying too heavily on words to explain or clarify photographs. This discourages our mindful reading of visual images and downplays photographers' agency in the actual making of pictures. It is Lynn's photographic portrait, after all, that tells us what she wants us to know about her; we see Lynn as a pensive, serious person—a thinker and a writer.

Lynn's portrait is crafted intentionally. This very agency represents another value of naming the young women's photographs as knowledge claims. Decoding the meaning of images, a common goal of media literacy lessons, is substantially different from actually creating images and thereby deliberately communicating with the language of photography. In addition to choosing their subject matter, the Sistahs decided exactly how to frame their subjects—what to include and exclude, from what angle and distance to shoot, and at what precise moment. In other words, they used cameras as tools to represent a subject or scene in precisely the way that communicates their own understanding of and feelings about their subjects. Whereas the photographs the students brought in from home furnished evidence with which the young women could relate stories of their families, communities, and histories, when they made their pictures they *produced* evidence of who they are.

Moreover, it is significant that Wissman's students made photographs from their own standpoint as young women of color. Portraying themselves as strong, intelligent, complicated, and multitalented young women, the Sistahs disrupted stereotypical cultural representations. Their work challenged conventional knowledge as well as traditional ideas about who possesses and creates knowledge.

What's at Stake for Teachers

Having discussed the value for students of Wissman's alternative pedagogy and broadened notion regarding what constitutes knowledge, I believe it is also worthwhile to consider, in closing, what is at stake for teachers. Wissman acknowledges that her reflective field notes included entries about "the tensions and complexities of pursuing this work as a white woman . . . [and] moments of discomfort . . . as well as moments of open exploration and trust." Likewise, during our LTP trainings, teachers anticipate both the possibilities and challenges of introducing new modes of representation. They are curious as well as hesitant about what their students´ photographs will reveal.

Some teachers, for instance, shy away from the idea of students using photography to represent the interior world of their dreams (one of LTP's core themes) when they see the gruesome nightmares occasionally revealed in some students´ pictures. They worry that the photographic assignment will evoke bad dreams or possibly memories about the death of a parent, an abusive situation, or any other family struggle. This hesitation may represent a desire to preserve a simplistic image of young people's innocence or a preference to remain outside students´ realities. It may also imply a fear of losing control.

Student-centered pedagogy requires that teachers acknowledge their power and relinquish some of it. It demands that teachers see themselves as learners and their practice as an inductive process.

Educators must embrace the unexpected so they may skillfully excavate and come to understand new and sometimes unsettling information.

Photographs elicit stories and provoke questions. When teachers allow their role to shift temporarily to that of a learner, they gain a more nuanced understanding of their students' home lives and personal histories. Although at times challenging, this openness to learning from students is essential, especially when teachers' own cultural reality differs from that of their students. Photographic representations provide teachers with an innovative and effective way to connect with their students—an outcome as fundamental as strengthening students´ visual and written communication skills and providing them with an opportunity for self-representation. In the end, despite uneasy moments, pressure regarding test scores, fears of the unknown, and endless other demands, teachers, too, stand to gain when they do something different, when they allow students to create complex and knowing self-representations and bring their worlds into the classroom.

References

Collins, P. H. (2000). *Black feminist thought: Knowledge, consciousness, and the politics of empowerment* (2nd ed). New York: Routledge.

hooks, b. (1994). *Teaching to transgress: Education as the practice of freedom.* New York: Routledge.

Response to Wissman

Valerie Kinloch

I appreciate Wissman's efforts to cross boundaries by incorporating technology and theory into her work. She discusses literacy as a process of engaging learners in an exploration of complex issues of identity and representation, photography as a social practice and an act of political resistance, and autobiographical engagements as sites where cultural representations of meaning making are interrogated. Her work is important.

Wissman's work with urban female high school teenagers who comprise "Sistahs" is situated in an ideological framing of literacy as social practice that insists, as Street (2005) tells us, "the ways in which people address reading and writing are themselves rooted in conceptions of knowledge, identity, being" (p. 418). This way of seeing literacy values people's lived experiences, identities, and "funds of knowledge" (Moll & Gonzalez, 2001). Or, as Wissman argues, literacy as a socially transformative practice invites "the texts of students' lives [to] become the texts of the class" and the "illustrious literary and artistic traditions of socially marginalized groups serve as both backdrop and inspiration." Contributing to a vision of literacy as social practice, Wissman uses an arts-based approach to encourage teenagers to examine public and private conceptions of self through technology (i.e., digital cameras) and storytelling (i.e., autobiographical texts).

Throughout her chapter, Wissman provides an important example of how technology can be used to establish connections, narrate stories, foster collaborative learning, and, quite provocatively, cross seemingly challenging racial divisions. She is aware of how the teenagers, identifying as Puerto Rican, black/Grenadian, African American, and multiracial, use technology to expose aspects of their lives to an "outsider" instructor: a white woman who recognizes her "limitations in perspective and experience." Wissman encourages Madonna, Jasmyn, Renee, and the other teenagers to use personal experiences to comment on the worlds in which they live. The use of technology involves the teenagers in meaning-making processes where family photographs, poetry, and narrative writing take center stage, where the art that is created is not decorative but expressive in its documentation of autobiographical selves.

Readers of this essay are able to witness that there is nothing too daunting or complicated about employing technology to investigate lived experiences. Cameras of all sorts are attention givers and have the power to transform fixed understandings of identities. Whatever is receiving attention in the lens of the camera is important and requires attention; no one seems to realize this point more than the teenagers, who demand attention be paid to their lives. For example, Madonna and Jasmyn understand the work of Sistahs as responses to the lack of opportunities in schools for young females "to make a way" and "be represented in society." Maria views her photographs as symbolic of her Puerto Rican culture, identity, and family— photographs that portray the value of belonging to a familial network. All in all, the dynamic teenagers in this group challenge traditional notions of identity by experimenting with the interconnections of photography and writing, which are useful in their pursuit to create meaningful relationships and advocate for social change in and out of school.

The teenagers utilize the camera to capture temporal-spatial conditions of everyday life. Exploring identities as socially situated in front of and behind the cameras, the teenagers demonstrate "the limitations of the routinized ways we engage in the process of sense making through visual means." They construct images, they use language, and they search for ways to represent themselves in opposition to "the deficit and deviancy discourses circulating in the educational field that reinforce images of all urban young women of color as living in the midst of crisis and despair." The work produced by the teenagers, and Wissman's documentation of the experience, are breathtaking. The insistence that teenagers can use technology to participate in autobiographical experiences while re-producing representations of self is an important idea that contributes to research on literacy as social practice.

On another level, Wissman's work speaks to young people's participation in democratic engagements (Kinloch, 2005), experiences that are grounded in reciprocity, mutual exchanges, and collaboration, experiences that are often ignored in schools. democratic engagements, I argue, have their roots in Deweyan thought and recognize education as a social process. In a recent study of my own, I describe two abbreviated creative writing experiences with urban middle school students in Texas. In particular, I investigate pedagogical practices, strategies, and relationships that resulted from students' involvement with poetry. Much as Wissman frames photography as a social practice, I frame creative writing, poetry in particular, as a transformative act and activity that encourages democratic forms of engagements among learners. Such work can encourage us to think about how to use creative techniques to help students express themselves in multiple ways.

Whether students are interacting in a poetry workshop, a photography planning session, or an after-school program, their engagements with one another, however democratic, can enhance their vision of themselves in the world. Through democratic engagements and supportive relationships, youngsters can challenge multiple complex discourses (i.e., mainstream cultural messages, dominant ideologies, representations of hopelessness) as they experiment with multimodal forms of learning. For Wissman, this happens when the teenagers share photographs and autobiographical texts with one another, or when they "claim their identities as artists." For me, this occurred when my former middle school participants listened to and offered feedback on poetic texts created by their peers, or when my current high school participants in Harlem (New York City) use their digital cameras to capture images of a black community undergoing rapid gentrification and share their images/narratives with family, friends, and community members. The youngsters use cameras to connect their lives with the world they had previously felt disconnected from; in doing this, they produce autobiographical texts (Wissman) and experience democratic engagements (Kinloch).

References

Kinloch, V. (2005). Poetry, literacy, and creativity: Fostering effective learning strategies in an urban classroom. *English Education, 37*(2), 96–114.

Moll, L., & Gonzalez, N. (2001). Lessons from research with language-minority children. In E. Cushman, E. R. Kintgen, B. M. Kroll, & M. Rose (Eds.), *Literacy: A critical sourcebook* (pp. 156–171). Boston: St. Martin's.

Street, B. V. (2005). Recent applications of New Literacy Studies in educational contexts. *Research in the Teaching of English, 39*(4), 417–423.

Chapter Three

"Are We Our Brothers' Keepers?": Exploring the Social Functions of Reading in the Life of an African American Urban Adolescent

Jeanine M. Staples

> It is necessary that we move beyond the familiar notion of reading as an isolated encounter between reader and text . . . and look not so much at the relationships between the reader and the text as at the ways in which meanings are socially established and circulated. Rather than merely concentrating on how young people read particular texts, we also want to consider the *social functions* that their readings perform. Broadly speaking, we want to move away from a notion of reading as merely a matter of individual "response," and to redefine it as part of a broader process of social circulation and use, which we might term culture. (Buckingham & Sefton-Green, 1994, p. 18)

Understanding the social functions that reading performs in the lives of urban adolescents placed at risk of academic failure is of particular interest to literacy educators and researchers. If, as Buckingham and Sefton-Green (1994) suggest, reading acts as an aspect of culture and provides ways for individuals to make sense of social situations that affect lived experiences, then struggling urban students have ways of making meaning from texts and assisting their understanding of the world they live in. Grasping students' ways of understanding is crucial because they provide points of entry to student motivation and authentic recommendations for teacher practice. As a high school teacher in an inner-city school, I sought these points of entry and attempted to construct venues both in and outside of schools where my students could share the social functions of their readings. Most recently, I assumed the roles of teacher and researcher when, over fifteen consecutive months, I (co)developed an after-school program in an inner-city high school called Youth Leadership.

The program comprised twelve low-income young men and women ranging in age from fifteen to eighteen. Most of my students were described as "disengaged readers" by their regular teachers. They disassociated themselves from individual engagements with traditional print texts. They were uninterested in exercising literacy skills (such as print recognition, phonological awareness, syntactic rules, and vocabulary usage) (Dean, 2000). They were also not interested in sharing their literacy practices—the socially situated, culturally informed, and politically loaded modus operandi by which people move beyond decoding, site recognition, or rote memorization of words on printed pages to "observable and ideological patterns of behavior across literacy events" (Hornberger, 2000, p. 344). Such practices lead to knowledge production, critical analysis, and interpretation of words, images, ideas, and (re)presentations embedded within texts (Gee, 2000, 2001; Moje, 2004; Moje & Young, 2000). As a way to motivate students to share the ways they disassociated themselves from the "disengaged" category outside of school, I shared power and authority in our after-school community.

For example, my students and I worked together to select media as world-texts; some included movies, television shows, Internet websites, and a number of popular periodicals. Students helped develop the structure of our meeting time after school by choosing activities we participated in (such as opening exercises, media reading, journal writing, community conversations, and closing reflections) and the appropriate times to execute them. In researching our experiences with media texts, many students also assumed the responsibility of scheduling audio recordings of whole-group conversations, initiating individual interviews, and completing member checks of participants' transcripts, journals, and field notes. As a result of this inclusion, the intermediary space of after school doubled as a space of freedom within which literacy practices could be expressed with very little prescription. It is within this context that students read differently and I explored the social functions their reading performed through their literacy practices.

For instance, several young women I worked with routinely used magazine articles (from *Ebony, Teen People,* and *Black Girl Magazine*) and television situations (from shows such as *Girlfriends* or *The Parkers*) to think through social and political issues relative to African American women discussed in their English or History classes. Many young men I worked with read periodicals such as *Vibe* and *The Source* and made interesting correlations between music artists, actors, sports figures, and ideas about masculinity and sexuality. I carefully observed what happened and noted that students used the narratives and images found in media to connect scholarly ideas and personal understandings. The same students who would not (or thought they could not) read "well" and initiate complex conversations about social constructs and cultural phenomena (such as race, class, and gender) became consistently engaged with media texts and eventually integrated more traditional texts to explore their interests. Media acted as a sort of common ground, and the students' interpretation and understanding of the nuances, images, and representations found in these texts were discussed at length among all members of the group. They used the latest rap lyrics, magazine and newspaper articles, Internet websites, films, and television show episodes as springboards for conversations with each other and with me.

Initially, I did not call the teaching and learning that took place around media "reading." Neither did I consider my students' habits of work "literacy practices" (Barton, Hamilton, & Ivanič, 2000). I did not name our work this way because we did not focus on reading in a traditional sense. For instance, we did not access texts in a typical teaching/learning context. We did not exclusively engage traditional print texts. Nor did we value individual experiences with texts over communal ones. We also did not objectify texts as singularly prescriptive documents. That is, we did not "study" media texts to tease out stereotypical images, violence, or gratuitous sex scenes as examples of socially detrimental imagery. Instead, we read media as popular culture narratives and engaged them receptively, remaining open to whatever stories provoked or challenged us. I attempted to (co)create respectful and receptive reading spaces within (co) constructed after-school communities with students who might not consider themselves successful readers (Lee, 2004; Street, 1995). These communities were intentionally open to the texts that moved students intellectually, culturally, politically, emotionally, socially, and, often, spiritually. I encouraged their questions and critical conversations about the texts we chose and began to see them as indicators of the social functions of their reading. I used their pondering as segues for their conceptual and analytical development as readers.

I found that searching for the social functions of students' reading within this framework—one of deliberate invitation, support, facilitation, and advisement—activated my teaching/learning life in unexpected and meaningful ways. Through my work as an after-school teacher, I came to deeper realizations about the social functions of reading in my students' lives. I also began to see the pedagogical benefits of being a student of students. I thought differently about the value of the after-school space as a site for urban literacy education and reading research. I learned to rely on unconventional visions of literacy to motivate students, thereby gaining insight into their literate worlds and capabilities. In addition, I thought deeply about the levels of interaction in the communities that were co-constructed by talking openly about purposes, intentions, objectives, and outcomes with students. I argue that examinations of the social functions reading performs in the lives of urban adolescents can inform ideas about student motivation and teacher practice. To this end, I examine the contributions made to our after-school program by a student named James.

Theoretical and Interpretive Frames

I use the Freirean theory of reading the world and the word to consider the social functions James's reading performed. Freire (1987) first coined the provocative notion that reading the world precedes reading the word. He suggested:

> Reading does not consist merely of decoding the written word or language; rather, it is preceded by and intertwined with knowledge of the world. Language and reality are dynamically interconnected. The understanding attained by critical reading of a text implies perceiving the relationship between text and context. (p. 11)

The Freirean conception of reading—as ever emerging, cyclical processes of oral, visual, aural, tactile, social, emotional, cultural, and cognitive understandings that bear up, manipulate, and affect knowledge production through contextual and textual awareness— relies heavily on the notion that one's perceptual awareness is key to reading deeply. Freire theorizes that there is a "movement from the world to the word that is always present" and that movement is often navigated through reflective, responsive discourse (1987, p. 12). Verbal responses to world-texts (such as media) reveal the "word universe of people who are learning, expressing their actual language, their anxieties, fears, demands, and dreams" (p. 13). These responses suggest that "reading the word is not preceded merely by reading the world, but by a certain form of writing it or rewriting it, that is, of transforming it by means of conscious, practical work" (p. 13).

According to the Freirean theory, critical readers perceive and conceptualize the world before the word, establishing a movement between the texts of each. They also create discourses to respond to world- and word-texts and navigate activity between them. Freire (1987) contends that "surveying the word universe gives us the people's words, pregnant with 'codifications,' pictures representing real situations" (p. 13). When the word universe of learners is realized, the possibility of transforming world- and word-texts becomes apparent because social functions performed by readings become apparent. The kinetic energy promised by these social functions invokes a type of authorship that may (re)position "at-risk" urban adolescents, who are routinely placed at risk of social, academic, and political failure by schools and teachers who misunderstand their literate identities and literacy practices, into stances of power.

My description of the social functions James's reading performs is shaped by my interpretive framework, which is defined by theories of adolescent literacies, critical black feminism, and critical race theory. Theories about adolescent literacies explore the role of media and alternative teaching/learning spaces in the lives of adolescent readers and writers, particularly those who are resistant to traditional conceptions of literacy and the confines of school (Gee, 2000, 2001; Hull & Schultz, 2002; Moje, 2004; Moje & Young, 2000). As these theories gel, it is apparent that attention to the relationship between literacy practices and the social functions reading performs is inadequate. Instead, there is a great deal of focus on the ways technology, popular culture, and social situations cooperate to affect adolescent literacy development. On the other hand, critical black feminists attend to the social functions that reading performs for the *individual*, who is traditionally assumed to be oppressed by social and political marginalization (Canon, 1995; Collins, 1990; hooks, 1989a, 1989b). They consider literacy as uniquely tied to cultural and social awareness because it is often cooperatively generated between genders, age groups, and socioeconomic classes. Critical black feminists also centralize the notion of voice as a valid instrument of authority and call for teaching and research that honors situated student and teacher voices as integral informants, without which little truth and understanding about education can be attained. Because my work revolves around African American urban adolescents, I also draw on critical race theory a great deal. Ladson-Billings (1999) identifies three features of a critical race theory of education. These are acknowledgment that American life is institutionally and structurally racist, the understanding that civil rights laws in America are inadequate, and the realization that all people have a responsibility to acknowledge and challenge these inequities. The work represented here was, in part, informed by these theories.

I echo Blackburn (2002/2003) in noting that these theories influenced my research not only insofar as it is critical, with respect to the literacy of historically marginalized students, but also insofar as it is activist. When I identify my research as critical I mean that I "paid attention to issues of power, particularly inequitable power dynamics" in students' responses to world- and word-texts (Blackburn, 2002/2003, p. 314). By activist, I mean that I worked to help students change such dynamics—through the instrumentality of their literacy practice and the social function of their reading. When I state that this study is both critical and activist, I am thinking not only of working for social justice on a grand scale but also about what St. Pierre and Pillow (2000) called "modest resistance and freedoms [that] are offered to us on a daily basis," particularly through literacy work (p. 4). Drawing from this understanding of critical and activist stances, I embarked on the study (re)presented here.

"Are We our Brothers' Keepers?": Cultural Criticism as a Social Function for Understanding and Resistance

James was a 16-year-old teenager in Youth Leadership. Like other students, he was not interested in traditional reading and writing inside of school. However, when engaged with media and discussing the implications of media stories with his peers, James began to locate some inspiring social functions for reading. Because many of my students' responses to texts were audiotaped, James had access to several transcripts in which he articulated thoughts about various characters, plot development, vocabulary and word choice, social stratifications, and so on. As he conducted member checks of these transcripts, he began to notice a recurring theme in his interests. He discussed with me his attention to the circumstances of African American men as they were (re)presented in media we read. He noted that he frequently discussed "brothas and the stuff we be goin' through" and that he "always seem[ed] to be talkin' bout brothas" (individual interview, January 18, 2002). As James became more interested in his own voice as it was documented in our community transcripts, he developed a strategy for dealing with difficult media stories involving African American men.

James began to copy his own words from transcripts and use them as inspirational or provocative quotes. He began to revise sentences and paragraphs that he spoke and eventually became interested in juxtaposing them with other voices. He worked to pull our transcripts apart like puzzle pieces and put them back together again in ways that were interesting to him. I seized the opportunity to capitalize on his interest and asked him to coauthor a poem with me. I wanted to use our transcribed words to flesh out conflicting responses James and I had in regard to our reading of the death of a local African American young man in the city. After nearly two weeks of poring over two sets of transcripts and several journal entries, teasing our voices out and rearranging them, James and I developed a poem depicting our disparate reading experiences. The poem is titled "Are we our brothers' keepers?" It is in response to a story students in Youth Leadership read in a local newspaper and on the local news.

The media story (covered in newspapers and evening news programs) had to do with the murder of a young man who had attended The High School and lived in the western part of The City— our local neighborhood. Several students brought the story to the attention of the group for reading and discussion. It was predicted that the boy would be a powerhouse rap artist. He was described as influential in local circles and well connected to powerful names in hip-hop. He was admired by many of the students in Youth Leadership. Also, he was (re)presented warmly and solemnly in media texts we surveyed, being characterized as a promising individual who was struck down as he neared his prime as an artist. I was interested in students' processes of constructing meaning about the life and death of this person as a native son, a fellow African American, and as a an urban adolescent. After we read the televised news broadcast of the MC's death and the newspaper's tribute to him, I asked students to respond verbally or in writing. James's reading was particularly critical and defiant. He resisted affiliation with the murdered artist, even after admitting to knowing him as a close acquaintance. His articulations about the importance of segmenting one's affairs, isolating individuals, and absolving oneself from community interdependence struck me as an informed political decision that contested his familial, social, and cultural connections. His references to lyrics from a popular rap song that toyed with the homonyms "piece" and "peace," "cents" and "sense" showed his appreciation of irony and satire within the language of texts' stories. And his dismissal of the possibility of African Americans being "written, produced or directed differently" in media texts demonstrates some experientially informed disbelief in the possibility of effecting change (Jeanine, whole-group conversation, January 30, 2002).

No inert passivity existed within his response to the text. James clearly thought critically about his stance. He made his meaning from the story of the text. He vocalized his awareness without wavering and after a great deal of personal reflection. He was lucid about not only the story of the text but also the deeper social, political, cultural, and ideological nuances it alluded to and he rejected. We cut and pasted a mosaic of our voices with spoken words from transcripts and journals. We aligned ourselves with our views, remained true to our individual reading experiences, and developed a collaborative literacy practice to make sense of the story. James's words are represented *in italics*. My words are represented in regular font. The piece was written in March 2002. In our discussion of the murdered artist, I prompted students to consider whether they believed in taking some responsibility for each other as African American people, young men and women, or because of any other unifying social or personal identity. James conveyed the most visceral reading and response.

The first poem:

I asked:
"Are we our brothers' keepers?"
You said,
"No.
I'm not."
I said,
"Yes.
We are."

Peace brother. Remember that day? We were talking about who to look out for, who to stay clear of. I asked you how you felt, what you know from the story that was shared, what you could tell us about brotherhood, sisterhood, and the hood. It was whatever. It was whatever you wanted to talk about. You didn't have much to say. So,

I asked you, again: "are we our brothers' keepers?" You said "*naw.*" I thought some more.

And later, I re-read the news on channel six and remembered your voice ringing in my head because I saw that three Black ~~brothers~~, black men were arrested yesterday. One for rape. One for murder. And, the other for armed robbery. I think two of them were around your age. 16. Damn. You said, "*Ms. J., you drawlin'. It's not that deep.*"

I remember how you shared your reading of the Center City rapist sometime last week. You said the relevance was that we all had "*to be aware of crazy niggaz on the block.*" Do you remember that James? Remember how I asked you not to use that word in that context and you groaned and nearly fell out of your chair (insert long, heavy, dramatic sigh) and said, "*Ok, ok, ok Ms. J.*" Remember how I said, "we all have to look out for one another," how I said, "we all have to have each other's back?" And you said, "*I ain't down with that. Cause Niggaz is crazy. Niggaz out here ain't got no cents. Get it? Jus like Outkast say, "Niggaz always out here talkin' bout 'peace my brother', 'peace this and peace that'. I got my peace. You got your piece. But niggaz always tryin' to get a peace a mine, so now I'ma go on and grab my piece.*" You started to laugh again, but continued. "*I'm sayin', Ms. J. . . . . I'm sayin' the kid was nice, but he wasn't kin to me.*" You were laughing so hard you almost fell out of your chair brother. Your laughter still rings in my ears.

Remember how I said "community" was what it was "all about," and you reached for the paper and pointed to it and started to (almost) shout . . . "*Ms. J., niggaz is crazy! Niggaz is crazy! I'm tryin' tell you, they crazy Ms. Staples.*" I squinted at you. You squinted back. You chuckled and said, "*look, it's all around us. Niggaz posted everywhere. Ain't nobody posin'. Niggaz is poor, raw, they drawlin', they hustlin'. I ain't gettin' in it.*" Then I asked you who you were. I asked you, "are you a part of the we, us, ours or a part of the they, them, those? Who are you in the picture? Where do you fit in the story?" You said, "*Ms. J., I know what you tryin' to do, but if they ain't my blood or my bol' my name is Binitt and I ain't in it. That's my word.*"

That broke my heart a little bit. But I pushed a little further. Wanted to dig a little deeper, see if I could get at the why, which always lies beneath. I asked you if you thought "things might be different if the stories we're surrounded with were written differently produced differently directed differently." I asked you how you might feel "if you read us in a different light." A light that casts shadows on wounds and dirt and other outwardly things, sometimes undesirable things, but shines beams of itself on goodness and beauty and honor as well. "What then?" I wondered aloud.

You said,
"huh?"

I said, "what do you think might happen if we were written differently, if we were storied differently in the stuff we're reading?" You said, *"what . . . you mean them?"* I said "us." You said, *"them?"* I said, "James, why do you separate yourself from Black people in trouble?" You said, *"Ms. J., you're losin' me."* I said, "what separates us from the brother you just read about?" You said, *"this."* You pointed to the paper crumpled in your hand. It looked like it had breath. It constricted in your fingers. *"He ain't here. He ain't mine. He ain't nobody. See?"* Then you tossed the ball into the trashcan. I heard it lightly thump the bottom of the rusted tin. I said, "what does it mean to abandon our people (yourself) because of what you read instead of what you live?" You laughed again. You said, *"look around you Ms. J., I'm livin' what I read. It ain't just what they write about niggaz, or how they talk about niggaz. It's about how we do. Look around you Ms. J. Keepin'? Keepin' what?! It ain't no keepin' nothin'. You gotta look after ya self. I know that's right."*

We locked eyes in disagreement for a minute. You did not let up. You stood inside the knowledge you shared about social stratifications, and communal separations, and the struggle between yourself and the (un)certainty in your reading. You told me how you made your meaning and you were done.

I was wondering how to (re)read and (re)present the texts.

You were ready to pass the shot. (Jeanine and James, journals / transcripts from whole-group conversation, March 2002)

Discussion

The social function James's reading performed was one of resistance and criticism. He relied on his reading experiences, layered within transcripts, journals, and the poem above, to make sense of his visceral reaction to the idea of alignment with a talented but troubled African American young man not unlike himself. As James moved between world- and word-texts, his reading functioned as a tool, useful for discerning and sense making. He assigned meaning to his beliefs and reflections. He engaged the stories from media texts that portrayed Black men as endangered, violent, destructive, and crazed.

He married the information he read with his personal experiences. And he carved out his own understanding. Finally, he defended his ideas and responses successfully. That is, the reception of his impressions and ideas caused me to rethink my own approaches to the story and to the group's interaction with it. This social function for reading should not be disregarded because it exists with respect to a media text as opposed to a traditional one. Rather, it should be coupled with other readings in an effort to support literacy in all its variation and in light of all texts.

By (co)authoring this poem, James positioned himself with more power and by sharing it he invited others to support him in his understanding. In this regard, his reading also performed the function of social leverage. That is, it moved him from a marginal position, bearing the intimation of victimization or endangerment as an African American male, to a central position, bearing the intimation of empowerment and authority. In the weeks that followed our (co)authorship, James worked to perfect his strategy for understanding. He continued to review the critical, responsive voices of Youth Leaders in transcripts and journals. He remained focused on his concerns about African American men and further questioned their (re)presentations in media texts. More than a month later, James discussed his strategy with me:

> Jeanine: So why are you so interested in these transcripts and journals Bubba [James]?
>
> James: 'Cause I can hear myself in 'em. I like that. I couldn't hear myself before.
>
> Jeanine: What do you hear?
>
> James: I can hear me talkin' about things I be thinkin' about when we readin'. I like to hear what I think . . . I mean read what I think after we finished readin' a text.
>
> Jeanine: Ok. So, what about the poems and letters you write from the transcripts and journals? Why do you do that? What does that do for you?
>
> James: It make me hear myself in another way than the original. When I can take the voices apart and put 'em back together again it help me hear myself again but in a different way. That makes me think about my response different[ly]. I like that. It keeps me thinkin' about stuff in

a different way when we readin'. That's what I wanna do. (Individual interview, April 11, 2002)

Performing the social functions of resistance/criticism and empowerment/authority, James's reading supported his desire to "think about stuff in a different way" (individual interview, April 11, 2002). By countering my perception (as an authority figure) of the slain local MC and criticizing my suggestion that he commit to a sense of community based on race and culture, James's reading performed the social function of resistance/criticism. By arguing his stance effectively in juxtaposition with my voice, without yielding to attempts at coercion, James's reading performed the social function of empowerment/authority. These social functions reflect what St. Pierre and Pillow (2000) called "modest resistance and freedoms [that] are offered to us on a daily basis" (p. 4). In this way, reading acted as a way for James to alter his stance as a social and political individual. Through his own ingenuity he capitalized on our reading experiences and texts to develop his own position and (re)write his role in world- and word-texts.

After the interview above James gave me another poem he wrote on his own. It provided an additional layer to the reasoning he presented in "Are We Our Brothers' Keepers?" He titled it "Can't Keep Nothin'." James spent several days revising the poem on his own and asked me to check and correct it through three drafts. In it he paralleled his voice with that of another student in Youth Leadership named Bashir. The young men reflect on questions they have about African American men in the city. Keeping with the social function of his reading, James resisted/criticized what he called "lost losers" and initiated empowerment/authority with his suggestion to "try and keep ya self" (whole-group conversation, April 11, 2002). James's voice is in *italics*. Bashir's voice is in regular font and in quotes.

The second poem:

Can't keep nothin'
"'Cause niggaz is crazy and ain't got no sense."
That's what I'm always tryin' to tell people. You can't trust everybody, just because they look like you.

But my bol says,

"We gotta try Bub. We gotta try to keep shit together."

But I'm always tryin' to tell people niggaz ain't Black people. "*Niggaz is niggaz. And a nigga will kill you.*"

But my bol says,

"Everything ain't lost Bub. We ain't lost everything."

But we lost a hell of a lot. Black people lost a lot because of niggaz. It's the losers that lost our stuff. The damn losers got lost and they lost our stuff in the meantime. So, "*no. I ain't my brothers' keeper. I'm keepin' my own stuff.*"

But then my bol says,

"That's selfish. That's real selfish Bub."

And I tell him, "*But it's real Bash. We got to try and keep our stuff. You got to try and keep yaself. That's my word. My word is my bond. Niggaz is crazy. Can't trust 'em. They don't keep shit.*"

Though I was bothered by James's stance against other African Americans, I was impressed by the ways he used his reading as a social function for his personal expression. He found a way to become critical and activist in a manner that suited him as an individual and also as a member of our ethnic group. Though controversial, he filled our reading community's word universe with codifications that appealed to him and allowed him to foster understanding about the topic that provoked his interest. As a result he became motivated to read more and, eventually, write more. He was motivated because

- our community supported his interests;
- alternative texts existed for him to utilize and transform as he saw fit;
- with support, he began to see himself as a cultural critic with potential for social action;
- he was able to identify a viable and personal use for literacy work;
- though an important part of a reading community, James saw opportunities to cultivate individual agency in his reading experiences.

Reading/Teaching Media as Texts

James's motivation informed my professional practice as a teacher. By exploring the social functions his reading performed I discovered the pedagogical stance that now informs my actions requires that I foster opportunities "not to guide [my] students to engage in work for particular kinds of change" but to be "willing to create space or respect space that students create where they can read and write for social change in ways that matter most to them" (Blackburn, 2002/2003, p. 323). It also requires that I cultivate lenses to perceive world- and word-texts in the ways students do; seek out the social functions of students' readings to encourage motivation in literacy education for urban adolescents who are placed "at risk"; and consider the social and political issues that urban adolescents are interested in and moved by so that in- and out-of-school spaces are punctuated with authentic impetuses for reading engagement among these youth.

A "next wave" of literacy education and research for urban students will encompass media as texts that can show us the myriad possibilities for teaching and learning with adolescents who struggle with decoding skills, sociocultural understanding, and political resistance through inquiry and action and the pursuit of "lived questions" (Palmer, 1998/1999, p. 10). This wave will parallel media education among adolescents that focuses on the "effects of media texts" or "media text production" with more indigenous inquiry into adolescents' unprescribed reading experiences and literacy practices (Gauntlett, 1998, p. 12). The next steps in considering what is possible with African American urban adolescents as engaged readers include attending to media as texts, (co)constructing multiple and variant teaching/learning spaces within which to read dynamically and divergently, and working with novice and in-service teachers in the development of professional practices that conceive and build adolescent reading experiences in line with student desires. In so doing, we will be able to meet students where they are, pull them to where we want them to be, and perhaps learn something of our own assumptions and directions in addition to their unaccessed and deeply valuable abilities as we go. In the weeks and months that followed our (co)authorship, James continued to watch and read news of hip-hop artists and neighborhood dramas on television and in popular print periodicals. He began to see himself in the texts and, despite his established boundaries, started to wonder about ways to express himself more. Adding to his repertoire of reading experiences and literacy practices, his list of texts and modes of expression grew. If not for the inclusion of the texts of his "desire," I am not sure I would have been privileged to witness and assist his reading (r)evolution.

References

Barton, D., Hamilton, M., & Ivanič, R. (2000). *Situated literacies: Reading and writing in context* (2nd ed.). Mahwah, NJ: Lawrence Erlbaum.

Blackburn, M. V. (2002/2003). Disrupting the (hetero)normative: Exploring literacy performances and identity work with queer youth. *Journal of Adult and Adolescent Literacy, 46*(4), 312–325.

Buckingham, D., & Sefton-Green, J. (1994). *Cultural studies goes to school*. London: Taylor & Francis.

Canon, K. (1995). *Womanism and the soul of the black community*. New York: Continuum.

Collins, P. H. (1990). *Black feminist thought: Knowledge, consciousness and the politics of empowerment*. New York: Routledge.

Dean, G. (2000). *Teaching reading in secondary schools*. London: David Fulton.

Freire, P. (1987). *Literacy: Reading the word and the world*. South Hadley, MA: Bergin & Garvey.

Gauntlett, D. (1998). Ten things wrong with the "effects model." In R. Dickinson, R. Harindranath, & O. Linné (Eds.), *Approaches to audiences: A reader* (pp. 10–24). London: Arnold.

Gee, J. P. (2000). Teenagers in new times: A new literacy studies perspective. *Journal of Adolescent and Adult Literacy, 43*(5), 412–420.

Gee, J. P. (2001). What is literacy? In P. Shannon (Ed.), *Becoming political too: New readings and writings on the politics of literacy education* (pp. 1–9). Portsmouth, NH: Heinemann; London: Lawrence Erlbaum.

hooks, b. (1989a). Pedagogy and political commitment: A comment. In b. hooks (Ed.), *Talking back: Thinking feminist, thinking black* (pp. 98–104). Boston: South End Press.

hooks, b. (1989b). Toward a revolutionary feminist pedagogy. In b. hooks (Ed.), *Talking back: Thinking feminist, thinking black* (pp. 49–54). Boston: South End Press.

Hornberger, N. H. (2000). Multilingual literacies, literacy practices, and the continua of biliteracy. In M. Martin-Jones & K. Jones (Eds.), *Multilingual literacies: Reading and writing different worlds* (pp. 353–368). Philadelphia: John Benjamin.

Hull, G., & Schultz, K. (Eds.). (2002). *School's out! Bridging out-of-school literacies with classroom practice.* New York: Teachers College Press.

Ladson-Billings, G. (1999). Just what is critical race theory and what's it doing in a nice field like education? In L. Parker, D. Deyhle, & S. Villenas (Eds.). *Race is . . . race isn't: Critical race theory and qualitative studies in education* (pp. 7–30). Boulder, CO: Westview.

Lee, C. D. (2004). Literacy in the academic disciplines and the needs of struggling adolescent readers. *Voices in Urban Education, 3*(Winter/Spring), 14–25.

Moje, E. B. (2004). Powerful spaces: Tracing the out-of-school literacy spaces of Latino/a youth. In K. M. Leander & M. Sheehy (Eds.), *Spatializing literacy research and practice* (pp. 15–38). New York: Peter Lang.

Moje, E. B., & Young, J. P. (2000). Reinventing adolescent literacy for new times: Perennial and millennial issues. *Journal of Adolescent and Adult Literacy, 43,* 400–410.

Palmer, P. (1998/1999). Evoking the spirit in public education. *Educational Leadership, 56*(4), 6–11.

St. Pierre, E. A., & Pillow, W. S. (2000). Introduction. In E. A. St. Pierre & W. S. Pillow (Eds.), *Working the ruins: Feminist post-structural theory and methods in education* (pp. 1–24). New York: Routledge.

Street, B. V. (1995). *Social literacies: Critical approaches to literacy in development, ethnography, and education.* New York: Longman.

Response to Staples

Renee Hobbs

Jeanine Staples describes her work with young people in an after-school program where media and popular culture texts provide rich opportunities for dialogue, reflection, and writing, a setting where it is possible to examine closely the social functions of reading media texts as a part of the identity work of urban adolescents. She shares her experience of one student who discovers the power of his own voice through a creative process that involves engaged dialogue, reflection, and the respectful clash of ideas through a unique compositional process. Here I will consider the historical context in which this work exists and apply communication theory to comment on the authentic learning experience described in the chapter.

What educator can ignore the role of screen activity in the lives of children and young people? Media use is a major activity in the lives of American young people, who spend an average of three hours a day watching TV—and nearly four hours when videos, DVDs, and prerecorded shows are included. Teens average nearly two hours a day listening to the radio or to CDs, tapes, or MP3 players, and they spend over one hour a day on the computer outside of schoolwork. Another fifty minutes a day is spent playing videogames. On average, outside of school, teens consume media messages for an average of forty-four hours per week, with African American youth among the most active consumers (Kaiser Family Foundation, 2005). Media consumption serves many functions for young people, including as a common-ground experience to facilitate peer interaction and an opportunity for mood alteration, relaxation, and escape from the pressures of daily life. As we see in Staples's essay, the media also provide opportunities for ongoing social surveillance, affecting the cultural context of adolescent identity development for urban youth.

Both in and out of school, educators have long sought opportunities to explore the possibilities of using popular culture and media in work with young people in urban settings; in the United States, such efforts began in the early 1960s as artists and educators established after-school programs to explore film, television, and popular culture through media analysis and production experiences (Halleck, 2002; Moody, 1999). The serious study of film and academic explorations of popular culture entered high school and college classrooms as educators in the United Kingdom, Australia, Canada, and the United

States, inspired by the work of Marshall McLuhan, began exploring how the critical use of film and popular culture could enhance literacy skills, provide opportunities for rich classroom dialogue about contemporary social and personal issues, and build aesthetic appreciation. More than forty years ago, one scholar wrote:

> At their best, films communicate valid and significant human experiences which illuminate our common humanity and which we should want to share with our students. At their worst, and they share this fault with all media, they present a dehumanizing view of man against which the best defense is trained intelligence and aesthetic judgment. The power of the moving image to manipulate, to editorialize and to form values and attitudes makes it imperative in this age of film and television that the audience be equipped with the competence needed to understand the rhetoric of the projected image. (Culkin, 1964, quoted in Center for Media Literacy, n.d., para. 2)

This argument, now usually identified with the concept of *media literacy,* positions educators as responsible for helping young people understand the rhetoric of the image, stemming from the belief that audiences need skills, tools, and knowledge to "read the word and the world" by understanding the manipulative power of mass media and popular culture.

Without formally introducing methods of rhetorical or textual analysis as a component of the program, Staples indirectly emphasizes this perspective when she and James engage in dialogue about the murder of a young man in their community. In interrogating James's lack of empathy and identification with the murder victim, Staples asks him whether things might be different if news stories were written differently, in ways that did not position African Americans as perpetrators of crime and/or victims of crime. She invites James to see that media representations are inevitably implicated in the personal and cultural construction of identity.

For James, his fascination with the representation of African American men in mass media is challenged by the murder story, because in his eyes it is not just a media representation—it reflects his lived experience and confirms his existing beliefs and attitudes. Instead of reflecting on the power of communications media to shape cultural identity, James is provoked by the news story to think about the nature of personal responsibility. As an adolescent just beginning to explore what it means to be responsible for oneself, James actively rejects Staples's ideas about shared social and community responsibility.

Through dialogue and creative play with language, the process of engaging with the author helps James to clarify his own position about the role of personal responsibility as he navigates the real-world challenges of urban life. What is particularly intriguing about Staples's essay is the way that we get such a clear sense of the author's own journey of reflection and discovery: when James articulates values that are at odds with her own, she finds a way to respond authentically and personally that clarifies her own moral position while simultaneously challenging him to extend his literacy skills. This is culturally responsive teaching, tuned in to the opportunity of the moment and empowering the learner, not by flattery or self-esteem stroking but by respecting the learning process and inviting the learner to stretch (Nieto, 1996).

I will conclude with a point about the composition process described in the chapter. It is not surprising to see James and Staples collaboratively using bricolage to assemble a work of creative expression and resistance through piecing together the phrases of their own transcribed voices, thoughts, and ideas. In a culture stuffed to the brim with multiple, often competing voices, images, sounds, and ideas, bricolage is an ideal way to conceptualize the inherent creativity of the meaning-making process in contemporary life. We are continually exposed to bits of ideas and images that we must use to form a coherent world view. In this essay, we see an adolescent and a teacher both discovering and clarifying their ethical positions through the reassembling of their own voices, a process that demands time—and provides an opportunity for self-reflection and questioning. Such practices necessarily include various asymmetries of knowledge and information in a complex discursive network, and this demands from participants a self-aware, critical stance (Habermas, 1984). Educators must continue to examine how the multiple, dynamic texts of mass media and popular culture can help provide opportunities for engaging learners in these kinds of authentic learning experiences.

References

Center for Media Literacy. (n.d.). Why study media? Thoughts from John Culkin. Retrieved May 23, 2006, from http://www.medialit.org/reading_room/article430.html.

Habermas, J. (1984). *The theory of communicative action*. Boston: Beacon Press.

Halleck, D. (2002). *Hand-held visions: The impossible possibilities of community media*. New York: Fordham University Press.

Kaiser Family Foundation. (2005). *Generation M: Media in the lives of 8 to 18 year olds*. Washington DC: Kaiser Family Foundation.

Moody, K. (1999). *The children of Telstar: Early experiments in school television production*. New York: Center for Understanding Media; Vantage Press.

Nieto, S. (1996). *Affirming diversity: The sociopolitical context of multicultural education*. White Plains, NY: Longman.

Response to Staples

Audra Price

Where are you in the picture? Where do you fit in the story?

When Staples posed this question to James, she helped him perceive and visualize himself within the greater context of the reading. Staples not only tapped into James's motivation but also enabled him to develop richer responses to the work he analyzed. Throughout this study, Staples produced insights into the ways that educators can develop reading literacy for adolescents. Staples first focused on personal narratives, then pointed to a need for bridging the sociocultural context to the learning experience, and concluded with an illustration of the students' ability to critically analyze and respond to texts. After situating myself as a teacher into this study, I found implications for linking visual literacy strategies to the literacy practices detailed in the chapter.

Personal Narratives

Staples's call for more professional practices, aligning reading experiences with the desires of the student, immediately made me think of my own experiences as an instructor at Florida State University. Teaching the course "Art in the Elementary Schools" affords me the opportunity to engage preservice elementary educators in developing *visual literacy*. Visual literacy is the ability to understand and comprehend the expressions and compositional devices used in visual images (Feldman, 1976). During my course, students learn ways to develop arts-integrated curricula that tap into the many modes of thinking and learning. Similar to Staples's study, I look at strategies that will motivate students to react to, interpret, evaluate, and produce works of art. Like Staples, I am trying to develop cultural critics who will have the desire to enact change in their social worlds.

Staples began her study by trying to understand how the students defined themselves through narratives and images found in the media. Once James discovered his connection to the text, he gained power and control over the information that prompted him to reflect, respond, and seek alternative texts to support his claims. One can only imagine how an illustration of James's poem would prompt further discussion of the reading and its implications regarding social action. Perhaps the illustration could propel James to continue the story and propose what actions might occur in the future. One technique to engage students of any age in comprehending certain ideas is to have them perform an activity that I will call "Before, During, After." In this activity, a student such as James could create an illustration of the events he thought led up to the printing of the article. Then he could create an illustration of what occurred in the article he read. Finally, James could create a drawing of what he thought might occur in the future as it relates to the article. Having students process these ideas can also help teachers understand how students associate symbols and visual images with ideas that are presented in reading material. Instructing students to share their illustrations with the class will help others develop visual literacy *and* reading literacy in an effort to understand both the students' artistic creation and the reading that the drawings were based on.

Sociocultural Learning

Students learn best when ideas are translated across different contexts (Byrnes, 2001). Staples helped James transfer knowledge from the classroom to his outside world. By integrating the contexts of the classroom and the sociocultural world of the students, Staples helped the participants in the Youth Leadership program understand how reading reflects their everyday lives. Participants in the program found personal meaning in their readings and subsequently developed responses to the texts by reflecting and sharing their ideas with others. If connecting the written texts to the sociocultural worlds of students proved effective, how could adding the arts enhance this learning?

Perhaps developing both visual and reading literacy could help student readers challenge, respond to, and re-articulate texts in a more efficient manner. Vygotsky (1997 [1927]) stated that effective teaching centers on educators collaborating with students and addressing the social environment. Unearthing metaphoric images found in the students' environment could elicit more responses to ideas also found in written texts. Vygotsky also stated that any form of education must address the perception of a stimulus, the ability to process that stimulus, and a reaction. In Staples's study, literacy strategies focused on ways to help students perceive the text, process ideas, and find personal meaning, which in turn allowed them to re-articulate and respond to texts in new ways. So, to continue Staples's study, I suggest creating more strategies for students to analyze and produce visual images that support ideas found in written texts. Analyzing visual images may also help students further understand the importance of the material they are reading.

The analytic model created by Anderson and Milbrandt (2005) is a set of questions that teachers can use in the classroom to prompt students to respond to, describe, analyze, interpret, and judge works of art and literature. First, the teacher has students discuss their initial reactions, feelings, and first thoughts regarding the work at hand. The description phase of the model asks the viewer to look at and describe the basic elements of the work, which could include discussion of the colors and materials the artist may have used, shapes, size, and placement within the work. For a text, this could involve asking students to give a general synopsis of the text at face value. "What are your initial responses to the text?" Interpretation asks the viewer to look more deeply into the work and make inferences and ask why certain things are presented the way they are in the work. "How would you feel if you were part of the work? What do you think this means? If you were the artist, what would you name the piece?" With regard to text, the teacher can ask the students to place themselves in the position of the author or reporter who covered the story. "What else would you include in the story? What would you determine to be the most important part of the story?" Finally, the viewer or student is asked to evaluate the work. Evaluation asks the student to make informed critiques regarding the work while asking questions such as "How clearly was the story or idea communicated? Does it move you to create or write a piece?" These types of evaluative questions move beyond yes and no and suggest that students offer reasons and rationales behind their statements or judgments.

Conclusion

Critically analyzing artwork and connecting it to themes relevant in literature can help students develop the ability to use metaphors and analogies (Gardner, 1999). For James to produce a poem, he needed to visualize ways in which he would symbolically reproduce key points and ideas relevant to both the text and his personal experiences. What might happen if James extended his original ideas and thoughts of symbolic representation to the production of photographs, illustrations, or video montages? Developing comprehension and helping students understand symbolic methods of communication may help students realize the importance of analyzing written texts.

Art is said not to exist within the artist's own personal bubble; works of art are created through an accumulation of experiences and conversations with friends, family, and strangers. The immediate effects of these experiences are not always present in the work but can help people find personal meaning within it. Staples's ideas on effective literacy practices center on ways to help students understand the production of knowledge, develop strategies for critically analyzing and interpreting texts, and find new ways of representing the content found in coded verbal and visual texts. To find personal meaning within texts, James discovered the power of responding, reflecting, and rearticulating his own story to fit within the context of those he read. James responded to his text in the form of a poem, but what could happen if he produced an image to further support his claims? An extension of Staples's study could begin by allowing students to seek and analyze images from their everyday lives. Then, instruct students to find a written text that supports the major ideas and themes revealed through the analysis of the image. Finally, have the students reflect on both the text and the image through a visual or written text that is shared with classmates. If visual literacy strategies are incorporated with reading literacy, students might perceive the importance of understanding various forms of symbolic communication that represent the narratives of the individual and the community.

References

Anderson, T., & Milbrandt, M. (2005). *Art for life*. New York: McGraw-Hill.

Byrnes, J. P. (2001). *Cognitive development and learning in instructional contexts*. Needham Heights, MA: Allyn & Bacon.

Feldman, E. (1976). Visual literacy. *Journal of Aesthetic Education, 10*(3–4), 195–200.

Gardner, H. (1999). *Intelligence reframed: Multiple intelligences for the 21st century*. New York: Basic Books.

Vygotsky, L. S. (1997 [1927]). *Educational psychology*. Boca Raton, FL: St. Lucie Press.

Chapter Four

Influencing Pedagogy Through the Creative Practices of Youth

Leif Gustavson

My motivation to conduct the study on which this chapter is based came from teaching middle school students and witnessing the creative work they were doing outside of school. Before returning to university to pursue a Ph.D., I taught English/language arts for seven years. In that time I established numerous work relationships with students who were engaged in what I thought was interesting learning outside of school. On the basis of this recognition, I eventually organized my seventh-grade class so that many of the students would bring their projects into class to develop and share with others. These projects included writing computer code for online adventure games, writing and illustrating comic books, composing music for various instruments, publishing zines, sculpting, drafting scripts for one-act plays, painting, and building stereo speakers. Many would call what these youth did "hobbies" or "passing fancies," but in conversation with these youth and through watching them work, I could hear and see that they were incredibly passionate about what they did and eager to discuss it. In addition, the craft involved in this kind of work was technically sophisticated and disciplined.

As I came to know their "out-of-school" work better, I could see how their ways of working within my class were often prescriptive and unimaginative. They would go through the routine of writing an essay, for example, and the result would be adequate. However, it would lack that personal touch or distinctive voice that sets powerful writing apart from merely adequate writing. At the same time, the same students were constructing sophisticated processes to do their out-of-school work. They were fashioning discourses in which to communicate with others. They were continuously representing themselves in refreshing ways as readers, writers, and thinkers. They were also evaluating their work and performing it. These sophisticated processes were not foreign to the ways of working that I valued in my class. In fact, I could see how the ways in which they worked outside of school often complemented skills and work habits that I wanted them to develop in my class. They were simply idiosyncratic and personally relevant to the students when they worked "on their own terms." I saw these youths' ways of working as an untapped resource for my teaching and as having the potential to transform the look and feel of the way we worked and learned in my classroom. With this in mind, I set out through my Ph.D. research to investigate particular creative practices to see the ways in which youth engaged in them and made them a part of their lives.

I understand the term *creative practice* to be a hybrid of Aristotle's notion of *tekhne* and Paul Willis's "grounded aesthetic." Aristotle defines *tekhne* as "the art in mundane skill and, more significantly, in day-to-day life . . . an intrinsic aesthetic or crafting that underlies the practices of everyday life . . . 'a reasoned habit of mind in making something'" (Cintron, 1997, p. xii). According to Willis (1998), grounded aesthetic is "the everyday application of symbolic creativity to symbolic materials and resources in context, whereby new meanings are attributed to or associated with, or seen in them, thereby re-organizing them and appropriating them to common concerns and issues" (p. 173). Willis argues that to understand the way youth understand and live in the world, we need to shift our focus away from products that they consume or make (e.g., CDs, websites, jewelry) to the "social practice" of making these products. The creative practices of youth, whether skateboarding, gaming, redesigning cars, or Parkour, are part of their everyday lives. They literally carry the practice with them wherever they go. Youth spend hours and days practicing their craft, swapping techniques, and scrutinizing their own practice. These creative practices take youth to all different kinds of spaces: friends' houses, conventions, skate parks, studios, concerts, clubs, and stores where they know they will find people and texts that are interesting and will inform their work. This characteristic of youth engaged in creative practices, to me, is the "intrinsic aesthetic or crafting that underlies the practice of everyday life" that Aristotle speaks of. And through this conscious and unconscious "mapping" and constructing of their everyday lives, youth employ a "grounded aesthetic." Their creative practices are part of who they are and how they understand the world around them. The way they live their lives informs their practice, and their practice influences the ways in which they live day to day.

In this chapter, I show how the creative practice of Gil, a fifteen-year-old turntablist, can serve as an analytic frame for thinking about how teachers can use the ways in which youth work in the everyday to inform pedagogy. I first show how performance, improvisation, self-reflection, interpretation, and evaluation are a part of the everyday practice of Gil as a turntablist. I then translate these aspects of practice—what I call habits of mind and body—into pedagogy. Through this approach, I wish to build on the critical work in "everyday" learning of scholars such as Schultz and Hull (2002), Heath (1998, 2000; Heath & McLaughlin, 1994), Lave (1997), Csikszentmihalyi (1991), and Wenger (1998) by turning my newly constructed knowledge of how youth work "on their own terms" back on to the classroom, in essence having youth inform us what a productive learning environment would look like if it were more finely tuned to the ways they work.

The Participant

At the time of the research, Gil, fifteen years old and African American, lived with his mother just within the western border of Philadelphia, a stone's throw from the elite private school that he attended. Gil's mother sold medical insurance to senior citizens—an incredibly demanding and stressful job because of the weekly quota that she had to fill. Gil worked hard during the summer before the research to help pay for an exchange trip to Spain offered through the school that coming year and for equipment he wanted to buy for his turntablism. He also worked during the school year, picking up a few hours bagging groceries at a nearby store as well as DJing for parties. In terms of academics, Gil was doing very well. He registered for an advanced class in math, to his mother's surprise and pleasure. At the beginning of the research, Gil took his studies seriously and appreciated the positive feedback he received from teachers and peers regarding his schoolwork.

During my Ph.D. program, I worked with Gil on a research project investigating student identity formation in school. He proved reliable, working with me on multiple drafts of the report. What I found most invigorating about this work with Gil was his ability to challenge me on observations that I was making about him and his willingness to question the research and its purpose. Not so coincidentally, this study provided insight into the creative practices of youth and exposed ethical difficulties inherent in collaborative research (Gustavson & Cytrynbaum, 2003). Perhaps the most challenging aspect of researching with teens is designing a study that indeed supports and utilizes their wisdom, not only in the collecting of data but in the writing of the manuscript as well. After the project, Gil spoke with me, critiquing the products and processes of the work and outlining what he felt could be done to improve it in the future. The study from which this chapter comes implements many of Gil's suggestions.

Turntablism

Turntablism, the art of manipulating vinyl records on turntables, is one of the four elements of hip-hop. Hip-hop began in the Bronx at a time when the area was undergoing dramatic and traumatic social change. The early 1960s were a time of racial unrest and economic inequality. The established African American and Hispanic communities in the Bronx of the early 1960s began to disappear with the introduction of an expressway that cut a swathe of asphalt through the Bronx—or, more specifically, directly through Hispanic and African American homes and neighborhoods. With this intrusion into their lives, people started to leave the Bronx for other boroughs such as Queens. With the exodus of people the businesses followed, and by 1965 the Southside of the Bronx was a picture of urban decay. Not surprisingly, without the vibrant and supportive neighborhoods of the past, both crime and unemployment rose. Soon, street gangs followed. Within this bleak context, hip-hop was born.

Turntablism, like all the elements of hip-hop, is a distinctly youth-oriented art form. It was created by mainly African American and Puerto Rican American youth in the 1960s and is sustained by youth of diverse cultural and class backgrounds today. Turntablism is a form of music: by remixing and reassembling sampled sounds, beats, and melodies on records, the turntablist creates a new piece of music. Turntablism perhaps most thoroughly embodies Kress and Van Leeuwen's (1996) and Street's (2000) theorizing on the multimodality of literacy. Kress and Van Leeuwen define multimodality as "a range of representational modes . . . a range of means of meaning-making, each affecting the formation of their subjectivity" (p. 39). When Gil composes, for example, he takes a form of representation—the vinyl record—and manipulates it with turntables to produce a new sound, a new form of representation. The "interactive elements," the found sounds on records, are "made to relate" to each other in new ways, thus creating new texts and new meanings (Kress & Van Leeuwen, 1996, p. 176).

For further explanation of how a turntablist works and what kind of work is produced, I defer to Sam, another young turntablist who taught me a great deal about the art form. Gil thought of Sam as a mentor. They would often get together to talk shop about their practice. Sam was a senior in the same high school as Gil. I knew him because he used to spend time in my classroom before school started. We shared similar musical tastes. We would spend the fifteen minutes or so before the bell rang swapping names of bands that we were listening to at the time. Part of Sam's way of educating me on turntablism was through giving me writing he had done on his creative practice. His essay entitled "Turntable Philosophy" clearly draws the connection between turntablism, multimodality, and the act of writing:

> The DJ represents this idea of reassembly in its purest form. Pieces from the past are put together to arrive at a present purpose, thus creating the aural collage that is called the mix. In this way the turntable/mixer combination is a tool, no different in its elemental sense than the pen and paper, for they provide a means to pull "words" and "quotes" from records and place them in a consistently new and different context.

> The idea of turntable language may seem farfetched, but when the roots of the language are examined, it is seen that it was not only an essential, but inevitable part of the guerilla-art social reaction (i.e. that of Black America), similar to the origins of many arts and humanities.

There is a certain kind of reading and writing involved in turntablism. Sam suggests that manipulating records is a form of language. There is the interpretation of words. There is the fashioning of a message out of words, phrases, and sentences that have been captured from other sources. The turntablist's "referencing" of words and phrases and the manipulation of preexisting words and notes on record resemble the way in which teachers expect students to quote from the work of scholars within their essays, for example. In addition, the sampling of phrases from various albums to construct a new text reminds me of the way Shakespeare "borrowed" themes from Ovid to write his plays. Like writers of more traditional texts, turntablists make meaning out of language and ideas they did not create or conceive. Sam also mentions that turntablism is a means of social action. Turntablists create music in part to subvert the status quo. We will see this in Gil's work later in the chapter.

While rap still garners all the media attention within hip-hop culture, the turntablist is back in style now and in high demand. One needs only to watch television for an hour or so to see the influence of

turntablism on our broader society. Zima ads feature turntablists. Lee
Jeans and Gap ads use turntablists. IKEA catalogues represent posh
adolescent bedrooms with two turntables and a mixer. MTV has a
turntablist how-to show. The Internet contains hundreds if not
thousands of turntable websites.

The creative practice is global as well. There is an international
federation for turntablists—the International Turntable Federation
(ITF). This organization and others host international turntable
competitions, including Disco Music Competitions (DMCs) and the
ITF World Championships. Even jazz artists such as Steve Coleman
and Medeski Martin and Wood are now recording with turntablists as
part of their bands—not to mention all of the popular bands that
have a "turntablist," if only the sampled sound of someone
scratching. Turntablists such as QBert, DJ Shadow, and The Invisibl
Skratch Piklz have attained rock star status among many youth. Gil is
a product of this renewed interest in the art form, and it is informing
what he reads, the messages he chooses to "write" on his turntables,
and how he works and learns in his everyday life.

I would like to illustrate through two vignettes the ways in which
Gil works in his chosen creative practice. These glimpses into the
ways he works on his turntables highlight specific habits of mind and
body that have the potential for influencing how work and learning
are conducted in classrooms. The first vignette focuses on Gil at work
on his turntables in a school space. The second vignette shows Gil at
home practicing. In both spaces we can see how performance,
improvisation, self-reflection, interpretation, and evaluation are
essential habits of mind and body within Gil's craft as a turntablist.

Playing at School: Turntablism as Performative,
Self-Reflective, and Interpretive

Through the jazz teacher's generosity, Gil and other students
interested in turntablism had a room off of the main music room
where they could set up their equipment, practice, and record
together. It was through this space, and the community of practice
formed therein, that Gil and others were able to transport their out-of-
school creative practices into school. The room was a popular place
at the end of the school day. The sound of needles scratching vinyl
always drew a crowd. Within this space, Gil had the opportunity to
observe other turntablists at work, to share his playing with others, to

talk about turntablism as art and craft, and to use his skills to think about and comment on his own life experiences.

This small room off of the jazz room had several tables of equipment. One held two turntables with a mixer between them. A sampler and drum machine faced the turntables. There was also a four-track machine and tape recorder. Facing all of this equipment was an electronic keyboard. All of this material rested on top of an old Persian rug. A mic stand stood at the ready to the right of the four-track machine. The rest of the room was filled with a worn Victorian-style couch, a baby grand piano, and a fairly new computer with laser printer. Bookshelves, haphazardly stocked with all kinds of records and sheet music, lined the walls. Posters hung on these walls. Two advertised the movie *Goodfellas*; one *The Godfather*. Others included a *Superfly* movie poster, a poster of Bob Marley smoking a large joint, a poster of Tupac Shakur, and one black-light print of two people standing on a mountain with their arms upraised.

Del, a senior and mentor for Gil, sat behind the table that held his turntables. He was rapping to a beat, half to himself. When Del saw us, he took the headphones off his ears, rested them around his neck, and asked, "What's up?" Gil walked over to him, shook his hand, and introduced me. Del nodded at me. He then asked, "You want to listen to the intro to the album?" Gil nodded, "Definitely."

Del turned around to the DAT player and put in the tape. The intro blasted an aural collage of phrases from recent rap albums out of the speaker to the side of the turntables: *My sound surrounds you like racism. You feel it all around you.* The three of us stood and nodded to the beat, made sounds of agreement when we recognized particular phrases or rappers: *I'm trying to catch my people in all different stages, all different phases.* No phrase was repeated: *If knowledge is the key then show me the lock.* Each blended seamlessly into the next. At the end of the intro, which was about two minutes in length, both Gil and I said, "Damn." Del smiled. I asked, "How long did it take to put that together." Del sighed, "Over eight hours."

Del checked the clock and realized that he had to go. Gil pointed to his turntables, "Can I spin for a while?" Del said, "Sure, just take care of my babies and put away any albums you use." On the way out the door, he added, "And yo, don't let anyone else mess with them, OK?" Gil put the headphones on, "Promise." With that, Del left. Gil told me that this was usually what he did: went up to this room and played for hours before catching up with his friends at around six.

As Gil warmed up, by scratching various phrases on two albums that he found in the stack of vinyl on the floor, we talked about the ubiquity of turntablism in the media. I sat on the couch and asked, "You ever see that Zima ad where that dude is spinning at a party so intensely that the records on the decks melt?" At this point in the ad, the turntablist picks up a Zima that miraculously cools everything off, and he is able to get back to spinning records. Gil winced, "That ad's corny: corny because Zima is corny and because Zima has nothing to do with hip-hop." He added, "Zima's not advertising with turntablism because they care about hip-hop. They're just out to make money." Gil, like Sam, felt strongly that playing on his turntables was in part a political act. Honing his craft helped sustain hip-hop as a cultural form that avoided commodification. The commercial, on the other hand, was only capitalizing on the rising popularity of the art form, with no recognition of its roots and cultural significance. Through ads such as this, turntablism ran the risk of being merely a product.

About a half-hour into spinning, he looked up from the turntables and said, "Guess I'm not going to practice." I asked him what he meant. Gil said, "I was supposed to go to track practice." The conference championships were this weekend, and the team was traveling to the track to check it out. Gil did not seem too concerned about missing what sounded like a fairly important practice. I asked, "You want to run and catch the bus?" He shrugged, "Nah," and went back to the turntables.

A few minutes later, three long-haired eighth-grade boys came in and lounged on the couch to listen to Gil play. One of them leaned against the table, "Can I spin? Gil? Gil? Gil?" Gil smirked and shook his head no. With this audience, Gil accentuated the physicality of a turntablist. He put the headphones on and rested them on his temples when he was not using them. When checking for a phrase on a record, he would hold one earphone to his ear with his shoulder. At one point, the eighth-grader who wanted to use the turntables said half-sarcastically, "Gil! I love you!" as Gil played. He smiled.

Students would drift in and out of the space, sometimes staying for only a few minutes, other times hanging out for an hour or so. When the eighth-graders eventually left, two seniors entered the room and flopped down onto the couch. Gil was experimenting with several albums that he had recently acquired. The first one was entitled *Mr. Noisy*, a children's novelty record that contained mini morality plays. He sampled phrases such as "must try harder" and "the police." He played a break beat behind what he scratched, meaning that he manipulated one of the records on the turntables to maintain a consistent beat as he scratched phrases on the other album. Gil looked over at me while experimenting with the beat he found: "Sounds like a car chase." It was subversive. He smiled, "Runnin'," like evading the law. The seniors nodded in agreement. Other students drifted in while he played. They sat down on the sofa and nodded to this beat. Sometimes they would laugh at phrases Gil selected to scratch. Other times they would walk over to the table and watch Gil spin.

In the midst of this activity, Gil and I, and the two seniors who had come in earlier, talked about the ability of the turntablist to, in the words of one of the seniors, "tell a new story out of one that already exists." For example, Gil experimented with the soundtrack to *The Rescuers,* a children's movie from the 1970s about two mice that rescue an orphaned girl from an abusive woman, and scratched certain phrases that created a completely different story from the original, particularly with the break beat behind it.

Later, I asked the two seniors and Gil, "Why are the samples that you pick so interesting when you take them out of context?" This came up while Gil spun the soundtrack to *Raiders of the Lost Ark*. While experimenting with various voices and sounds on the album, Gil found the sound of a gunshot. Through scratching this sound, he transformed the gunshot into something different—a drum beat. Through the improvisational freedom of reappropriating this sound, Gil took a dominant discourse (gunshot as violent act) and invested it with his own particular inflection (gunshot as rhythm). One senior suggested, "It's the timing of the phrases." The art of phrasing to him was the element of surprise, catching the listener off-guard with a quirky or familiar pop culture reference or found sound. The other senior added, "You got to be able to kinda recognize where the sample's coming from or from what kind of music." The comfort of the familiar perhaps makes it possible for the listener to suspend his or her disbelief and create an alternative reality of sorts. The pleasure is in recognizing the familiar sound, voice, passage, or beat juxtaposed with another sound, voice, passage, or beat from a disparate source. For example, at one point, Gil scratched the phrase "Sunday school," playing it over and over again. By taking this easily recognized idea in the form of a phrase out of context and placing it within the context of that music room at that moment in time, Gil essentially made the familiar strange. He suggested, "Sampling's a lot like wearing a *Sesame Street* T-shirt to high school. You're fucking around with what's expected of you."

In considering the applicability to pedagogy of Gil's craft as illustrated within this vignette, there are several points I wish to make. First, the kind of work that Gil enjoys doing on his own time is highly experimental, and it involves working to create something original. Second, there is also a subversive quality to it: the recognition that the composition challenges normative behavior or language use contributes to the desire to practice and play for others. Third, notice too that the practice of being a turntablist at times involves playing in a semipublic space, where people can see you practicing/performing. This semi-public space makes possible the occasional conversation that arises out of the work, a pause either to think about what has been playing or to consider what the most recent composition means. Fourth, work within this realm involves others coming up and looking closely at what Gil is doing, not necessarily to judge him, but instead to watch him work: to see the way he uses his hands, to understand the effect that he is making, and to check to see the album he decided to play. Finally, the everyday practice of a turntablist involves working in spaces where many things are happening at once. People are listening, watching, talking to each other and the turntablist, and flowing in and out of the space. It is this multiplicity that contributes to the vitality of the creative practice.

Toward the end, once the seniors left, just Gil and I remained, with the hum of the amps in the background. Gil said he wanted to play a song for me. "Have you heard 'E Pluribus Unum' by The Last Poets?" He pulled the vinyl out from the record jacket. I told him that I had. Gil smiled and placed it gently on the platter of the left turntable. He placed the needle on the outer edge of the record. The popping and hissing of a well-worn record filled the room.

At the time, as we sat and listened to this song together, the anger and frustration of the lyrics did not register with me nearly as powerfully as they do now, looking at this song on the page. In the midst of listening to the song, I was swept away by the raw and minimal beat. I "heard" the lyrics, but not as deeply as I think Gil wanted me to. When the song ended, Gil said only that he "agreed" with a lot of what they said and proceeded to put away the albums, much like someone would reshelve books in a library. I was struck by the image of Gil putting the records away and did not ask him to explain what he meant by agreeing with the song.

Reading the lyrics now, and hearing the beat only faintly in my head, I think I understand more clearly why Gil wanted to play me that song, at that particular time, in that particular place. I hear the way the song resonated with Gil, how it had a context beyond being just an interesting piece of music. Finally, I see how the turntable can be a place for Gil to be self-reflective and construct an interpretation of his current life situation through an important piece of hip-hop history.

The Last Poets brutally deconstruct the dollar bill, showing how money has corrupted those in power and how those in power—white men—have oppressed African Americans. Not a particularly new idea now, but the message of the song—originally recorded in 1972— is fresh to me because of the way they deconstruct the text and images on the dollar bill. The Last Poets take each image, each word, and explain its significance and culpability in the history of oppression in America: *so the people don't get any in the land of the plenty | because E PLURIBUS UNUM means One Out of Many*. What is perhaps the most powerful and lasting image of this song for me is the way in which The Last Poets show how racism is ingrained, even printed, in our society. The way money is used can be oppressive, they argue, but what is even more sinister is how images and text can be used to weave racism into the infrastructure of society: *Then there's the pyramid that stands by itself | created by Black people's knowledge and wealth | and over the pyramid hangs the devil's eye | that stole from the truth and created the lie.*

Back to that day, in the music room, listening to the song. *Racism and greed keep the people in need | from getting what's rightfully theirs.* The lyrics of this diatribe against racial and economic injustice poured out of the speakers and slid underneath the door into the second-story hallway of the auditorium, which is part of the campus of an upper-middle-class, predominately white private institution. *Seclorum is a word that means to take from another | knowledge, wisdom and understanding stolen from the brother.* By the time the lyrics made their way down to the end of the hall, they were probably faint, the message indecipherable to a group of students who may have been sitting on the faded Oriental rug. *And so the power is in the hand of the ruling classes.* However, through Gil's act of playing the song in this room, the lyrics were now a part of this institution. I interpret Gil's playing of this song as an acknowledgment of the subtle and not so subtle racism that he experienced at this school.

Gil came across this song *through* his work as a turntablist. He heard about The Last Poets through other hip-hop that he listened to as well as through other turntablists talking about the music that influenced them or that they used. He read about them in liner notes on albums in his collection. Gil learned through his practice that they are an important part of the lineage of hip-hop. By playing them, Gil signified his knowledge of their significance and in a way authenticated that he *was* a turntablist. He also connected his current life situation with the life experience of his hip-hop "ancestry."

About a year before we sat in that space off from the music room, listening to "E Pluribus Unum," Gil and I had worked on a different research project. In this project, Gil and I explored the concept of inscribed and chosen identities in his high school. In the process of working on this project, Gil shared with me that there were times when he felt he needed to prove himself academically as a young black man in a predominately white school. As a way of explaining this feeling, he sent me this e-mail:

> I always feel the need to prove myself . . . I was in the bathroom . . . Chris walks in, and says hi. He ok so far. Then out of the clear blue sky he says "All of the black teachers in this school were hired because they are black." Now I know that Chris is something of a mathematical genius, but his social skills are horrible . . . I don't want to prove to him that they are qualified, because its not so much what he said, but what it revealed about what he is thinking . . . One time I said to Dan [a friend of Gil's] "I think I might have gotten a 100 on the lit test." Right away two guys come over and ask me if I want to bet. They both bet $5, and even though I stay away from gambling, I took their money. Now if that's not having to prove myself I don't know what is.

Gil jumps to a conclusion in this story that the two guys who questioned whether he aced the test were in fact implying that because Gil was black, he could not possibly have scored that high. They could have just been teasing him like they would any other student or friend, regardless of his/her race. However, Gil's response to their taunt is indicative of the social climate in which we live. It is powerful and quite frustrating to think that regardless of the two students' motives, in the back of Gil's mind was the possibility that they were being discriminatory, and because of that, he had to respond defensively to prove his worth or intelligence.

Imagine for a moment the two incidents that Gil mentions in the e-mail above somehow being in that room on the day when Gil played "E Pluribus Unum" for me on that turntable. Perhaps they were in his head when he put down the needle. The song speaks to the discrimination and oppression present in those two stories. It makes me think of the money that changed hands in the story that Gil told in the e-mail. As in the song, money in Gil's story was used as a vehicle for forcing Gil to prove that what he said was true. The money was a mechanism for placing the two white students in a position of power over Gil. Through laying down five dollars each, they were in the position of being able to judge whether Gil was right. I would argue that Gil played "E Pluribus Unum" in part to tell the story of incidents such as this where issues of race, class, and power put Gil in the position of constantly negotiating his identity. It was an act of witness in a way. Playing the song provided Gil a way of articulating feelings, thoughts, and ideas that were swirling around in his head at the time. The turntable concretized those feelings, thoughts, and ideas.

Gil worked on the turntables for a good three hours on that day after school. In that time, he performed his skills on the turntables to those who came in. Instead of a formal performance, it was a series of mini/in-process performances where Gil tried out new moves to see the reaction he would get. He also reflected with other turntablists in the room about his practice, exploring with them why he does what he does, what hip-hop means to him, and why turntablism intrigues people. Finally, Gil used his turntables to make connections between certain pieces of music and his own life. On the way out I asked him whether spending that much time in the room was normal, and he said, "Definitely. One time my mom got so pissed at me because I was here until, like, 7:30."

Gil on the Decks at Home: Turntablist as Historian

Gil did not practice only at school. His primary place to practice was in his room at home, where he kept his equipment and records. When I would show up at Gil's house to watch him spin, he would greet me at the front door and ask whether I wanted to see what he had been working on on his turntables. We would then jog up the flight of stairs to his bedroom.

The first thing that inevitably grabbed my attention upon entering Gil's room was his enormous queen-size bed. It took up most of the room, the wooden headboard occupying the space between the two windows that looked out on to the street. Listening to Gil play, I often started off sitting on the edge of the wooden footboard of this bed until it became far too uncomfortable and I would end up sitting on the plush tan carpet.

Across from the footboard of his bed were Gil's turntables and mixer. They sat in his black *coffin*—the term used for the long, rectangular carrying case needed to lug around a turntablist's equipment—on top of his white chest of drawers. Gil said it was the perfect height for him. To the right of his turntables were his cardboard boxes of records: four in all. The records that he most often used when he spun stood stacked on their edges either directly to the left of his feet as he played or behind the mixer. To the left of his turntables was a wardrobe, on top of which sat his TV. Often, the TV was on when he played. Around the room were objects that represented his other interests. I got the sense that his room was a collage of many years of life and that some objects may have clashed with the way Gil thought of himself in the present. For example, there was the computer drawing of a human figure holding a guitar, resembling the symbol used to delineate the men's restroom from the women's. A pair of stilts leaned against a slim floor-to-ceiling bookshelf. Next to these stilts was his hockey stick. "I used to play when I was in sixth grade," Gil told me. His paintball gun hung over his bed, and an army helmet sat on one of the shelves of the bookshelf.

Next to his bed hung a corkboard with one small article from *Jive* magazine thumb-tacked to the bottom:

DJs: Perhaps the easiest parallel one can draw between the South Bronx mixing OGs and their effect on future generations is the legacy of the 1940s and '50s blues legends on the rock guitar gods of the 1960s and '70s. Just as the instrumental and compositional creativity of modern rock predecessors like Chuck Berry, Bo Diddley, and Muddy Waters inspired the amplified fretwork frenetics of Jimi Hendrix, Eric Clapton, and Jimmy Page (subsequently causing kids worldwide to pick up guitars), so too did DJ Kool Herc, Afrika Bambaataa, Grand Wizard Theodore, and Grandmaster Flash inspire the first wave of post-old school pyro-techno-theatrical phenoms: DJs Scratch, Cash Money, Jazzy Jeff, and Aladdin.

On one particular day, Gil wanted to show me some work he had been doing with two albums of Martin Luther King Jr. and Malcolm X speeches. A friend from school had loaned him the albums a few days before. He placed one album on each of the turntables, turned on the mixer, placed the headphones over his ears, and dropped the right turntable needle on the revolving record. Malcolm X's voice boomed out of the speaker:

> Malcolm X: . . . are waking up and they are gaining a new political consciousness, becoming politically mature, and as they develop this political maturity, they are able to see the recent trends in these political elections. They see that whites are so evenly divided that every time they vote, the racist polls have to go back and count the votes all over again . . . In fact I think we would be fooling ourselves if we had an audience this large and didn't realize that there were some enemies in it.

Gil started scratching the phrase "in it" from the Malcolm X speech and then allowed it to continue playing: *This afternoon we want to talk about the ballot or the bullet*. Gil then sampled and scratched "bullet" over and over again. At this point in his playing, I asked Gil what interested him about these two albums: "Well, like, it relates to today. I'll show you specifically with me and [my school] how it relates."

The turntable with Malcolm X continued to spin; however, with the cross-fader of the mixer moved over to the left, no sound came out of the speaker. Gil then placed the Martin Luther King album on the left turntable. He placed the needle on the album and flicked the cross-fader to the right again; Malcolm X's voice bellowed, *Well, this country is a hypocrite. They try to make you think they set you free by calling you a second-class citizen. No, you nothing but a twentieth century slave*. Gil flicked the cross-fader to the left, and Martin Luther King spoke: *This nation is wrong because it is nothing but a new form of slavery*.

Gil started juggling the phrases "You nothing but a twentieth century slave" from Malcolm X and "This nation is wrong" from Martin Luther King Jr. By juggling, I mean that he went back and forth between these two phrases, sometimes allowing the whole phrase to play before he spliced the other in, sometimes playing only bits and pieces of each. Sometimes, he played both at the same time, so that the voices overlapped or lay on top of one another. I asked him why he made the choice to juggle these two phrases:

The contrast between what they are saying and the similarities . . . They are talking about two different things. He is talking about colonization with the second-class citizenship [referring to Malcolm X]. And he is talking about segregation [referring to Martin Luther King Jr.] and they are sort of the same thing but they are kind of different names for it. They kind of look at it from a different point of view . . . segregation is sort of a name that is sort of geared toward the Sixties and the Civil Rights Movement. And second-class citizenship and colonization sort of like general and sort of like looking at history in general . . . so they are both saying that it is basically slavery. He's saying the new form of slavery or twentieth-century slavery [referring to Malcolm X] and he is saying new form of slavery [referring to King]. That is pretty good contrast and similarity.

The act of sampling from these speeches for Gil was not simply one of indiscriminately dropping the needle. Part of his personal work was hours of listening to the albums until he knew them inside and out. Thus, on the day he showed me this work, he constructed a spontaneous message out of bits of text he knew by heart, much like the improvisational playing of a jazz guitarist. Gil never "performed" this piece. In other words, he did not play it for a larger audience than me. However, this space served as more than a time to hone his technical skills as a turntablist. Through this space and time, Gil drew from other sources and manipulated messages to construct his own meaning. In this case, he also used his turntables to analyze a historic event—the civil rights movement—as well as the different connotations of the term "slavery" from the perspective of two of its leaders. Through playing these voices on his turntables, remixing them the way that he did, he was able to hear the rhetorical differences in the way Malcolm X and Martin Luther King Jr. understood the climate of racial injustice in the 1960s.

It is useful to compare Gil's work with the kind of writing work that many teachers expect of their students. In this case, the two ways of making meaning are surprisingly similar. Gil worked and learned the way we wish all of our students would when they write. For one, Gil conducted research. He first went *grave robbing:* the DJ's expression for finding albums to use in compositions. This search involved hours at various new and used record stores and yard sales, as well as trading albums with friends and fellow turntablists. Then Gil spent several more hours, over a period of days, listening to these albums, first all of the way through to get "the message," and then in bits and pieces, experimenting with particular scratches and phrases;

Gil deconstructed the vinyl texts. A part of understanding the messages of the albums also entailed conversations with Sam. He would document these conversations in a notebook he carried in his pocket. This notebook also contained ideas for turntable pieces, lists of records he wanted to obtain, and names and contact information of people associated with turntablism. After finding the phrases he liked, he would begin putting the new text together. To construct this new text, or new argument, Gil cited from other people's work—citing, in this case, the phrases that he sampled from the records. This whole practice created a way for Gil to make what he "read" personally meaningful to him.

After Gil played his piece, he told me that he had read the Malcolm X speech that he was manipulating in his English class that semester. But the act of reading the speech did not interest him nearly as much as playing it on his turntables:

> I think the idea of having a voice played of someone who's dead is really cool . . . Because it kind of brings them back to life, and not many things have that power. I actually feel that he is talking. I feel that he is alive when I hear the voice. We read the script of the speech in Lit class, the one where he's like, "I would be mistaken if we had a turnout this big and there weren't some enemies in here." And it was really cool to read that, but I felt like I was reading the speech of a dead guy . . . but when I play it on a record, it's almost like he's not here but he's over there (pointing to the corner of his room).

Through his turntables, the words of Malcolm X and Martin Luther King Jr. were no longer disembodied or "embalmed speech," to use Denzin's (1997) term. Rather, Gil had the power to resurrect their voices *and* embody their messages in the life he lived. In the quotation above, and through his process of work, Gil speaks to a critical characteristic of an effective teacher: the ability to work with youth to find ways to make the texts with which they interact feel like they are "not here, but . . . [right] over there" within arm's reach, malleable, and connected to their lives in relevant ways.

The amount of time and effort that Gil devotes to his creative practice is considerable, the envy of any teacher I would think. The interesting thing to me is that it is not only the subject that stimulates Gil to work long hours on his creative practice. It is also the way in which he gets to work, the *craft* of his creative practice, that makes him stay up all hours on the turntables. In fact, the physicality of the work, and the freedom he has in determining when he wants to do it, influence the meanings that Gil makes in and through it.

To return to my comparison between traditional methods of teaching English and Gil's ways of working, my experience in schools has shown me that often writing is taught as a linear skill. The writing process is presented as brainstorming, prewriting, first draft, sharing, editing, final draft, and publishing. Writing assignments are presented axiomatically as well. In other words, students are to work on one piece of writing at a time, finish that piece of writing, and then move on to the next piece, often with little to no connection between the two other than the fact that both pieces of writing involve commenting on something that they have read. This process seems artificial and manufactured in light of the ways in which Gil works. In the remainder of the chapter, I offer ways for teachers to develop complex understandings of how youth like Gil work and learn on their own terms as a means to move beyond these artificially constructed learning environments and into classrooms that take advantage of the skill and sophistication that students like Gil bring to school.

How can Gil's Way of Working Inform and Influence Pedagogy?

Because of my background as a teacher and my current work as a teacher educator, I am committed to forging linkages between my research and the ways in which teachers work and learn with students in classrooms. I make this commitment recognizing the real constraints that standardized tests, core curricula, class size, uneven distribution of funding, and other state and district mandates place on curriculum and pedagogy. However, I choose to believe that these constraints need not get in the way of allowing students to work and learn on their own terms. I say this because core curricula and other mandates more often than not merely emphasize which skills and concepts need to be developed within a certain time frame. While it may be difficult to cover those skills and concepts within the time allotted, this does not prohibit a teacher from teaching those skills and concepts through the ways in which youth work in their everyday lives. In other words, the curriculum is not the issue here; it is the way in which students and teachers interact with the curriculum that needs reexamination.

This idea of having the way youth work inform the practice of teaching is not new. In fact, John Dewey argued for this approach to teaching and learning early in the twentieth century. More recently, scholars such as Shirley Brice Heath, Donna Alvermann, Greg Dimitriadis, and Elizabeth Moje have explored this idea from various perspectives.

Heath (1997, 1999) shows how teenagers organize their personal time: they "take up mixed patterns of learning, working, and [take] seriously their leisure time" (p. 2). Often adults construe this work and learning as play. Heath argues that this "work" of teens is filled with risk and challenges and in many ways mirrors the work of adulthood. She describes how youth are involved in creating "developmental assets" to better themselves and their community (1999, p. 3). Heath argues, like Street and Barton and Hamilton, that "youth draw upon multiple symbol systems, engage several versions of themselves depending on circumstances, and call on multiple discourses according to need, motivation, and domains" (1997, p. 120).

Educational research that seeks to understand youth perspectives on work and learning also provides us with useful perspectives on how youth go about interpreting pop cultural forms. Alvermann (2003), for example, researches the way youth interpret the culture of rap and rap songs through observing them "in the action" of interpreting this art form. For instance, through his interest in the Goodie MOb, Ned, a fourteen-year-old African American eighth-grader, develops strategies for "acquiring facts" about the group. Alvermann also shows how he gains "independence" in pursuing information about the group. She writes of "Ned's command of several multiple and overlapping literacies gleaned through personal, familial, and social interactions both in and out of school that afforded him the opportunity to act like—and, just as important, to be recognized as—a competent and literate person."

Dimitriadis (2001) has done interesting work on how African American youth "mobilize" forms of popular culture to construct understandings of where they live, of generational identity, and of iconic rappers. Moje (2002) argues that the way to acknowledge "unsanctioned" forms of literacy such as graffiti in the classroom is to recognize their complexity and power. In addition, she recommends that teachers work with youth who are engaged in these practices to develop a critical understanding of why the practices are marginalized. She writes, "As educators, we need to work with youth to learn how the language and literacy practices they value might be used productively in other contexts to challenge dominant assumptions about literacy and social practice" (p. 48). Moje's suggestion recognizes the importance of the practice involved in these creative forms. In addition, she speaks to making connections between the seemingly disconnected phenomena of youth cultural forms and school learning.

This kind of research is extremely helpful in terms of understanding how youth make meaning with popular culture products that often have been produced by people other than the youth themselves or how youth-produced popular culture products could be used in classrooms. In this research, the cultural products of youth provide ways of expanding or exploding the literary canon in schools, for example. Novice and veteran teachers with whom I work are intrigued by the idea that they should be integrating songs by the Goodie MOb and Tupac Shakur into their units on poetry. It is not a difficult leap for them to see how their students could be reading the rap of the Goodie MOb or Tupac Shakur alongside *The Scarlet Letter*, for example. This orientation still positions books and other forms of literature as objects to be studied by students, not written by them, so it fits nicely with the way learning looks in traditional classrooms. What these teachers have a difficult time understanding is how the way a young rapper works, for example, could influence how youth *do* learning in their classrooms. Teachers with whom I work struggle with conceptualizing how the ways youth "draw upon multiple symbol systems, engage several versions of themselves depending on circumstances, and call on multiple discourses according to need, motivation, and domains" could alter the way they teach in a classroom setting.

Lave and Wenger (1991) argue that "there is a difference between talking *about* a practice from outside and talking *within* it" (p. 107). Teachers often make youth culture "work" in their classrooms by designing units of study around the products of the practice: graffiti, rap, zines, and so on. This pedagogical approach talks *about* the practice because it positions the teacher and students as outside observers of the cultural form, gleaning meaning from studying it rather than constructing meaning about the cultural form through *doing* it. Teachers who design these kinds of units are interested in and influenced by popular culture. They value popular culture as high art and potentially part of the "canon." For example, they believe that Tupac Shakur and Bob Dylan have a place in poetry. These teachers help their students to see that they can view anything as a source of learning. Placing popular culture at the center of the curriculum legitimates it and allows students to speak about their own experiences within the classroom.

Nevertheless, youth do not necessarily want their cultural practices to be legitimated or co-opted by schools. In fact, adult sanctioning of youth culture may ironically delegitimate it as an interesting world of experience. Youth might see through this practice as trying to trick them into learning: an attempt to motivate them to participate. If the teacher's interest in the practice is merely as a tool of motivation, students will read this as a dismissal of their interests, rather than as a "cool" way to learn. Also, not everyone is "into" turntablism, and not everybody needs to be into turntablism. If teachers head down this road, they could be setting up all sorts of obstacles for certain students to get involved with whatever it is that they are exploring in the classroom. Finally, making something a subject of study can "fix it" in such a way that it loses its vitality. In the same way that a Shakespearean play can be boring to read as opposed to *acted*, turntablism could be boring if it is something to study rather than something *lived*.

We need to think of other ways of informing pedagogy through youth creative practices. We need to look at the ways in which youth engage *in* the practices—how they do what they do—and have those habits of mind and body influence the way we design learning environments in classrooms.

Wenger (1998) writes that "what we think about learning influences where we recognize learning, as well as what we do when we decide that we must do something about it—as individuals, as communities, and as organizations" (p. 9). How can teachers teach in ways that capitalize on the need youth feel to develop communities of practice, to perform their work, to improvise, to self-reflect, and to assess work that they are committed to? Teachers can open their practice to these forms of youth work in two interconnected ways: as an ethnographer in her/his classroom and then as a conscious designer of the learning experience.

Teacher as Ethnographer

One way to get at answers to the questions above is through developing an ethnographic understanding of how youth make meaning in their own lives (Ben-Yosef, 2003; Dimitriadis, 2001; Goswami & Stillman, 1987; Schultz, 2003; Sitton, 1980).

Ethnographers approach their phenomena realizing that they know little and that the people who are part of the phenomena, the "natives," know a lot (Gallas, 1994). With this realization, ethnographers position themselves as the learners and the people who are part of the phenomena as the teachers. When we make this role recognition analogous to teaching, it is our job as teachers to figure out how our students are mathematicians, historians, writers, and scientists *in their lives,* instead of assuming that they are not or that they need to be taught how to be. Therefore, a teacher who is influenced by ethnographic practices would no longer look at Gil's interest in turntablism as simply a product. Instead, the teacher would recognize that he is involved in a practice—a craft, a habit of mind and body—that enables him to do the work. From a curriculum standpoint we would call this "experience" (Dewey, 1997). The teacher would realize that it is part of her or his job to understand the how and why of the practice because it is one of the ways in which Gil makes meaning in the world. A teacher who takes an ethnographic stance would find ways to understand the depth and complexity of Gil's turntablism. She would work to see how Gil is self-reflective, experimental, and analytic in the way that he works on his own terms. She would come to know the community of practice Gil keeps to be able to do his work. She would honor that sophistication through the way she teaches.

Understanding youth cultural practices as an ethnographer requires that we look at youth as inherently creative problem solvers, problem posers, solution finders, and so on. The teacher enters her room assuming that her students are already some form of mathematician, scientist, poet, architect. Karen Gallas (1994) writes that she "suspend[s] [her] disbelief as a teacher and [leaves her] judgment in abeyance in service of a child's development" (p. 96). She continues, "Rather than my 'teaching' . . . what science [is], we [struggle] together to understand [our] changing picture of science" (p. 96).

Edward Said (1996) would describe Karen Gallas as a "professional amateur," someone who does not limit herself through special knowledge of a discipline. Experts, Said contrasts, only feel comfortable approaching problems, issues, ideas, through their rarefied knowledge. He warns that specialization, as opposed to competence, can result in the "sacrifice of one's general culture to a set of authorities and canonical ideas" (p. 76). He adds:

Specialization means losing sight of the raw effort of constructing either art or knowledge; as a result you cannot view knowledge and art as choices and decisions, commitments and alignments, but only in terms of impersonal theories or methodologies. . . . In the end . . . you become tame and accepting of whatever the so-called leaders in the field will allow. Specialization also kills your sense of excitement and discovery . . . giving up to specialization is, I have always felt, laziness, so you end up doing what others tell you, because that is your specialty after all. (p. 77)

When people present an expert with a problem that grows out of their creative practice, the expert often feels that she or he cannot even discuss it because it is beyond the purview of her or his expertise. What the expert knows has nothing to do with the problem. Teachers often think of themselves or approach their subject as experts or specialists. For example, a math teacher may see her job as teaching students how to factor polynomials and therefore may not afford the time to link mathematics with presidential elections or even be able to entertain a provocative tangent related to everyday life. Said suggests that teachers who view themselves as specialists are not able to see the "raw effort" of work and learning. They are blind to the practice—the daily habits of mind and body—that lead to the construction of knowledge. Instead, they focus on the end result—the knowledge itself. This blindness may also lead to a lack of genuine interest or "excitement," to use Said's term, regarding understanding the world around us. Specialization makes it difficult for teachers to believe that youth are creatively intelligent human beings. It narrows a teacher's sense of what or who a mathematician, scientist, writer, historian can be and makes it difficult to connect turntablism, for example, to any of these disciplines.

On the other hand, teachers who view themselves as professional amateurs pounce on these opportunities to think about things differently and learn from others. Said defines amateurism as "an activity that is fueled by care and affection rather than by profit and selfish, narrow specialization" (p. 82). Teachers as professional amateurs relish the chance to get involved in conversations where they can take what they know and grow new understandings. They see their students as allies in a common project. They expect to learn from their students not just how to be a better teacher or how to understand fractions in a new way but also about the world in general. Said writes that teachers as professional amateurs "can enter and transform the merely professional routine most of us go through into something much more lively and radical; instead of doing what one is supposed to do one can ask why one does it, who benefits from it, how can it reconnect with a personal project and original thoughts" (p. 83). Teachers who see themselves as professional amateurs value a student's experiences in creative practices as resources for the their own understandings of academic subject knowledge in particular and the world more broadly.

Gil, like so many youth, is a professional amateur as well. What makes him a professional amateur is the range and variety of things that he does that somehow influence how he embodies a turntablist. For example, Gil reads widely and disparately. He plays guitar in his church band. He raps, break dances, and views films. He writes music and listens to music. Gil redesigns his car. He does not pursue these experiences solely because of his interest in turntablism. Nevertheless, they inform and influence what and how he decides to work on his turntables. Like Gallas, teachers who understand youth work as a craft provide a space where students can see for themselves that the skills and concepts they are developing within their creative practices are assets in the classroom. All of Gil's varied experiences can be used in the classroom to *do* the work of the class. Students as professional amateurs see their craft as informing and influencing the way they engage in the work of the class. They see academic disciplines and their creative practices as equal resources for their work. Youth already do this kind of work. For example, Gil used his skill as a turntablist to explore more deeply and thus make more relevant the class discussions on Malcolm X through manipulating one of Malcolm X's speeches on his turntables.

As teachers, it is difficult for us to see the classroom as a space to encourage these ways of working. Heath writes:

> Schools face imposing constraints of structure, disposition, resources and externally imposed guidelines for curricula and outcomes . . . teachers have to neutralize their methods and materials to satisfy a constituency of wide-ranging interests. . . . The constraints with which schools must wrestle and within which they must define practice make deep inroads into educators' autonomy, especially in areas most central to authentic curricula. (p. 485)

This "constituency of wide-ranging interests" often gets appeased by viewing teaching as always trying to find something to do with students instead of designing learning experiences that encourage enduring understandings of essential conceptual ideas. Wiggins and

McTighe (2005) describe this way of teaching as "engaging experiences that lead only accidentally, if at all, to insight or achievement" (p. 16). Another problem with this practice is that the search for the best activities is never over, and teachers are always hunting for more ideas to fill time. Jean Lave (1997) captures this perpetual crisis of teaching by comparing a curriculum that supports the creative practices of youth with a curriculum that delineates what that practice must be:

> The problem is that any curriculum intended to be a specification *of* practice, rather than an arrangement of opportunities *for* practice (for fashioning and resolving ownable dilemmas) is bound to result in the teaching of a misanalysis of practice . . . and the learning of still another. At best it can only induce a new and exotic kind of practice. . . . In the settings for which it is intended (in everyday transactions), it will appear out of order and will not in fact reproduce "good" practice. (p. 32)

Lave cautions us that the focus in classrooms should not be *about* practice, meaning an emphasis on learning how to do something out of the context of doing it. Instead, teachers should spend their pedagogical energy on designing experiences where students can learn through doing. Lave calls these experiences "ownable dilemmas." These are challenges, problems, obstacles that students want to take on, see the purpose in solving, and feel the need to overcome. A curriculum where youth utilize skills and conceptual knowledge developed through creative practices is designed around ownable dilemmas, for that is exactly the way in which Gil engages in his creative practice on his own terms. His daily practice places him in perplexing, confusing, or challenging moments where he must do more work to move forward in his art form. This orientation to work and learning is more sustainable than the kind of curriculum that focuses on covering material or is built from a collection of one-off activities. Instead, teachers design learning environments that encourage a way of being in the classroom, as opposed to a collection of methods of teaching.

Implementing this sort of curriculum gives teachers a "solution" to the problem of constantly trying to find one day, one month, or one hour of something to do in the classroom. Lemke (1997) reminds us that "practices are not just performances, not just behaviors, not just material processes or operations, but meaningful actions, actions that have relations of meaning to one another in terms of some cultural system" (p. 43). There is value in building a "common culture" of "professional amateurs" in our classrooms to enable our students to "learn not just what and how to perform, but also what the performance means" (p. 43). It is in this spirit that we can build with our students a "community of classroom practice" through the conception of creative practice—youth work—as craft.

Classroom as Youth Space

While it is important to develop a sense of the culture of work of one's students, it is just as important to translate that understanding into how one designs the learning experience. In fact, these two perspectives go hand in hand, with the ethnographic stance informing how one goes about designing a learning experience. In the case of classroom as youth space, I mean that informed by an ethnographic understanding of her students, the teacher now needs to open up space in the classroom for youth such as Gil to utilize the technical skills and conceptual knowledge acquired through their creative practices. She can do this in several ways: by allowing for multiple forms of performance, by embracing idiosyncratic ways of working, and by working alongside her students.

Multiple Forms of Performance

Performance often has a narrow definition in classrooms. In a classroom context, performance often means displaying some kind of product at the end of a unit. Performance is used as a sign of the end of learning a concept or set of skills: the culmination of several weeks of work. It could be a "public" reading involving students sharing their writing in front of the rest of the class. A performance could be a museum of artifacts produced through research students have done in a history class. The performance is polished and practiced. It is meant to be one's best effort. The performance is also a way for teachers to assess the work of their students. When the performance concludes, the class moves on to something else, and this something else is tied to curricular objectives that are often not connected at all to the learning that led up to that performance.

Gil's multidimensional use of performance in his turntablism pushes us to expand the ways in which we design performances in our classrooms. Many times, Gil developed a particular product out of snippets of ideas amassed over a period of time. In fact, Gil would purposefully perform works in progress designed in this way to push his creative practice forward. Recall Gil's layering of the Malcolm X and Martin Luther King Jr. speeches. He wanted to perform for me what he had been working on, not as a final product but as a work in progress that, by performing, he could think about more critically. He performed this work in progress to open a space where we could talk about the issues introduced by the material.

In addition to the end-of-unit culminating performances, we need to offer more informal forms of performance where our students can try their work out, in mid-production, as Gil so often does. These informal performances serve a crucial purpose: they provide essential feedback from peers to determine where to go next or even whether it is worth proceeding with the project at all. They also open up avenues for critical conversation about the craft itself and the meaning of the products being constructed. These performances provide opportunities for discussing the ideas within the work. Freedom must be given to allow students to decide, after such performances, to abandon works and move on to other ideas that they are pursuing.

How would this look in the classroom? Imagine a teacher teaching a unit on short stories. The teacher decides to have her students write their own short stories. This teacher, informed and influenced by the creative practices of youth, would not only have a culminating performance at the end of the unit where students would pick their "best" short story to read aloud or display. She would implement weekly performances, informal readings for example, where her students could try out stories as works in progress to see where to take them next or whether to drop them entirely for another idea. After all, isn't this self-reflection and assessment what many writers do? They work on getting ideas down on paper and then share those rough ideas with others whom they trust. In fact, this is different from sharing a rough draft of a piece that needs polishing. Youth and adults involved in a creative practice see feedback throughout the process of developing an idea. We need to enact this kind of practice in our classes.

Gil also performs widely. During the research, Gil performed in the music room, in his own room, in a studio, in a record store, in his friend's house, and at parties. If we want to design learning environments where the learning has the potential to be personally meaningful and resonate with how youth learn in the world, we must provide our students the chance to perform in small and large ways outside of the confines of our classrooms or schools. This pedagogical move creates the possibility of our students identifying multiple audiences for their work. These different audiences can push our students' work in new directions. For example, if students are investigating how to improve the safety of a local intersection in a math class, they should not perform their findings only to a high-level official in city government. They must also meet with urban planners, transportation advocates, and pedestrian advocates while they are doing the project. At this time, students perform what they are learning not just to show what they know but also as a way of figuring out what needs to happen next.

Embracing Idiosyncratic Ways of Working

Gil has an idiosyncratic work process. He has a peculiar and individual way of making work meaningful to him. When you spend time with any youth you will find that they have their own personal ways of understanding the world around them and they have personalized ways of working to construct that understanding. These processes are certainly not axiomatic or linear. They do not follow the regimented work patterns of classrooms: one day to brainstorm ideas, another day to read and take notes, another day to write a rough draft, and so on. Or study a topic for a prescribed amount of time and then take a test on it. Instead, Gil, like other youth involved in these kinds of practices, works in starts and spurts, sometimes dabbling, at other times working for many hours at a stretch. While at work, they experiment. They test out ideas by themselves and with members of their community of practice. They hone particular technical skills.

Gil told me that there were days when he came home from school and immediately got on his turntables. The next thing he knew he would look up at the clock and realize that he had been on them for six straight hours. By the end of the session, records would be strewn about the floor, evidence of intense work. Gil even rigged a cross-fader so that he could take it to bed with him and practice crabbing, a technique for moving the toggle switch of the cross-fader to create various effects as the record plays.

Another important characteristic of the work that Gil did was that when he came up against an insurmountable obstacle or was not satisfied with what he had done, he moved on. He may or may not have put the work away and come back to it at another time. This meant that Gil's work involved experimentation and partially completed projects. He had the freedom to determine when a project did not merit completion. For example, Gil used his notebook to scribble ideas for turntable pieces. Some of these ideas became compositions. Others did not. He also gave me several audiotapes of partially completed pieces. These starts and stops on their own may not seem to amount to much, but when put together they actually enabled Gil to bring other projects within his practice to completion.

This particular aspect of how youth work on their own terms can have direct implications in terms of the way we teach, for it turns upside down the idea that the goal in learning is the product. Gil shows us that the accumulation of attempts that lead up to an eventual turntable composition is where we should be focusing our pedagogical energy if we want youth to produce powerful and meaningful work in our classes.

The way we design learning spaces in schools needs to honor the idiosyncratic nature of real work. Instead of making everyone follow the same steps for a research paper, for example, teachers need to recognize everyone's personal way of exploring something by establishing a set of criteria that enable students to construct their own way of finding what it is they want to explore and how they want to explore it. These criteria should be shaped by listening to youth describe their ways of attacking a problem, exploring an issue, or developing an argument balanced by our understanding of the ways mathematicians, historians, writers, and scientists pursue their craft. In addition, teachers need to design ongoing conversations where teachers and students articulate to each other and themselves how they go about working. This form of work dialogue honors the ways youth are making meaning in their worlds and acknowledges that the classroom can be a place to put that understanding of practice to work as well.

Teachers Doing Work with their Students

Teachers need to be working *with* their students. One thing that struck me about Gil's practice is that he surrounded himself with others who were engaged in the same or a similar practice. This meant that when they got together, they were all speaking from experience. Gil played with and watched Del and others work on the turntables. He hung out with seniors who were part of the hip-hop scene in his school. He taped up articles about other turntablists in his room. These real and imagined communities of practice introduced new skills to be developed, books to read, movies to see, words to learn, places to go, and concepts to understand.

Too often in classrooms, work is assigned and the last thing that the teacher would ever consider doing is the work that her or his students are doing. School districts, schools, and teachers *package* learning in such a way that teachers would never want to do the work. It is boring, childish, contrived, and meaningless. This division-of-labor approach to learning contradicts the way youth, and I would argue adults outside of schools, do real work. Part of what makes Gil productive in his practices is the fact that his friends are actively engaged in the work as well. This egalitarian approach to the work provides a shared language in which the youth can communicate with one another and establishes a set of rituals and behaviors that are common to everyone. What keeps this community of practice together is a belief that the work they are doing is purposeful and meaningful as well as a sense that the work connects them to possibilities of meeting new people, exploring new places, and progressively getting better at what they do. Imagine if these qualities of work were the driving force behind curriculum.

Surprisingly, there is little writing to be found on this idea. Certainly, Dewey (1997) advocates for this kind of engaged pedagogy when he writes that "the very nature of the work done [is] a social enterprise in which all individuals have an opportunity to contribute and to which all feel a responsibility" (p. 56). This way of working resonates with people such as Kirby, Kirby, and Liner (2003), who suggests that writing teachers are readers and writers "modeling the life of a literate person" (p. 10). Foxfire's Core Practices include "The work teachers and learners do together is infused from the beginning with learner choice, design, and revision. . . . The role of the teacher is that of facilitator and collaborator" (section, para. 14). Even with this work we have somehow lost this idea in middle and secondary schools for the most part. It is a rare classroom space where the teacher collaborates with the students. Put simply, teachers need to write with their students, do scientific experiments with their students, and research alongside their students. This way of being a teacher in the classroom goes beyond modeling how we would like students to be working and learning. Often times modeling in classrooms is used simply to show students what to do or how to do something. It does not stem from real work that the teacher is engaged in. Del and Sam modeled technical skills through their work on the turntables. Their modeling was a natural outgrowth of their practice. Doing work *with* students meant that teachers are personally interested in the work. The modeling, then, is done not just to show students what to do but actually to help the teacher continue the work as well. Teachers need to be engaged in the act of *learning* within their classroom. With that, teachers need to engage in conversations with their students around what it means to work, how they do it, and so on. This discourse is a fundamental part of how youth work in the everyday.

The classroom should be a space of mutual work. Instead of the traditional "detached spectatorship" where teachers observe and evaluate the learning of their students, we need to shift to a classroom space of actors—both students and teachers engaged in the challenges, frustrations, and benefits of real work (Rorty, 1998).

Conclusion

> To engage with our students as persons is to affirm our own incompleteness, our consciousness of spaces still to be explored, desires still to be tapped, possibilities still to be opened and pursued . . . We have to find out how to open such spheres, such spaces, where a better state of things can be imagined . . . I would like to think that this can happen in classrooms, in corridors, in schoolyards, in the streets around. (Greene, 1986, p. 29)

Throughout this essay, I have been arguing that when educators investigate and acknowledge the creative practices of youth within their pedagogy, opportunities for authentic learning emerge: teachers tune their teaching practices more closely to the ways in which youth learn and make meaning in their everyday lives; they heed the clarion call of writers such as Maxine Greene who encourage educators to make the ways in which students work and learn in their everyday lives explicit in their teaching.

An ethnographic understanding of the ways in which youth perform, improvise, self-reflect, form communities of practice, and assess their work allows us to treat students as people with "desires still to be tapped, possibilities still to be opened and pursued"(Greene, 2003, p. 111). In classroom environments driven by prepackaged curricula or standardized testing, students are figured as finite, closed systems. These classrooms lack the open-ended fluidity of authentic, meaningful learning. They make it difficult or almost impossible for students and teachers to develop a shared sense of *how they can learn together.* In this chapter, I have argued that one of the most underutilized ways of weaving into the fabric of the class habits of mind and body that are at the heart of the work that Gil and so many youth choose to do is gaining a deep ethnographic understanding of how youth make meaning in their everyday lives. Indeed, by honoring the *personhood* of each of our students, we can reframe traditional questions such as "How can I (teacher) teach them (students) these skill and concept objectives?" as "How can we as a community of practice develop these skills and concepts, utilizing my (teacher) understanding of the creative intelligence at work in my students' daily lives?" While this reframing may seem insignificant, in fact it opens up the possibility of adopting curricular standards as a guide rather than a set of constraints to be slavishly followed. In this light, curricular standards are not the source of the problem as many teachers feel. Rather, they become useful tools for learning. We can then work with our students to meet the current high-stakes testing curriculum in the same ways these students meet challenges in the work of their daily lives—by implementing what I have discussed above as authentic forms of performance, improvisation, self-reflection, interpretation, and evaluation. Through this recasting of teacher and student roles as well as how learning looks, sounds, and feels, we transform the classroom into a space where the multisited nature of the ways in which everyone makes meaning is embraced and put to work.

References

Alvermann, D. (2003). Image, language, and sound: Making meaning with popular culture texts. Retrieved July 1, 2007, from http://www.readingonline.org/newliteracies/action/alvermann.

Ben-Yosef, E. (2003). Respecting students' cultural literacies. *Educational Leadership, 61*(2), pp. 80-82 .

Cintron, R. (1997). *Angel's town: Chero ways, gang life, and rhetorics of the everyday.* Boston: Beacon Press.

Csikszentmihalyi, M. (1991). *Flow: The psychology of optimal experience.* New York: Perennial.

Denzin, N. K. (1997). *Interpretive ethnography: Ethnographic practices for the 21st century.* Thousand Oaks, CA: Sage.

Dewey, J. (1997). *Experience and education.* New York: Macmillan.

Dimitriadis, G. (2001). *Performing identity/performing culture: Hip hop as text, pedagogy, and lived practice.* New York: Peter Lang.

Gallas, K. (1994). *The languages of learning: How children talk, write, dance, draw, and sing their understanding of the world.* New York: Teachers College Press.

Goswami, D., & Stillman, P. (1987). *Reclaiming the classroom: Teacher research as an agency for change.* Upper MontclaiR, NJ: Boynton / Cook.

Greene, Maxine. (1986). In search of a critical pedagogy. *Harvard Educational Review, 56*(4), 427–441.

Greene, M. (2003). In search of a critical pedagogy. In R. D. Torres, A. Darder, & M. Baltodano (Eds.), *The critical pedagogy reader* (pp. 97 – 112). London: Routledge.

Gustavson, L., & Cytrynbaum, J. (2003). Illuminating spaces: Relational spaces, complicity, and multisited ethnography. *Field Methods, 15*, 252–270.

Heath, S. B. (1997). Culture: Contested realm in research on children and youth. *Applied Developmental Science, 1*(3), 113–123.

Heath, S. B. (1998). Working through language. In S. Hoyle & C. T. Adger (Eds.), *Kids talk: Strategic language use in later childhood* (pp. 217–240). New York: Oxford University Press.

Heath, S. B. (1999). Rethinking youth transitions [Review of the book *Everyday courage: The lives and stories of urban teenagers*]. *Human Development, 42*(6), 376–382.

Heath, S. B. (2000). Seeing our way into learning. *Cambridge Journal of Education, 30*(1), 121–132.

Heath, S. B., & McLaughlin, M. W. (1994). Learning for anything everyday. *Journal of Curriculum Studies, 26*(5), 471–489.

Kirby, D., Kirby, D. L., & Liner, T. (2003). *Inside out: Strategies for teaching writing.* Portsmouth, NH: Heinemann.

Kress, G., & Van Leeuwen, T. (1996). *Reading images: The grammar of visual design.* London: Routledge.

Lave, J. (1997). The culture of acquisition and the practice of understanding. In D Kirshner & J. Whitson (Eds.), *Situated cognition: Social, semiotic and psychological perspectives* (pp. 17–36). Mahwah, NJ: Lawrence Erlbaum.

Lave, J., & Wenger, E. (1991). *Situated learning: Legitimate peripheral participation.* Cambridge, UK: Cambridge University Press.

Lemke, Jay. 1997. Cognition, context, and learning: A social semiotic perspective. In D. Kirshner & J. Whitson (Eds.), *Situated cognition:*

Social, semiotic and psychological perspectives (pp. 37–55). Mahwah, NJ: Lawrence Erlbaum.

Lyrics2. (2006). Retrieved March 14, 2006, from http://www.lyrics2.co.uk/The-Last-Poets-E-Pluribus-Unum-lyrics2-59608.php.

Moje, E. (2002). But where are the youth? On the value of integrating youth culture into literacy theory. *Educational Theory, 52*(1), 97–120.

Rorty, R. (1998). *Achieving our country: Leftist thought in twentieth century America.* Cambridge, MA: Harvard University Press.

Said, E. (1996). *Representations of the intellectual: The Reith Lectures.* Ne York: Knopf.

Schultz, K. (2003). *Listening: A framework for teaching across differences.* New York: Teachers College Press.

Schultz, K., & Hull, G. (Eds.). (2002). *School's out! A review of theory and research on literacy and learning outside of school.* New York: Teachers College Press.

Sitton, T. (1980). The child as informant. The teacher as ethnographer. *Language Arts, 57*(5), 540–545.

Street, B. (2000). Literacy "events" and literacy "practices": Theory and practice in the "new literacy studies." In K. Jones & M. Martin-Jones (Eds.), *Multilingual literacies: Comparative perspectives on research and practice.* Amsterdam: John Benjamin's.

Wenger, E. (1998). *Communities of practice: Learning, meaning, and identity.* Cambridge, UK: Cambridge University Press.

Willis, P. (1998). Notes on common culture: Towards a grounded aesthetics. *European Journal of Cultural Studies, 1*(2), 163–176.

Response to Gustavson

Greg Dimitriadis

Leif Gustavson's chapter opens up a critical space for youth culture researchers and activists today. Gustavson's great impulse here is to look at young people's creative practices—in all their multiplicity and unpredictability—from "the ground up." In his chapter, Gustavson follows a young man he calls "Gil," carefully exploring the ways in which Gil develops his skill at "turntablism," both in school and out of school. This is serious business for Gil—as it should be for us. As Gustavson shows, turntablism entails a range of creative practices—from carefully looking for new and unexpected resources (i.e., record albums), to calibrating the ways in which beats work with and against each other, to thinking through how song lyrics can be articulated in new and unexpected ways. Gil sees himself as in a long tradition of DJs—a lineage he very self-consciously draws upon as he thinks through and perfects his craft.

Gustavson's deep appreciation of the particularities of this creative practice is striking. While much work on young people tends to affirm or dismiss these kinds of leisure activities uncritically, Gustavson's accomplishment is to open up a nuanced, detailed discussion of this practice and its contours. We see intense moments of transformation here—a gunshot on a *Raiders of the Lost Ark* soundtrack turned into a drumbeat, an obscure song by the Last Poets opened up to critical reflection, sound bites from Malcolm X and Martin Luther King Jr. drawn together in mutually informing ways. All of this underscores the kinds of creative, emergent, and unpredictable learning that happens around the activities young people themselves gravitate toward.

Educators can learn much from Gustavson's focus. In particular, we can learn that learning itself does not always happen in the prescribed sites and settings preferred by educators. Gil's creative activity takes place in and across a range of sites—both in school and out of school. As Gustavson shows, all these sites are important for refining his art—his bedroom, the school music room, and the public club, among them. While some researchers have turned their attention to out-of-school activities, Gustavson's work is in many ways more profound. Instead of "flipping the binary" between in-school and out-of-school learning, he "works the hyphen" between and across the two (Fine, 1994). Gustavson recognizes the continuing value and importance of school sites, as he reads them against nontraditional sites. More than anything, Gustavson's work is intensely *relational*. He does not allow us to rest comfortably on any particular "node" in young people's lives.

All this points to a different model for educators and researchers—one that de-centers our authority and control without giving it up entirely and naïvely. Gustavson shows us a model for thoughtful pedagogy, one that looks toward authentic kinds of assessment and performance, interpretation and evaluation. These kinds of authentic practices are not the ones often foregrounded and valued in school. They are the kinds that take place in front of real audiences, around the kinds of activities young people value. While Gustavson points us toward one such practice here, his book (2007) opens up other such practices—zine writing, spoken word poetry, and graffiti—for discussion. More broadly, though, this work is a generous invitation to look at youth culture and creativity in all their multiplicity, heterogeneity, and specificity. In many respects, Gustavson has set the agenda for the next generation of scholars and activists concerned with youth culture today.

References

Fine, M. (1994). Working the hyphens: Reinventing self and other in qualitative research. In N. Denzin & Y. Lincoln (Eds.), *Handbook of qualitative research* (pp. 70–82). Thousand Oaks, CA: Sage Publications.

Gustavson, L. (2007). *Youth learning on their own terms: Creative Practices and Classroom Teaching.* New York: Routledge.

Response to Gustavson

Decoteau J. Irby

Leif Gustavson's chapter examines the educational and decision-making processes of Gil, a tenth-grade student and hip-hop "turntablist" whose educational contexts move from in school to out of school, from popular to traditional, from past to present. Through ethnography, Gustavson explores how these various contexts overlap in ways that allow Gil to perform, improvise, self-reflect, interpret, and evaluate—all processes of learning in which he participates in the "everyday." Gustavson suggests that understanding these learning processes from the youth perspective is useful in informing pedagogical practices and research and dares educators to rethink classroom practice and the process of educating youth.

As more educators recognize the value in everyday learning, significant challenges emerge as we bring the everyday into traditional learning spaces. The challenges include the "real constraints [of] standardized tests, core curricula, class size, uneven distribution of funding, and other state and district mandates." In addition to these clear and present challenges are those that require teachers to rethink the role of the teacher and consider the importance of students' out-of-school learning. This integral aspect of valuing the everyday in the classroom requires that teachers share the responsibilities of choice, time, and power and acknowledge that the(ir) traditional classrooms are not necessarily the only or most suitable sites of learning.

Gustavson's work illuminates the importance of such out-of-school sites of learning and provides teachers with a temporary glimpse of how students can and do work on their own terms in their own spaces. Moreover, he provides an analysis that suggests traditional teaching methods and processes do not match youths' processes of learning. Through a comparison of traditional ways of teaching English and Gil's work to perfect his turntablism, Gustavson illustrates the difference between the traditional process of teaching and the process by which Gil learns, the former being "artificial," linear, and restricted by time and choices, and the latter being more authentic, autonomous, and situated within a broader life narrative.

Incorporating such everyday practices into the traditional classroom context requires that educators and researchers explore new ways both to create learning opportunities and to assess the learning that takes place. Gustavson essentially asks that we become what he calls "conscious designers of the learning experience." This can be accomplished through first becoming ethnographers and using this knowledge of youths' learning processes to create authentic learning experiences. We must seek to understand *how* students are what they are academically through knowing their process of learning. It is here Gustavson's work is of particular importance for teachers and researchers.

Gustavson allows the roles of the researcher and the teacher to fade back and forth and overlap, so to speak. He calls for educators to act not as researcher or teacher but as professional amateurs willing to learn by discarding previous assumptions about how students learn. Much like Gil's performance of "cross-fading" on his turntables allowed for re-articulation of ideas, Gustavson essentially re-articulates traditionally bifurcated roles and asks teachers to rethink their process of creating learning opportunities that value preexisting knowledge and learning processes of youth by going back and forth from researcher to educator to imagine new possibilities of how to create opportunities for learning and to assess learning.

The metaphor of the turntable is particularly appropriate in Gustavson's analysis. On the turntables sit different, often but not always competing, ideas: the teacher and the student, the teacher and the researcher, standardized curricula and creative freedom, in-school learning spaces and out-of-school learning spaces. The future of what happens in education is largely dependent on how learning is re-articulated through mixing, sampling, and fading between these turntables to create something new. Undoubtedly, Gustavson's work will require us to think creatively about our own process of creating authentic learning opportunities for students and evaluating learning. He has provided us with much to consider as we begin drawing from the past to create better education for the future.

Chapter Five

"Kind of Like Emerging from the Shadows": Adolescent Girls as Multiliteracy Pedagogues

Rachel E. Nichols

I started working on [the literary/art annual] because if I wanted to get on NHS [National Honor Society], I needed an after-school activity. I liked the idea of creative writing, which is why I chose [the magazine] over yearbook or [the school newspaper]. . . . Besides meeting new people every year, I could develop my writing skills and have a bit of control over the magazine. (Beth Ann, personal interview, January 14, 2002)

Joining the staff of the school literary/art magazine in ninth grade, Beth Ann continued to work on the publication for four years, positioning herself as an editor during her senior year, when this study took place. Beth Ann's initial reasons for choosing to spend more than ten hours each week working on the magazine were both practical and personal: she could achieve her academic goal of being accepted into the National Honor Society as well as her personal goal of finding a space to develop her writing. However, these individual goals expanded when she came to embrace the vibrancy of collaboration as she built a community of practice and contributed to the delineation of a multiliteracy pedagogy. For Beth Ann, the magazine became a space unlike others available in school—it was one she considered "hers" (Beth Ann, personal interview, January 14, 2002).

The development of a multiliteracy pedagogy by the young women who worked in the multimodal space of this school-affiliated literary/art magazine is of particular importance in the increasingly visual landscape of adolescent literacy practices, including those that are privileged *in*, *out of*, and *of* school, especially as the in-school literacy practices tend to remain more focused on the verbal. In this chapter, I explore how literacy work happens in one particular school-affiliated context, the context of the literary/art magazine in which I participated as a teacher–researcher. The research described here took place from September 2001 through June 2002 at St. Vladimir,[1] an urban parochial high school for girls, where I was previously an English teacher for six years, as well as a literary/art magazine advisor for three. Each day as we worked together on the magazine, the girls and I also worked to build community through our shared words and actions. While I initially viewed it as a community that reflected the general sense of pride and ownership in the school, I came to notice ways that the space in which we created this magazine seemed different from other spaces in which I had spent time with students—including my own classroom.

Elizabeth Moje and David O'Brien "believe that secondary literacy theory and research must move beyond a focus on print" (2001, p. xv). In my experience as a teacher of high school English and a researcher of literacy, I have seen that adolescents construct knowledge and utilize multiple forms of literacy both to make meaning and to represent themselves and their worlds. Heather Bruce states in *Literacies, Lies, and Silences: Girls Writing Lives in the Classroom* that "little has been done to study the effects of writing in the education of adolescent girls" (2003, p. 7). Although Bruce looks at girls' writing entirely within the context of a for-credit women's studies class in a high school and is primarily interested in their written discourse as produced within and for that class, she convincingly asserts that girls' writing lives—and their lives as constructed through their writing—are underexplored. Of course, it is not the case that adolescent girls are not writing, and I remain interested in the relationships between their in-, out-of-, and of-school writing lives.

It is particularly noteworthy that during the period of this study, the eleven young women who voluntarily chose to work on constructing the literary/art magazine and who became my co-researchers demonstrated unfailing commitment, considering there was no academic credit or other tangible incentive offered for participation on the magazine. Clearly, the space itself, the activities experienced within the space, and the people who worked on this magazine were each important components to consider. Something significant was happening while we created and produced the magazine—and it happened in a setting that is associated with school.

In working with young women on a school-affiliated literary/art magazine, every day I saw them exhibit characteristics that Heath (2000) maintains are not pervasive in schools but are present in the arts programs she studied: for example, they demonstrated responsibility, they worked to make their ideas happen, and they utilized a variety of literacy forms. It seems to me that it is indeed possible to value the interests and talents of young people and to recognize ways that their involvement in a voluntary, *school-affiliated* arts program contributes to the development of individuals, groups, and larger communities. Just as Hull and Schultz (2002) implore literacy theorists and researchers to do, in this study I put my "energies toward investigating potential relationships, collaborations . . . and the informal learning that flourishes in a range of settings" (p. 53).

This inquiry started from my experience as a teacher–researcher in the context of this literary/art magazine. As I began to look closely at the construction of the magazine, I paid attention to the range and variation of the girls' literacy practices. I was interested in how the participants engaged with literacy while they were involved in the creation and publication of a school-affiliated literary/art magazine. I also wanted to explore how both the creative and the publication processes of making the magazine were socially constructed; that is, I wanted to see how the participants worked both individually and within the group, as well as within the larger school community.

As we worked together, I saw that as a multi-genre text of words and images, the literary/art magazine offered an opportunity to consider the concept of literacy as also including visual representations. Through the girls' multiple and broad literacy practices, I grappled with what it might mean—and to whom—to consider visual art as a multimodal literacy form, in line with Moje and O'Brien's (2001) call for action. Relatedly, I also sought to explore the relationships between the girls' literacy practices and their evolving identities as learners and participants in the process of creating and publicizing the magazine while also considering our evolving roles and relationships with one another.

Overview of the Theoretical Framework

This research was conducted within an interpretivist paradigm, in that I looked at the socially constructed, complex, and ever-changing realities of the participating adolescent girls and myself. Through our conversation and activities around the construction of a literary/art magazine and the close reading of tangible multimodal literacy artifacts created by the girls on staff and their peers, it was my hope that together, we would come to some interpretations and understandings of how the young women of this community construct their worlds and represent them through literacy forms. As I collected and interpreted data, it was from a stance of feminist ethnography: I worked toward a climate in which all participants (the girls—my co-researchers—and I) were encouraged to be reflexive in our discourse and our analysis, especially in the interrogation of issues of identity, gender, and power as evident in our daily work and as seen through the writing and art created by the young women.

The combination of feminism and education "has the potential to be subversive—encouraging not just 'exposure' to concepts, but participation in experiences that could change participants' perspectives" (Ropers-Huilman, 1998, p. 19). Through feminism, future possibilities are imagined and expanded. I perceive that if education is a nonviolent means of social change, then feminist education is an inclusive nonviolent means of social change that starts from within. Moje (2000a) suggests that part of teaching literacy processes and practices in secondary schools "needs to focus on the development of caring relationships that make spaces for young people to inquire, speak, read, write, and perform what they are interested in and care about" (p. 4). If attention is paid to the literacy practices embodied in spaces such as the school-affiliated one documented in this research, then we can transfer our newfound knowledge and understandings across settings, including within school. Moje also states that her research shows that "when kids feel cared for—when they believe they are working in relationship with a teacher—they tend to be more willing to try different literacy practices and strategies that the teacher offers" (2000a, p. 69). Similarly, O'Brien, Moje, and Stewart write that "[a]n often overlooked context for literacy researchers in secondary school settings is the relationships conducted among students" (2001, p. 42). They continue to underscore the important role that literacy learning has in adolescents' lives, especially in the construction of identities, and they echo those (Heath & McLaughlin, 1993; Hull & Schultz, 2002; Moje, 2000a, 2000b) who, like me, lament that out-of-school literacy practices are rarely recognized in school.

Studies of young people's literacy practices are beginning to offer expanded perspectives about where and how youth use literacy both in and out of school (Hull & Schultz, 2002; Moje, 2000a, 2000b; Schultz, 2002). I align myself with these researchers who resist the tendency to conceptualize literacy as being either a school-based or an out-of-school practice. Invoking theorists of youth culture, Elizabeth Moje also calls for further study of the literacy practices in the "in-between spaces" young people navigate, so that we might "understand more about conventional literacy processes and about how new literacies are invented and transformed in hybrid spaces" (2002, p. 118). I am particularly interested in these hybrid spaces that create and engage media texts. This research is explicitly aligned with those who seek further understanding of adolescents' multiple literacy practices as they are constructed in, out of, and of school, as well as with those who are concerned with the literacy practices of young women in general.

I locate my research as a feminist (Coffey & Delamont, 2000; Hauser & Marrero, 1998; Olesen, 1998; Shrewsbury, 1987), ethnographic (Ceglowski, 2000) practitioner inquiry (Cochran-Smith & Lytle, 2001; Lytle & Cochran-Smith, 1992). The collective framework that informed my research design and data analysis consisted of the juxtaposition of multiliteracies (Kress & Van Leeuwen, 2001; New London Group (NLG), 1996), practitioner inquiry (Cochran-Smith & Lytle, 2001; Lytle & Cochran-Smith, 1992), intertextuality (NLG, 1996), hybridity (NLG, 1996; Fairclough, 2003), and portraiture (Lawrence-Lightfoot & Davis, 1997). In this chapter, I argue that the participants in this project utilized social literacy practices predicated on dialogue to create their own pedagogy. In doing so, they determined the space, content, and production of a literary/art magazine, simultaneously establishing their own community of practice (Gee, 2000a, 2000b; Lave & Wenger, 1991). Finally, I discuss how our roles in the community of practice (Gee, 2000a, 2000b; Lave & Wenger, 1991) were constructed through our relationships. This culminates in a summary discussion of the implications of this study.

On Literacies, Art, and Aesthetic Education

This study is concerned with the literacy practices of adolescent girls, as constructed through their creation of a literary/art magazine. Since the practices involved comprise mainly two modes—namely, those that involve writing (verbal) and those that involve art (visual)—I examine both. While there is a considerable amount of related work in the area of verbal literacies from which to draw, it has been more difficult for me to locate the visual literacies mode. The already-named field of "visual literacies" as defined by Fransecky and Debes

(1972) presents a limited—and limiting—framework within which to work. However, I do find resonance in Maxine Greene's concept of "aesthetic education" (1995). I will further elaborate upon these positions following a discussion of how New Literacy Studies theory applies to this work.

In speaking of literacy as a social practice, Brian Street (2000) has said that using the term "literacies" challenges the dominant emphasis on a single form of literacy, one with a "big L" and a "little y". When we think of the plurality of literacies, the generic concept of "literacy" is expanded to include the many factors that influence one's practices of reading and writing. People, both individually and communally, engage in "literacy practices," or intersections of reading and writing with actions, values, attitudes, and relationships. Building on Shirley Brice Heath's concept of a "literacy event," or "any occasion in which a piece of writing is integral to the nature of participants' interactions and their interpretive processes" (as quoted in Street, 1993, p. 12), Street has further developed the concept into "literacy practices." This incorporates the idea of "literacy events" and what Street calls "folk models" of those events, as well as the ideological preconceptions that undermine them (pp. 12–13). Literacy practices are aspects of people and their relationships with culture and power structures in society.

David Barton and Mary Hamilton put forward a theory of literacy as a social practice, noting that "literacy is not the same in all contexts" (1998, p. 10). They write that "there are different literacies associated with different domains of life" and that associated with these "domains"—or structured contexts in which literacy is used and learned—are "discourse communities"—or groups of people who are "held together" through or perhaps because of their "characteristic ways of talking, acting, valuing, interpreting and using written language" (p. 11). In studying the verbal/visual literacy practices of adolescent girls, I consider both the "domain" of the magazine space and the "discourse community/ies" that formed throughout the process. I also notice that the "domain" of the magazine was a place in which literacies were not only used and learned but also constructed simultaneously. Similarly, not only do I focus on the spoken and written aspects of emerging literacies discourse, but, through my consideration of multimodal literacy practices, I include the visual as well.

Interpreting the creation of a magazine that fuses the writing and art of particular adolescent girls at a particular time can be done only through socially situated lenses. In this unique context, premised upon the coming together of the verbal and the visual, some narratives and identities are potentially being created, shared, or even dismissed. One notion embedded in New Literacy theory, that literacies are employed in the negotiating of identities (Street, 1995)—and I would add in the construction of identities—is particularly significant to this work. Furthermore, conceptualizing literacies broadly makes room for one to conceive of transformative understandings of the multiple and varied uses and meanings across reading, writing, and visual practices.

The area of visual literacy is still developing. In 1996, the National Council of Teachers of English (NCTE) board of directors passed a resolution supporting "professional development and public awareness of the role that viewing and visually representing our world have as a form of literacy." They continued that teachers should "guide students in constructing meaning through creating and viewing nonprint texts" (NCTE, as cited in Childers, Hobson, & Mullin, 1998, pp. ix, xiii). Even though they do not use the term "visual literacy," it appears that the NCTE are acknowledging the profound connections between verbal and visual practices here. As Lee Galda says, "[V]isual literacy and print literacy may be reciprocal: we use pictures to make meaning of text and we use text to make meaning about pictures. . . . The truth may be that writing and art are on a continuum as part of the same thing—a way to express meaning about our world" (as cited in Flood, Heath, & Lapp, 1997, pp. 790–791). By emphasizing the interrelated processes employed in the construction of a literary/art magazine, this research contributes to the area of visual literacy by presenting a case through which the concept of visual art as a literacy form can be reappropriated, redefined, or renamed through this exploration of adolescent girls' interconnected, hybrid, multimodal literacies. The belief that literacy as a social practice includes reading, writing, and discourse practices, as well as visual practices, and an emphasis on the social, multiple, and dynamic characteristics of literacies and identities remains vital to this work.

In light of this, I work toward a definition of literacy that includes art. Writing about and reinterpreting John Dewey's views of the arts, Philip Jackson (1998) mentions that art has the power to be genuinely transformative, both for artists and for audiences. Art itself is experience occasioned by both the production and the encounter; that is, art is a social practice. Jackson expands Dewey's description of experience, saying it is "transactional," a conglomeration of "self, object, and event" (p. 3). Just as an artist may change through the process of creating art, so may the individual who becomes an audience for it; both "experience" the art, and both are affected by it. In conceiving of "art as experience," Dewey portrays the arts as providing people with moments of "delight," expanding horizons, "contributing meaning and value to future experience," and modifying ways of perceiving the world, thereby changing both the person and the world (Jackson, 1998, p. 33). In addition, neither producing nor engaging with art is a passive occurrence, and there are social and individual constructs that come into play during every art "experience." Jackson, building on Dewey's 1934 *Art as Experience*, makes much use of the term "aesthetic," which Dewey proprietarily defined (p. 45ff.). The common interpretation of the term "aesthetic" is not appropriate when conceiving of visual art as experience: to harp on aspects of form or beauty would be to impose value on the art objects themselves. In my work, I am more interested in the processes through which art is created and encountered and in the "transactions" that occur within/between artists and audiences. Embedded in this is an understanding of art as a literacy form with meanings that are socially constructed and that are not fixed.

It is for these reasons that I find words of Maxine Greene so appealing. Building on Dewey, she states that the way to get individual expression is to have a sense of community, which is made "through dialogue, through doing things together, through shared concern" (Weiss, Systra, & Slater, 1998, p. 27). Greene sees the arts as invitations to explore identity and as calls to social criticism (Grumet, 1998, p. 134). Through the notion of what she has termed "aesthetic education," Greene champions the "deliberate efforts to foster increasingly informed and involved encounters with art" (1995, p. 138), envisioning an emancipatory pedagogy that enables students to "live within the arts, making clearings and spaces for themselves" (p.135). As a "mode" of education, aesthetic education involves seeing the arts as a means through which students can articulate their stories and create their identities; inherent within this is an emphasis on process over product. Michelle Fine echoes Maxine Greene's call to action and vision of possibility through aesthetic education and community: "[T]he burden is on us, on adults, to carve out 'spaces,' to inspire a sense of the 'not yet,' to reinvent schools and communities that are engaging for young people" (1997, pp. 214–215).

A Pedagogy of Multiliteracies

A pedagogy of multiliteracies is "based on the assumption that the human mind is embodied, situational, and social" (NLG, 1996, p. 82). From a multiliteracies perspective, knowledge is therefore "situated in sociocultural settings and heavily contextualized in specific knowledge domains and practices" (p. 84). Defined in this way, literacy pedagogy includes negotiating a multiplicity of discourses, and it also entails accounting for a variety of text forms and understanding representational forms, including visual images (NLG, 1996, p. 62). According to the New London Group, a pedagogy of multiliteracies "focuses on modes of representation much broader than language alone" (1996, p. 64).

The New London Group authors delineate six elements of the meaning-making process and suggest four components of multiliteracy pedagogy that build upon one another, each structured within the concept of design (1996). Although I will not utilize all of their arguments, I will say more about the design of the literary/art magazine as I specifically discuss the New London Group's notion of "situated practice" (NLG, 1996, p. 85) within the context of this study. It is important to note here, however, that a pedagogy of multiliteracies was an essential methodological component of this study. As a practitioner–inquirer working with a community on a literary/art magazine—the design and production of a multi-genre text via multimodalities—I had to consider my research and teaching practices in ways that allowed for multiplicity. Multiliteracies create "a different kind of pedagogy, one in which language and other modes of meaning are dynamic representational resources, constantly being remade by their users as they work to achieve their various cultural purposes" (NLG, 1996, p. 64). As a practitioner–inquirer, I helped to create a context that valued multiliteracies, and I looked at how all of the participants, including myself, made meaning through creating and engaging with texts.

All of these concepts directly contributed to the foundation of the methodology for the research design and the interpretation of the data in my study. Specifically, the multimodal meaning-making terms of hybridity and intertextuality, initially explored by Norman Fairclough (1992, 2003) and discussed further by the New London Group (1996) and others, are key to my understanding and interpretation of the happenings in this research.

Multimodalities

The methodology and interpretation of this study were predicated on these core tenets of multimodalities: all meaning making is multimodal, and all written text is also visually designed (NLG, 1996). Knowledge is situated in sociocultural settings and is contexualized in specific practices; this is reflected in the written and visual aspects of texts. A multimodal text, such as a literary/art magazine, is one that mixes words and images. In multimodal texts, "the images often communicate different things from the words. And the combination of the two modes communicates things that neither of the modes does separately. Thus the idea of different sorts of multimodal literacy seems an important one" (Gee, 2003, p.14).

Addressing the "digitization" of today's society, Kress and Van Leeuwen (2001) purport that multimodality is that in which "common semiotic principles operate in and across different modes," such as images encoding emotion (p. 2). They delineate how discourse, design, production, and distribution are central to communication and representation, noting that "[t]he basic assumption is that meanings are made, distributed, received, interpreted, and remade in interpretation through many representational and communicative modes—not just through language—whether as speech or as writing" (Jewitt & Kress, 2003, p. 1). Put simply, multimodality is the use of different modes or ways of creating and shaping material for the representation of meaning. Multimodal meanings and the relationships of different designs of meaning can be further described through the concepts of hybridity and intertextuality (Fairclough, as cited in NLG, 1996).

Hybridity

There are several meanings currently associated with the term "hybridity." According to the New London Group, hybridity is the articulating of established practices and conventions in new ways within and between different modes of meaning (NLG, 1996, p. 82). A hybrid product can be said to be something that has shattered the text's origins, centers, and essences (Angermüller & Bunzmann, 2000). People create and innovate different cultural forms and traditions by constantly recombining and restructuring, enabling new relations to be created through linguistic and visual meanings. Hybridity, then, can result in a blurring of boundaries (Fairclough, 2003), encompassing the processes of fragmenting and mixing established constructs to create new ones.

Intertextuality

As the term implies, intertextuality is meaning making through a cross-referencing of texts. It deals with the "potentially complex ways in which meanings (such as linguistic meanings) are constituted through relationships to other texts (real or imaginary), text types (discourse or genres), narratives, and other modes of meaning (such as visual design . . .)" (NLG, 1996, p. 82). Intertextuality encompasses the presence within a text of elements of other texts, broadly defined. These texts speak to and influence one another as meaning is created. My analysis will show not only that the participants in this study created a volume of a school-affiliated literary/art magazine but that in the process of doing so, they also constructed meaning through multimodal, hybrid, and intertextual literacy practices. In turn, the young women established a multiliteracy pedagogy through which they both taught and learned from one another.

The Literacy Practices of *Camouflage*

In this section, I describe and analyze the social literacy practices that the participants used to determine the theme and content, to orchestrate production, and to navigate the physical and virtual spaces of the literary/art magazine. I utilize narrative description and examples of these processes that I argue built our community of practice (Gee, 2000a, 2000b; Lave & Wenger, 1991) and produced collaborative knowledge while leading to the production of the magazine. James Gee states that

> [w]ithin a community of practice all members pick up a variety of tacit and taken-for-granted values, norms, cultural models and narratives as part of their socialization into the practice and their ongoing immersion in the practice. Tacitly accepting these values, norms, cultural models and narratives (in mind, action and embodied practice), and sharing them with others, is just what it means to be a *member* of the community of practice. (2000a, p. 186)

To look at the work of members of this community of practice, I use concepts of multimodalities, including hybridity and intertextuality, to examine the ways in which the members of this group read, wrote, and learned together as we constructed meaning in the process of creating a literary/art magazine and ultimately developed our own pedagogy. I argue that social literacy practices were central to this group and that it was through, by, and because of the utilization of various modalities that both the context and the magazine came into existence. I find that there was a recursiveness to our work: members of the community of practice developed and used six specific social literacy practices (described below), which resulted in the creation of an emergent multiliteracy pedagogy. In turn, the social practices, the modalities, and the multiliteracy pedagogy contributed to the creation of the community of practice and the collaborative knowledge production that was typical in our work together. This analysis sheds new light on adolescent girls' literacy practices and extends the knowledge base related to multimodalities and the development of school-affiliated multiliteracy practices, from which the participants developed their own literacy pedagogy.

As previously explained, I designed this study with an explicit personal understanding of and commitment to feminist educational practices. In this chapter, I show how the girls responded to my initial invitation to be involved in a student-centered research project in ways that cogently illustrate the productive possibilities of feminist educational practices in an adolescent setting. Given the opportunity and initial modeling, the girls developed their own agenda for our work together, which resulted in the development of six pedagogical dimensions, namely, dialogue, structure, negotiation, collaboration, critique, and representation. I begin by examining the ways in which we collaboratively established the theme of the magazine primarily through the dimension of dialogue. I then consider the selection processes that we mediated through dialogue by establishing a structure for the reading of written and visual texts. Next, as we began to explore aspects of design and production, several social practices amalgamated in our simultaneous work with writing and images through the negotiation of meaning and responsibility and the resulting collaboration. As we shifted our perspectives outside of the regular physical space in which we worked, the social practices employed during several field trips expanded our educational environment, providing new vistas for retrospection and critique. Finally, I underscore the notion that the girls were the ultimate pedagogues of their own community of practice, as evident in the critique and metaphorical and physical representation of their epistemologies in the published volume of the literary/art magazine.

All of these dimensions were informed by and infused through the ongoing dialogue of the community of practice; in one sense, then, dialogue was both a central pedagogical practice and a modality through which the other five dimensions came to be (Figure 4).

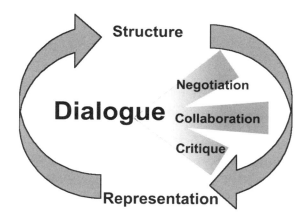

Figure 4. Six Pedagogical Dimensions

The discussion unfolds according to the six emergent pedagogical dimensions realized by the girls through their social literacy practices. The analysis is presented in rough chronological order to show the development of the dimensions; however, it must be emphasized that in most cases, once established, the categories were traversed simultaneously. That is to say, the emic dimensions of the girls' pedagogy of this community of practice were constantly recursive. I incorporate some lenses of a pedagogy of multiliteracies as defined by the New London Group (1996) as I examine the social literacy practices that the girls invent alongside those that they maintain within this literacy community. In doing so, I address the overarching question that I carried with me as I conducted this work: that is, what is the range and variation of the literacy practices that adolescent girls engage in while involved in the creation and publication of a school-affiliated literary/art magazine? I also explore this related subquestion: How are both the creative and publication processes of making a literary/art magazine socially constructed?

As a community of practice that was of school but not in school, the experiences in this context complicated the in-/out-of-school dichotomy because the girls simultaneously drew upon and extended schooled literacy practices. Their literacy practices were uniquely developed for this project in terms of their use of collaboration, consideration of multiple audiences, and attention to word/image relationships. The community of practice provided rich, student-centered, arts-based opportunities for girls' literacy engagements and created a setting for more democratic uses of voice, knowledge production, and social relations among the girls as well as between the girls and myself.

Dialogue: "Camouflage" Is a Verb and a Noun

It is a tradition that every year, the girls who work on the St. Vladimir school-affiliated literary/art magazine rename it. Though the publication has a general moniker, which also functions as the name of the after-school activity, a new title is determined for each year's edition. In 2001–2002, as well as in each of the three previous years that I had been affiliated with the magazine, the girls carefully selected a title that served as a thematic organizing metaphor for the entire publication. My field notes from the fall of 2001 reveal that we spent the majority of our first two months together discussing what that year's book would be called. Early in our work together, the girls established their parameters for what the magazine would include and they began developing some procedures for how to go about its creation. From the start, the social practice of dialogue was central to the group's process of coming to know things. Related to the New London Group's concept of "situated practice," which draws upon "the experience of meaning-making" in the "lifeworlds" of the participants (NLG, 1996, p. 65), the initial parameters were namely those experiences anchored by school.

Starting from ways that had worked in the past, the girls proposed that we should go about obtaining submissions through direct solicitation in English classes and through general school advertisements and that we should organize the book with one unifying theme and related division titles. After hours of dialogue, one of the first major decisions the girls made was to name and structure the magazine thematically. Having done so before, they were comfortable with maintaining many of the social practices of the literary/art magazine established in previous years; they began discussing themes almost immediately. I saw this as being as much reflective of their schooled literacy practices as it was a tradition of the magazine; as students in English literature classes, the girls were familiar with the notion of writing to a theme. In this instance, however, they were turning the tables a bit. In the first instance of their emerging multiliteracy pedagogy, the girls flipped a familiar construct on its head: they determined the theme through dialogue— as opposed to absorbing it, as so often happened in school—and they went on to interpret and represent it through the art and writing they selected and created for the magazine. By reinterpreting what it means to work with a theme, the girls reclaimed a familiar schooled literacy practice for their own purposes. Those who had mastered the familiar thematic practices of their English classes began to talk about them and to teach others how to apply them in the new domain of the magazine. As they began to establish their multiliteracy pedagogy through dialogue about the creation of the magazine and how they would organize its contents, the girls drew upon schooled literacy and claimed agency to extend the use of the concept of theme in a way that was generative for them.

The social literacy practice critical to the girls' initial meaning making was dialogue, and it remained the primary means through which the other practices came into being. Though some of the girls were hesitant to talk in the group in the beginning, their reticence to share their ideas did not last. The transcripts reveal countless times when girls spoke simultaneously and when they also engaged in side conversations related to the matter at hand, not to mention the incessant friendly interaction that grew out of our familiarity with one another. It was not long before all of the magazine production procedures were established through verbal and written dialogue about what had happened in the past and what would be necessary to achieve the desired outcomes that the girls rapidly established. Even at times of disagreement, they negotiated through their dialogue—proposing, questioning, and clarifying every idea as they built upon one another's words. Embracing the opportunity to redefine the use of a theme, the girls chose to work within yet another commonly schooled frame: the metaphor, which they also adapted across contexts. Again, familiar with how metaphor can be used to open up possibilities of meaning, the girls sought a word or phrase that evoked both rich figurative and literal associations. After agreeing upon what would become the metaphorical theme and the title of the magazine, *Camouflage*, the girls then teased out some layers of its meaning thorough their discussion of the word. I, Rachel, played the role of mediator throughout this lengthy discussion, presented here to illustrate the girls' processes of making meaning through dialogue:

Rachel: Now, if we're thinking about the theme, now it seems pervasive—camouflage seems to be what people are working from. Can you tease out how you see that?

Beth Ann: Didn't you break it down before?

Lynda: I have like two.

Rachel: What are some of them?

Lynda: like the whole idea of hiding and then emerging. 'cause then there could be a middle one about like—

Beth Ann: —the process of hiding?

Lynda: —thinking about emerging but not actually doing it, —head out—

Beth Ann: —what about like, hiding, the emergence and how you changed? Like, one is you're totally hidden, one is you're totally exposed, and the middle section is the transition period, like when you're coming out, when you're—

[?²]:   —while—

Beth Ann: —yeah, while you're coming out, your reasoning behind it. Not that you're hidden, not that you're emerging, you're in the middle.

Suzie: I need a dictionary.

Rachel: Turn around.

Suzie: Dictionaries are like my favorite book. [*She grabs a dictionary from the table.*]

Beth Ann: Hiding/fully/fully exposed.

Rachel: So you're kind of looking for something at the end. Fully exposed— to me I hear revealing. Is that what you mean?

Beth Ann: Yeah, kind of that, like what was there to begin with that *nobody* saw?

(Excerpted from whole-group transcript, November 26, 2001)

As the girls reintroduced their understandings of the word "camouflage," I encouraged them to explain what they were thinking by asking two probing questions. Beth Ann and Lynda took up the invitation by splitting up the word into various forms, through which they seemed to be expressing the word's active properties. Suzie, wanting to enter the dialogue, turned to yet another familiar schooled practice—she looked up the word in the dictionary and shared what she found. Summarizing what I heard the girls saying, I reentered the conversation and encouraged Suzie to continue her engagement with the group:

Rachel:	It sounds to me like when you're looking at camouflage, you're playing with it in the verb sense.
Beth Ann:	Yes, the process more so than the noun . . .
Rachel:	Can you look up camouflage for us again, please? And tell us what it says?
Lynda:	We wrote it down last week! In the book.
Suzie:	I want to have something to do, please.
Lynda:	OK.
Rachel:	[*looks in group dialogue book*] There was a word . . . I remember now that I see it. But Suzie can read it to us.
Suzie:	I just want to have something to do . . . eh! A spider! [*flicking if off the page while reading from the dictionary*] "Camouflage. The disguising of equipment or an installation with paints, nets or foliage."
Lynda:	—foliage will be the first section of our book. [*laughter*]
Suzie:	—"a disguise so applied, concealment by means of disguise" ding ding ding [*she mimics the sound of a bell*], "behavior or an expedient design." I don't know, let me try this again.
Beth Ann:	We got the word we were looking for.
Suzie:	OK.
Rachel:	Disguising . . .
Suzie:	Goodbye, spider book.
[?]:	Concealed . . . and revealed? . . . disguised/concealing/revealed?
Beth Ann:	Now, I like the way that sounds, the -ed, -ing, -ed so you can see the middle one as the process of going between?

Rachel: What did you say? Say it again.
Justine: I forget.
All: Concealed! Revealed! Revealed!
(Excerpted from whole-group transcript, November 26, 2001)

The thematic negotiation was quick and communal; the girls listened playfully to one another's spoken contributions and built upon them. Sometimes they even repeated what had been said, in effect reifying it. Very little was contested; consensus seemed to emerge with each new idea. This is where the social practice of dialogue was used in a different way: unlike in their typical classroom conversations, the girls participated freely and worked off one another's ideas, instead of relying on the teacher for questions or direction. Conversely, as a teacher, I listened to and reinforced the girls' words, pointing to the students as meaning makers. As I continued to listen to the girls, and to partake in the dialogue, I named what I heard them working through. After someone had suggested "disguise," I interjected: "Wait a minute: disguise is a verb and a noun. Maybe we can find all words that are verbs and nouns." Suzie rolled her eyes, smiled, and said, "Uh oh." I continued: "Like camouflage, it's a verb and a noun; disguise is a verb and a noun." As I negotiated my own in- and out-of-school teacher identities, Beth called out "Homework!" in her most teacherly voice. Such playful banter characterized much of this one-and-a-half hour conversation; it was regularly interspersed with a democratic process of listening and responding to one another's thoughts about the theme and its possible permutations. As the girls collectively agreed upon their theme, Beth Ann calmly relinquished her early entry into the theme discussion, as others reassured her that her ideas had been heard and that the discussion was running its course:

Beth Ann: All the "normalcy of madness" advocates [a previously suggested theme] are gone, so right now it's 100% camouflage.
Suzie: That's alright; we hear your voice, ringing—
Beth Ann: No, I'm good with camouflage.
[*3]:   For me, I didn't care, I liked both . . . I'm oscillating . . . that's how I feel about it, too.
[?]:   These words are making me crazy!
(Excerpted from whole-group transcript, November 26, 2001)

Yet before we moved away from the subject completely, I wanted to recap what the girls had said, so as not to lose sight of what they had accomplished by determining a metaphor/title and to clarify how they might use the metaphor in the book. Recalling their earlier discussion of dividing the thematically unified book into three related divisions, I asked them to think toward that end. Lynda responded by taking it in a visual direction, further expanding the modalities that might be employed in the representation of these ideas:

Rachel: . . . How do you see the three divisions? What are they?

[*Individual conversation ensues.*]

Lynda: Do you mean like ways to visualize?

Rachel: Anything.

Lynda: I see weird things—

Suzie: —I see some guy hiding behind a bush . . . peeking out . . .

Rachel: So you see someone hiding and jumping through?

Lynda: —tentative at first, to get out.

[?]:   —black, gray, and white.

Rachel: When you say "revealing, revelation"—can you say that in some other ways?

[?]:   Reveal

[*Lynda and Suzie turn on the computer and open the thesaurus.*]

(Excerpted from whole-group transcript, November 26, 2001)

They moved back to the words themselves, consulting another resource and calling out; only now they began to talk about how they might also show the metaphor through images along with the assumed written text of the magazine. We thought aloud:

Suzie: Divine manifestation? bombshell . . . disclosure . . . discovery . . .

[?]:   Discovery, I like that . . .

[*They continue to read words aloud from the Microsoft Word thesaurus for a minute.*]

Rachel: The neat thing about discovery is that there's two parts to it, it can be the discovery of the person, him or herself, who has been camouflaging *or* it can be the discovery of that person—

Suzie: —I like the word obscure.

[*The girls engage in several minutes of commentary about a test that had been given that day, testing in general, make stuff up on an essay, etc.*]

Suzie: Anyhoo, back to this *Camouflage* thing—

Kathleen: —put emerging—

[*All throw out words and try to match them in threes for a few minutes; they talk about how to "show" the ideas in the book; one that gets repeated is "disguise/emerge/discover" . . .*]

(Excerpted from whole-group transcript, November 26, 2001)

As talk of the school day crept in and I heard the girls repeating the same words over again, I suggested that we might move on to something else. Tired from the work, someone responded with gratitude, "Yeah, maybe something will pop into my head." The girls did keep "disguise/emerge/discover" as the section titles for *Camouflage*. It was through both guided and unstructured dialogue that the girls came to agree upon the title and subdivisions of the magazine, carefully fielding ideas and consulting one another and other resources such as a dictionary and a thesaurus to broaden our understandings. They examined the words for what they might mean, define, represent, and contain. Their dialogue reflects a central means of their meaning-making practices and remained a central tenet of their developing multiliteracy pedagogy. Collaborative knowledge building was typical in our work together; it was often through dialogue that schooled literacy practices were drawn upon and transformed into new meanings to be shared with others.

Structure and negotiation:
The selection process for *Camouflage* poetry

On the same day that the girls determined the theme and its divisions, they reviewed past processes for selecting poetry. This was when the girls first began to develop a structure for accomplishing their intended work. In our community of practice, this structure continued to be established through dialogue, and it was extended through the creation of specific criteria and processes for selecting the magazine content. As part of their pedagogy, the girls assumed and blurred the roles of teachers and learners, valuing the input of the experienced staff members and building upon it.

The Monday after the theme had been determined and the selection criteria discussed, eighteen girls were present and ready to begin reading and evaluating the poetry submissions they had received. I asked Suzie to begin the meeting by telling everyone what we had discussed the previous week, since she had taken the responsibility of keeping the notes in our group dialogue notebook. After reminding everyone that the poetry would be selected by a blind review process, primarily to avoid personal bias, Suzie began reading the summary notes she had written:

Suzie: When you're selecting the poetry, you'll be in a small group, and you'll read each poem. Most of the time we'll read it out loud. And each person will give it a rating from 1 to 5, 1 being lowest and 5 being highest. And you'll rate it on different things, like your own personal reaction, your opinion if you like it or not, style and language, like if the writing transitions and stuff like that are all factors that should be considered when selecting the poetry. And the only other thing I have written is untitled poetry is always asked for a title from the author.

(Excerpted from whole-group transcript, December 3, 2001)

Reading the group's notes, Suzie continued in the role of teacher as she listed the process (be in small groups, read poem aloud, rate from 1 to 5) and criteria (personal reaction, opinion, style, and language) for poetry selection. On one level, the process and criteria she described were orderly and school-like: there was a defined routine to follow and an established set of factors to consider as student writing was evaluated. On another level, the process and criteria were also quite different from those utilized in school: the routine and criteria had been established by the girls themselves, and the material being considered was to be read blind. As designers of the magazine, the girls were both "inheritors of patterns and conventions of meaning and at the same time active designers of meaning" (NLG, 1996, p. 65). They actively sought to eliminate the potential bias associated with name-attributed writing, and they aimed to consider each submission on its own merit and its relationship to their selected theme.

Suzie remained a knowledge source for the other girls throughout that and many other conversations, and she looked to me to jump in when she was unsure how to respond. By the time the girls had determined the structure of the magazine and had negotiated the major aspect of poetry selection, it was evident that they were responding to affordances made possible through a feminist educational space. The following transcript excerpt shows our negotiated process for poetry selection, as constructed through our dialogue about the texts we had received, and it reveals some emerging feminist educational practices of the literacy community:

[?]:   On the writing, if things are spelled wrong—

Suzie: —You don't have to count that—

[?]:   Even if they have something incorrect, could you still, like, rate it higher and they could be able to fix it?

Suzie: It depends on what you mean by incorrect . . . Like if it's grammatical or spelling errors just ignore that, 'cause we correct all that. But if it's like, I don't know, incorrect like—

Beth Ann: —it doesn't make sense—

Suzie: —it doesn't make sense then it's just . . . [*She looks at me.*]

Rachel: That's a great question. Once we select what we're doing, what we put in the book, we will work on it together. And generally, if it's spelling or grammar, or sometimes punctuation, depending on how they're using things, we will make editing choices on how to fix that. If it's something significant that will alter the content or meaning of the poem, we go back to the authors to ask them, "Did you mean to use this word here?" Or, like if we change the spelling, like sometimes it's invented spelling to get a meaning across or to make up a word, sometimes it's just an error, like if it's handwritten or something. So, if it's going to change the meaning of the poem, we like to go back to the author, with our suggested change, and say, "Is this OK with you?" But, that is a really good question to bring up because you're reading. You're reading for content, you're reading for general

> impressions, you're reading for how you see it
> fitting into our book—the overall theme and
> maybe our working titles . . . OK? Any other
> questions about poetry selection?
>
> (Excerpted from whole-group transcript, December 3, 2001)

Drawing upon the girls' prior discussion and my understanding of how they wanted to work, I restated what they said and added some explanation of my own. They looked to me as a member of the literacy community, one who would draw not only upon our social literacy practices but also upon my experience as a meaning maker in another of my lifeworlds, that of an English teacher who clearly values and espouses feminist educational practices. Through my participation in this particular dialogue, I hear myself acknowledge vital feminist processes of the work, including the girls' shared authority and the confrontation of bias, which had been raised initially by the girls themselves. Although it was not discussed explicitly, there was an implicit understanding that the girls would continue one long-held tradition: they did not want to share the theme with anyone outside of the staff until the day of publication. What this meant was that while the girls would be actively designing, creating, and selecting the contents of the magazine around the theme of camouflage, scores of their peers who had submitted their work for consideration would not be aware that the book would have this particular thematic orientation. Thus, the girls established not only a structure for how they were going to create the magazine but also one for how they would build its contents by selecting pieces from the submissions and writing that fit a particular theme.

Collaboration: The Way We Worked in the *Camouflage* Community of Practice

It is fitting that the fourth pedagogical dimension, collaboration, falls right in the middle of the six emic constructs, for it held together all that we did. The girls' pedagogy was rooted in their shared literacy community. They made nearly every decision together, and they actively sought to work communally as opposed to competitively, yet another characteristic of feminist educational practice. The girls cared deeply about their work, but they cared about the people involved with it even more. Continuing the earlier poetry discussion, Suzie asked me what was to become a critical question. When I responded,

I was sensitive to her concerns and I attempted to return the focus to emphasizing the girls' own agency in the construction of the magazine.

Suzie:	Oh, I have a question. If we notice that our poem is in the stack that we're selecting, then you have to bring that up so your group doesn't read that, 'cause last year we had an incident where someone got really upset.
Rachel:	That's a good point. The poems are just numbered from 1 to 65 or something. What we're going to do is just break into groups—I haven't figured out how many people we have, it looks like we have about 18 or 16 or something—we'll break into 4 or 5 even groups and we'll give you like 1–10, 11–20 to start reading through. By chance, you might get your own poem. What you need to do is say, "I wrote this." It doesn't mean you can't read it, 'cause it might be nice to get the feedback while you're sitting there if you want to, but please don't rate it. Because it's not that you can't rate your own, but we want to avoid, as Suzie said, any uncomfortable situations for the authors where some people go, "No, no, no, don't like it." We'd rather just have a more objective reading of it, so we'll just kind of put it aside and move it to another group. OK?
[?]:	And how many can be chosen overall?
Rachel:	That's another good question. You will decide the layout of your book, hopefully in two weeks, after you decide how much of this poetry you want to put in there. So, you're going to choose what you want first and then say how you want to make it fit in the book. Suzie did a count last week—how many poems?
Suzie:	I think it was something like 48.
Rachel:	Yeah, there are a lot . . . If you read all of them, and you really feel strongly positive or strongly negative about all of them, it could just be that you're getting a batch that's not speaking to you. That's OK, too. I mean, you want to go with what

> you're thinking. We'll do a sample one together
> and then it might be a little bit clearer.
> (Excerpted from whole-group transcript, December 3, 2001)

As the girls began to delineate their pedagogy through the establishment and experience of the poetry selection process, they also began to move in a direction in which the students' own theory became reflective practice. The poetry evaluation continued over a period of two months, with more than seventy peer-submitted poems eventually read for consideration. The nature of the process, in small groups scattered across many days and multiple readings, meant that it was not possible for me to capture the girls' exact words as they read, discussed, and evaluated the poetry. Unlike for the longer pieces, many of which were written by staff members and on which we conferenced repeatedly, there are no transcriptions of their discussions. But I do have traces in my field notes, often in the form of my own responses to what I saw and heard. I think that my own passion was stirred by the girls' eagerness to engage with this work and their commitment to their own literacy community. They were hungry for the opportunity to utilize multiple modes of meaning making and to be part of this literacy community. This excerpt from late January reflects my awe at their emerging pedagogy:

> Today was one of those days where I felt I could sit in this room forever, listening to the girls read their peers' words aloud and discussing the nuances that separated the poems into our forced metaphorical divisions. I forgot my tape recorder today; it is sitting on my desk at home, probably still on pause from last night's unfinished transcription attempt. I wish I could have captured verbatim what they said about their "readings" of each poem, what was in there, what wasn't—and who was willing to concede her opinion sooner. There will always be more poems, and we will do this again; heck, we do it everyday. (Excerpted from field notes, January 23, 2002)

Nearly every decision regarding the content of the magazine was made collaboratively, and the collaboration was conducted primarily through dialogue. Our dialogues about texts helped us become clearer about what each person was thinking, and over time and through reflection they enabled us to see things differently. We established a forum in which we talked about everything, sometimes maybe too much (as evidenced by the lengthy transcripts), but this came to be a practice that was essential to our creating the magazine. Collaboratively fusing dialogue with the reading and writing of text was a significant component of the emergent pedagogy, and, as we continued to create the magazine, the relationships between this dialogue and text—both words and images—became increasingly important in the determination of how the girls would express their newly found meanings through the design of the magazine itself. This also made it possible for the girls to interrogate written and visual texts in ways that were not normally recognized in their schooled literacy experiences.

Critique and representation: Designing a magazine through the *Camouflage* community of practice

The selection of camouflage as a thematic metaphor, referenced in the previous sections of this chapter and examined at length in the following pages, became the impetus for the overall design of the magazine even while it symbolized the community of practice itself owing to its being a product that mediated an of-school space. It was by expressing and representing the theme that the girls further interrogated relationships between written and visual texts and their multiple modalities became even more intertwined. In addition to utilizing dialogue and text to make meaning, this aspect of the project required the girls not only to use spoken and written language to evoke what the magazine was about but also simultaneously to negotiate images, symbols, and design. The hybridization of these modalities stretched the girls' understandings of camouflage, their selected metaphor, while also constraining it. To represent these understandings, they chose to make explicit critiques of school and the world. Arguably, the metaphor is a problematic one, as are some of their representations of it within the magazine, and I by no means imply that the girls interrogated it to its fullest extent while utilizing it. However, what is most significant is the fact that the girls envisioned the space and product of the magazine as places where such critique could begin. Knowing the school, the girls, their families, and the neighborhoods within which they live, I see this as a major step. In many cases, they expressed to me that it was a newfound opportunity to express themselves in school, and I believe that the essence of camouflage, the word itself, resonated as much for the girls in their daily living as it did for their magazine.

Reading the Word and the World through *Camouflage*

The metaphor of camouflage was taken up, explored, and complicated in myriad ways within the community of practice. Lynda, a senior who had worked on the magazine staff for three years, originally suggested the theme of camouflage at our first meeting of the year. Before its selection by the whole group in late November 2001, the word camouflage had been deeply probed in conversation during the preceding weeks. Just before we were about to vote on the organizing theme, Lynda talked about the origins of her idea:

> The whole thing came up because, well, me and Suzie were just goofing off. But the word camouflage, if you think about it, on the surface it is that green material or whatever. But if you think about how it relates to what's goin' on in the world today, even like, it doesn't even have to be that way, but because it does relate, it fits. And umm, the whole thing about camouflage is that you're hiding, it's hidden but not seen, like no one can see you, but you can see them and things that go on for you. And there's the other part of it, which is kind of like emerging from the shadows, the risks that you take, like when you emerge from the camouflage and show your true self, like your personality.
> (Excerpted from whole-group transcript, November 19, 2001)

During that meeting, as we discussed the magazine's potential title, the girls said that they were drawn to camouflage because of Lynda's passion about it and also because of its potential for double meaning. Some found it interesting that the word is associated with war, especially in connection with September 11 and the then-potential war in Iraq. Camouflage's potential connections to aspects of self resonated with others. Then, as we read and edited poetry submissions and conducted writing conferences on staff-produced pieces, the girls continued to play with their chosen metaphor, twisting its possible meanings and arranging the magazine according to their interpretations. They were immersed in talk about ways of structuring a visual and interpretive metaphorical rendering of camouflage, organizing the design and content of the magazine into three sections they had named disguise/emergence/discover. They suggested ways to articulate the meanings of the metaphor in words and images for their readers even as they constructed them for themselves. And they hotly debated whether they should try to make a cover that looked like fabric—army fatigues to be precise (Figure 5). They did, though not in familiar shades of green—they favored a melon color, indicating that to make it a pinkish color would be the opposite of what people would expect (field notes, December 3, 2001 and January 29, 2002).

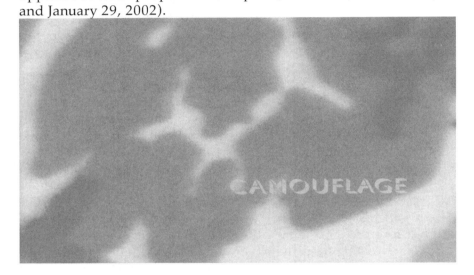

Figure 5. *Camouflage* Cover (original in pink)

As they worked, the girls spoke of interpreting the metaphor both for themselves and for their readers, the school community, through their choosing to select certain pieces of writing and art over others. In a Freirean sense (1970), their metaphor was used as a way both to make and to represent meaning. As Lynda indicated, this magazine was a means through which the girls were rendering an emergence from the shadows (transcript, November 19, 2001). They told me that this was not only their magazine; it was also the school's, and they were attempting to construct something that would be representative at once of their individual and collective identities. For example, they knew from the outset, even before they had begun to review submissions, that they wanted to devote a two-page spread specifically to art and poetry about the memories and impact of September 11. As it happened, there were plenty of fitting submissions to choose from, and the first layout decision made was for the September 11 spread to be placed on pages 24–25, directly in the middle at the staples, so that when the book fell open it would honor those pieces. Thus, in one way of reading, book-ended by the camouflage covers, the entire publication became a collection of their emotional responses to living in post–September 11 America. By designing the structure of the magazine in this way, the girls asserted their desire to foreground the social and political impact that the event and its aftermath had on them. Through the multiple modalities incorporated into the design, the girls were representing their readings of the world (Freire & Macedo, 1987).

Redesigning the Word and the World through *Camouflage*

The girls explored and redefined their understandings of the world through their representation of the camouflage metaphor. According to the New London Group, writing of the "designing" component of a multiliteracy pedagogy, "the process of shaping emergent meaning involves re-presentation and recontextualization" (1996, p. 75). While at times the girls certainly relied on "available designs" (p. 74), or familiar discourses of the literary/art magazine, it was through the conception and representation of the metaphor of camouflage that the girls transformed its meaning. They "redesigned" or created a product that was "founded on [the] historically and culturally received patterns of meaning" of the magazine while making something out of their own agency (p. 76). They created new meaning and represented it through multimodal representation.

In addition to serving as a word that encompassed their feelings about living in the world, camouflage also resounded as a metaphor for how the girls sometimes perceived their internal lives as young women. The girls talked at length about how the concept of camouflage was multifaceted for them, and they wanted to explain their interpretations of it in writing. Therefore, the three editors-in-chief, Lynda, Beth Ann, and Suzie, offered their analysis and interpretation of the title in the Editors' Notes that they placed on the opening pages of the magazine:

> *Camouflage* can be separated into three distinct and continual stages: disguise, emerge, and discover. Anything hidden will eventually be brought to light; the content within these pages illustrates this process in words and images, separating each unique step and clarifying its literal and figurative definitions.

The façade that many hide behind can be convincing and effective, but it cannot withstand the truth and integrity within each individual. There are many ways in which truth can be concealed. The use of blatant lies and gratifying self-deception are common in today's society, where the world itself can be looked upon as a combat zone between what is "accepted" by its standards and what really exists. Whether intentionally hidden or instinctively suppressed, the barricades of disguise are unable to withstand the ongoing battle of life.

As one in battle hesitantly decides to reveal her cover and move into her surroundings, she takes that first step toward making her presence fully known to the universe. As Sir Isaac Newton once said, "What goes up must come down." Human disguise is no exception. When the barricades of deception crumble, truth begins to emerge. A bridge toward revelation appears, as if with the dawn a new world has come. It is in this second stage that the idea of camouflage as a continuum is fully understood, and is able to manifest itself as a movement toward clarity. The mask of any disguise has been removed and it becomes the mission of the courageous and strong-willed to fully uncover the mystery.

As the masquerade comes to an end, all costumes are removed, guards are let down, and individuality shines through. Truth is discovered and reality is exposed. As the battle comes to an end, one becomes aware of her surroundings. She learns valuable lessons about herself and no longer desires to camouflage herself to the rest of the world. But as one revelation comes to a close, a plethora of obscurities and false appearances present themselves. The cycle of camouflaging does not conclude with the discovery; it merely frees the explorer to begin the journey once again. Our lives are full of self-discoveries and revelations, displays of knowledge and integrity. It is through our journeys that we learn from our mistakes and gain wisdom and insight. It is through our natural quest for sincerity that we obtain independence, freedom, and respect.   Though   we   have   chosen   to differentiate the stages of this metaphor in our book, it is only when camouflage is taken as a whole that the progression of disguise, through emergence, and eventually toward discovery is made apparent. ("Editors' Notes," *Camouflage,* p. 3)

Envisioned as a growth process, camouflage also served as a guiding metaphor for how the girls saw themselves, as well as for how the staff selected and represented the writing and art they included. In their community of practice, they represented these meanings in hybrid ways, articulating established conventions in new ways. Through the intertextuality, or cross-referenced meaning relationships, of the magazine's contents, they also furthered their emerging multiliteracy pedagogy.

An Emic Pedagogy Predicated on Multimodal Literacy Practices

Individually and collectively, the girls' literacy practices were broad and varied across modes, but they were all sanctioned within the space of the magazine. This resulted in the girls establishing greater understandings about the relationships between school and their own social literacy practices through the emic pedagogical dimensions of dialogue, structure, negotiation, collaboration, critique, and representation. By creating their own pedagogy of multiliteracies (NLG, 1996), some girls not only gained new understandings about writing, art, and design, but also reinformed what some of them they already knew. Informal learning made additional social and multimodal literacy practices possible, and it was by using these that the girls created and documented a process that could later serve as a model for other students.

As the girls spoke and listened to one another, and I to them, I increasingly saw the need to recognize the importance of the hybrid and intertextual literacy practices that the girls established to express meaning while creating the magazine. Nearly all of them were linked either to our community of practice or to other lifeworlds of the students, or to both. By hybridizing genres and creating new forms to express themselves, the girls extended and enriched their intended messages. Likewise, drawing upon other texts from the magazine, the school, the world, and even our own experiences and transcribed conversations, the girls added layers of meaning to their work through the use of intertextual dialogue, words, and images. Maxine Greene advocates that students find a way to "live within the arts, making clearings and spaces for themselves" (1995, p. 135). Considering dialogue as both a pedagogical practice and a modality allowed for individual expression within a shared literacy endeavor through which the girls were able to construct meaning and to further explore their own individual and collective identities through the hybrid and intertextual practices and spaces of *Camouflage*. Our relationships, both with the texts and with one another, were central to the practices and the space.

Realizations

The young women who comprised the *Camouflage* staff—and who were co-contributors to this research through their documenting of practices and events, reviewing transcripts, and participating in group conversations and interviews—created a literacy community through the social multimodal literacy practices they enacted while creating this magazine. Their ownership and involvement resulted in the creation of six dimensions of their social literacy practice—dialogue, structure, negotiation, collaboration, critique, and representation—through which the girls built both the community and the project, developed leadership, and paid close attention to one another, ultimately establishing their own pedagogy. Varying views of reading and writing were affirmed, questioned, challenged, and established as the girls read their peers' writing, looked at their art, and created their own multimodal text. Likewise, by employing principles of art and design in the creation of the magazine, they also broadened their understandings of the relationships between images and ideas, and they developed their ability to represent concepts in ways that were new for them. All of these were essential elements of the girls' own multiliteracy pedagogy, which they developed through their own social practices and their embracing of feminist educational practices.

By enacting feminist educational practices that were constructed from the girls' own agenda, including creating a collaborative community in which they shared authority and validated one another's perceptions of the world, the participants created an environment in which they determined the educational work to be done, and, through doing so, they developed their own pedagogy of multiliteracies. The project of creating this magazine provided a context through which the range and variation of the girls' social literacy practices could be utilized, developed, and explored, while recursively helping to create the community of practice. To construct this magazine, the girls made use of different modalities; some girls knew these already, and others needed to be taught them by their peers. In creating the magazine, the girls used different modalities to say things, and they were consequently able to say different things because of the multiple modalities they employed. Sometimes they moved from an idea to a modality and other times from a modality to an idea. The girls' co-constructed knowledge about art and writing grew primarily from their interactions with one another and with one another's work across time and space. Looking at it now, I clearly see the resonance between the girls' in-, out-of-, and of-school literacies as utilized through their creating *Camouflage* and the feminist educational practices they enacted to accomplish their work.

Implications

The girls and I began this work together one week after September 11, 2001. Several years later, we are all still grappling with the aftermath of September 11. With each passing day, the death toll rises for members of the U.S. military and civilians of all nationalities in Iraq, and we remain a nation at war. These happenings resonate deeply with me as I consider the implications of the work of *Camouflage*. Look at that word: camouflage. From the moment we met, the girls were preoccupied with the concept; they repeatedly voiced a desire to reflect a post–September 11 world in their magazine. Initially, they just seemed to want to document the event, to preserve it on record in some way. But over time, and through dialogue, they moved beyond mere documentation by choosing to interpret and represent the layers and complexities they were associating with living in a world at war.

Admittedly, I see now that there was room for us to take the dialogue about September 11 and its resonant camouflage metaphor much further, to take a more critical look at both the word and the war it represented. I think this now, as a teacher–researcher, though I am not certain I was able to see it while I was in the midst of the research. It stands as an example of how dialogue can also move along a particular path, even to the point of shutting out dissonance or divergent viewpoints. The question of whether I should have done more to interrogate the metaphor lingers, and, having discussed it with my colleagues, I see now that by foregrounding the girls' interpretations of camouflage throughout the text of this study, I leave space for certain implications of how it might be read. In line with my own political ideologies, the girls' work on *Camouflage* begs me to think about what it can mean to teach and to learn literacy so that people will stop killing each other (to paraphrase Mary Rose O'Reilly, 1993)—or at least to create a space where such work can begin. Engaging with media texts within a learning space that is built on relationships affords the opportunity—and the accompanying responsibility—to be critical and reflexive.

Through creating learning spaces with students, whether they are in, out of, or of school, we can better teach for openings (Greene,

1995) and work for individual and social change. Certainly, the objectives in classrooms are usually different from those in an *of-school* space such as this magazine. While classroom teachers must concern themselves with school, district, and state standards—at an alarming rate—adults who work with adolescents in other contexts usually do not have the same accountability concerns. As one who traverses both arenas on a daily basis, I can speak to the positive interplay of the two. Without the externally imposed constraints of proficiency testing, for example, the girls who worked on the magazine felt free to take risks with their writing and to try out new things. They created a space—an of-school space—in which they established and enacted their own pedagogy, one that was enabled by their engagement with multimodal texts. The hybrid genre of the literary/art magazine made it possible for them to participate in an arena otherwise unavailable to them in school, however omnipresent in their out-of-school lives. This was possible, however, only because we all worked hard to create a climate in which such risk taking was valued and supported. This can also be reciprocated in a classroom: when students have agency in their own learning, they will push themselves, their peers, and certainly their teacher further.

bell hooks argues that serving our students is a form of political resistance. As educators, we can see what becomes possible when we forge relationships with our students and create a "learning community that values wholeness over division, disassociation, [or] splitting" (2003, p. 49). There is no better time than now for us to deliberately create learning spaces—both formal and informal—that value and respect our students while fostering their literacy development.

Notes

[1] St. Vladimir is a pseudonym for the school that was selected by the students who participated in the study.

[2] The presence of [?] as a speaker indicates that the identity of the speaker could not be discerned from the audiotape.

[3] The use of [*] indicates the voice of a student who was present at that particular time but who was not a regular participant and therefore had not signed a consent form to participate in the research. I include her comments so as not to interrupt the conversation as well as to acknowledge her contribution to the discussion.

References

Angermüller, J., & Bunzmann, K. (2000). Hybrid spaces—Theory and beyond: An introduction. In J. Angermüller, K. Bunzmann, & C. Rauch (Eds.), *Hybrid spaces: Theory, culture, economy* (pp. 1–11). New Brunswick, NJ: Transaction Publishers.

Barton, D., & Hamilton, M. (1998). *Local literacies: Reading and writing in one community*. New York: Routledge.

Bruce, H. (2003). *Literacies, lies, and silences: Girls' writing lives in the classroom*. New York: Peter Lang.

Ceglowski, D. (2000). Research as relationship. *Qualitative Inquiry, 6*(1), 88–103.

Childers, P., Hobson, E., & Mullin, J. (1998). *ARTiculating*. Portsmouth, NH: Heinemann.

Cochran-Smith, M., & Lytle, S. (2001). Beyond certainty: Taking an inquiry stance on practice. In A. Lieberman & L. Miller (Eds.), *Teachers caught in the action* (pp. 45–58). New York: Teachers College Press.

Coffey, A., & Delamont, S. (2000). *Feminism and the classroom teacher: Research, praxis, and pedagogy*. New York: Routledge.

Dewey, J. (1934). *Art as experience*. New York: Minton, Balch and Company.

Fairclough, N. (1992). *Discourse and social change*. Cambridge, UK: Polity Press.

Fairclough, N. (2003). *Analysing discourse: Textual analysis for social research*. New York: Routledge.

Fine, M. (1997). Greener pastures. In W. Ayers & J. Miller (Eds.), *A light in dark times: Maxine Greene and the unfinished conversation* (pp. 209–218). New York: Teachers College Press.

Flood, J., Heath, S., & Lapp, D. (Eds.). (1997). *Handbook of teaching literacy through the communicative and visual arts*. New York: International Reading Association.

Fransecky, R. B., & Debes, J. L. (1972). *Visual literacy: A way to learn—a way to teach*. Washington, DC: AECT Publications.

Freire, P. (1970). *Pedagogy of the oppressed*. New York: Seabury.

Freire, P., & Macedo, D. (1987). *Literacy: Reading the word and the world*. South Hadley, MA: Bergin & Garvey.

Gee, J. P. (2000a). The New Literacy Studies: From socially situated to the work of the social. In D. Barton, M. Hamilton, & R. Ivanič

(Eds.), *Situated literacies: Reading and writing in context* (pp. 180–196). New York: Routledge.

Gee, J. P. (2000b). Teenagers in new times: A new literacy studies perspective. *Journal of Adolescent and Adult Literacy, 43*(5), 412–420.

Gee, J.P. (2003). *What video games have to teach us about learning and literacy.* New York: Palgrave Macmillan.

Greene, M. (1995). *Releasing the imagination: Essays on education, the arts, and social change.* San Francisco: Jossey-Bass.

Grumet, M. (1998). Restaging the civil ceremonies of schooling. In W. Ayers & J. Miller (Eds.), *A light in dark times: Maxine Greene and the unfinished conversation* (pp. 134–144). New York: Teachers College Press.

Hauser, M., & Marrero, E. (1998). Challenging curricular conventions: Is it feminist pedagogy if you don't call it that? In M. Hauser & J. Jipson (Eds.), *Intersections: Feminisms/early childhoods* (pp. 161–173). New York: Peter Lang.

Heath, S. (2000). Imaginative actuality: Learning in the arts during the nonschool hours. In E. Fiske (Ed.), *Champions of change: The impact of the arts on learning* (pp. 19–34). Washington, DC: Arts Education Partnership and President's Committee on the Arts and Humanities. Retrieved November 27, 2001, from: http://www.aep-arts.org/Publications&Resources.html.

Heath, S., & McLaughlin, M. (Eds.). (1993). *Identity and inner-city youth: Beyond ethnicity and gender.* New York: Teachers College Press.

hooks, b. (2003). *Teaching community: A pedagogy of hope.* New York: Routledge.

Hull, G., & Schultz, K. (Eds.). (2002). *School's out: Bridging out-of-school literacies with classroom practice.* New York: Teachers College Press.

Jackson, P. (1998). *John Dewey and the lessons of art.* New Haven, CT: Yale University Press.

Jewitt, C., & Kress, G. (Eds.). (2003). *Multimodal literacy.* New York: Peter Lang.

Kress, G., & Van Leeuwen, T. (2001). *Multimodal discourse: The modes and media of contemporary communication.* New York: Oxford University Press.

Lave, J., & Wenger, E. (1991). *Situated learning: Legitimate peripheral participation.* Cambridge, UK: Cambridge University Press.

Lawrence-Lightfoot, S., & Davis, J. (1997). *The art and science of portraiture.* San Francisco: Jossey-Bass.

Lytle, S., & Cochran-Smith, M. (1992). Teacher research as a way of knowing. *Harvard Educational Review, 62*(4), 447–474.

Moje, E. (2000a). *"All the stories that we have": Adolescents' insights about literacy and learning in secondary schools.* Newark, DE: International Reading Association.

Moje, E. (2000b). "To be part of the story": The literacy practices of gangsta adolescents. *Teachers college record, 102*(3), 651–690.

Moje, E. (2002). But where are the youth? On the value of integrating youth culture into literacy theory. *Educational Theory, 52*(1), 97–120.

Moje, E., & O'Brien, D. (Eds.). (2001). *Constructions of literacy: Studies of teaching and learning in and out of secondary schools.* Mahwah, NJ: Lawrence Erlbaum.

New London Group (NLG). (1996). A pedagogy of multiliteracies: Designing social futures. *Harvard educational review, 66*(1), 60–92.

O'Brien, D., Moje, E., & Stewart, R. (2001). Exploring the context of secondary literacy: Literacy in people's everyday school lives. In E. Moje & D. O'Brien (Eds.), *Constructions of literacy: Studies of teaching and learning in and out of secondary schools* (pp. 27–48). Mahwah, NJ: Lawrence Erlbaum.

Olesen, V. (1998). Feminisms and models of qualitative research. In N. Denzin & Y. Lincoln (Eds.), *The landscape of qualitative research: Theories and issues* (pp. 300–332). Thousand Oaks, CA: Sage.

O'Reilly, M. (1993). *The peaceable classroom.* Portsmouth, NH: Boynton/Cook.

Ropers-Huilman, B. (1998). *Feminist teaching in theory and practice: Situating power and knowledge in poststructural classrooms.* New York: Teachers College Press.

Schultz, K. (2002). Looking across space and time: Reconceptualizing literacy learning in and out of School. *Research in the Teaching of English*, 36(3), 356–90.

Shrewsbury, C. (1987). What is feminist pedagogy? *Women's Studies Quarterly, 15*(3–4), 6–14.

Street, B. (Ed.). (1993). *Cross-cultural approaches to literacy.* Cambridge, UK: Cambridge University Press.

Street, B. (1995). *Social literacies: Critical approaches to literacy in development, ethnography and education.* London: Longman.

Street, B. (2000, July). EDUC 724 class notes, University of Pennsylvania, Philadelphia.

Weiss, M., Systra, C., & Slater, S. (1998). "Dinner with Maxine." In W. Ayers & J. Miller (Eds.), *A light in dark times: Maxine Greene and the unfinished conversation* (pp. 22–32). New York: Teachers College Press.

Response to Nichols

Michele Knobel

Rachel Nichols's chapter documents and analyzes the decision-making processes and collaborative work of a group of students as they produce a literary/arts magazine for their all-girls private school. These student editors were responsible for soliciting and selecting content and for developing a unifying theme for the magazine. Nichols uses her research to argue that schools can become productive spaces for effective literacy learning and text production when young people are provided with opportunities to engage seriously with selecting and publishing literary and artistic works for an authentic purpose and audience.

Nichols's study aims at developing a model of literacy pedagogy that draws on a number of complex theories. For the purpose of this review, I have chosen to focus on two key elements within her chapter: multiliteracies pedagogy and the young women's commitment to producing a high-quality magazine.

Nichols's teacher-research study is a fruitful contribution to the field of adolescent literacy and media studies because, among other things, it encourages readers to ask all kinds of important questions about putting theory into practice. Nichols argues, for example, that the young women in her study were co-constructing a "pedagogy of multiliteracies," a concept based on the work of the New London Group (1996; see also Cope & Kalantzis, 2000). The theory of "multiliteracies" itself was generated out of a commitment to "multimodality" (i.e., textual visual, aural, and other meaning modes) and to using functional grammar—originally out of systemic functional linguistics—as a metalanguage for learners to talk about language, meaning, and texts (Cope & Kalantzis, 2003). Multimodality and metalanguage or "grammar" are brought together by the concept of "design," where design is considered to be both structure and process. That is, designs can be available structures that come "ready made" for use, such as curriculum documents, text genres, and social procedures (New London Group, 2000, p. 20). These available designs can also be modified by the user or designer That is, elements and conventions of these designs can become resources for transforming available designs or for creating new designs. The process dimension of designing focuses on how resources from available designs, along with elements of the grammars of various semiotic systems (e.g., grammars of language, film, gesture), are selected and brought together to meet a specific purpose within a given social context or discursive order (ibid.). The multiliteracies pedagogy itself is a four-part process comprising analysis of situated practice, overt instruction (in designs, grammars, etc.), critical framing, and transformed practice (Kalantzis & Cope, 2003, p. 24).

In Nichols's study, we see the student editors engaging carefully and seriously with design-as-structure and design-as-process. The magazine on which the girls are working comes with a history that has given it a particular purpose, thematic structure, mix of visual and textual content, and reputation for being a professional-quality production. The young women seem well aware of this history and keen to maintain this available design. In terms of process, Nichols documents the ways in which this group of young women arrives at a cohesive theme for the book that draws on resources and social contexts from outside the existing available design of the magazine. On paper, this process is perhaps not quite as analytical, collaborative, or transformative as Nichols claims, and this raises interesting questions for further discussion and exploration: for example, if the analysis of social or situated practices, overt instruction, and transformation are components of a multiliteracies pedagogy, does this require some expertise on the teacher's (and, in this case, the students') part in terms of an ability to identify and articulate component grammars and situated discursive dimensions of relevant available designs? To what extent does a multiliteracies pedagogy lend itself seamlessly to a student-centered, collaborative approach such as the one advocated by Nichols? Are the students in this study constructing themselves as multiliteracy pedagogues—that is, as discursively knowledgeable and design savvy—or is something else going on here?

Interestingly, subsequent work by members of the New London Group has focused on developing the theory of multiliteracies into a curriculum design (Kalantzis & Cope, 2003). Nichols's study focuses more on documenting and analyzing elements of this theory in practice. This is no easy task, and Nichols's refusal to supply neat and tidy evaluations of her application of multiliteracies theory makes her account all the more useful to the research community. Indeed, her study breaks important ground in helping educators more fully to realize the pragmatic implications (and complexities) of multiliteracies theory and pedagogy for classroom practice.

While the theoretical and pragmatic dimensions of this study are important, Nichols also speaks directly to the value of literacy tasks that are meaningful to students and are authentically purposeful in a real-world sense. It is clear that these young women took seriously their responsibility for selecting high-quality, thematically linked poems and artwork to be included in the final publication. Admittedly, Nichols's study is small in scale and set within a context—a girls private school—often considered to be one of material and social privilege. All the same, the scale and context do not detract from the challenge this study presents to broadcast media and even some government claims that young people's literacy proficiencies are much less developed than they should be. For example, a study by the National Association of State Boards of Education (2005) argues that the United States is facing a national adolescent literacy crisis. Newspapers are replete with frightening reports on low literacy levels in middle and high schools across the United States and elsewhere (e.g., Aratani, 2006; Beauchamp, 2005; PR Newswire, 2005). George W. Bush has pledged to push the No Child Left Behind Act into middle and high schools in response to low or plateaued scores on a range of international literacy tests. Crisis-couched pedagogical advice on "essential elements" of a literacy curriculum and a range of commercial programs are available for helping educators to address this adolescent literacy "crisis" (e.g., Alliance for Excellent Education, 2004; Fleishman, 2004; Glencoe/McGraw-Hill, 2006; National Association of Secondary School Principals, 2005).

However, there appears to be little evidence of a general literacy crisis in the school that provides the context for Nichols's study. The popularity of the school's annual literary/arts magazine speaks to a general interest in reading/viewing, creating, and writing high-quality texts. It would be easy to say that this interest is a matter of course in a girls private school. However, a growing body of research evidence suggests strongly that young people *are* reading and writing in myriad ways in their everyday lives—much more so than "literacy crisis" talk would have us believe (Alvermann, 2002; Black, 2005; Chandler-Olcott & Mahar, 2003; Lam, 2000; Mackey, 2003; Steinkeuhler, forthcoming; Stone, forthcoming; Thomas, forthcoming). For example, literary, visual, and procedural modes are especially popular "fan practices" among a wide range of adolescents (Black, forthcoming; Jenkins, 2004; Lankshear & Knobel, 2006). An important component of many fan practices includes reviewing others' texts in constructive ways to help authors/artists improve or refine the quality of their work. In this study, the young women's close attention to theme, the development of selection criteria, and their careful evaluations of peer submissions resonate strongly with popular practices in the online and offline reading and writing worlds of many young people. Nichols's study usefully reminds us that educators have much to learn from observational studies of young people's media engagement and literacy practices, even when these practices are occurring within school contexts.

References

Alliance for Excellent Education. (2004). *Reading next: A vision for action and research in middle and high school literacy.* A report to Carnegie Corporation of New York. Washington, DC: A4Ed.

Alvermann, D. (Ed.). (2002). *Adolescents and literacies in a digital world.* New York: Peter Lang.

Aratani, L. (2006). Upper grades, lower reading skills; Middle, high schools find they must expand programs for older students. *Washington Post,* July 13, Metro Section, p. B01.

Beauchamp, P. (2005). State reading crisis; Kids among nation's worst. *Herald Sun,* June 1, p. 9.

Black, R. W. (2005). Access and affiliation: The literacy and composition practices of English language learners in an online fanfiction community. *Journal of Adolescent & Adult Literacy, 49*(2), 118–128.

Black, R. W. (Forthcoming). Just don't call them cartoons: The new literacy spaces of animé, manga, and fan fiction. In D. Leu et al. (Eds.), *Handbook of new literacies research.* Mahwah, NJ: Lawrence Erlbaum.

Chandler-Olcott, K., & Mahar, D. (2003). Adolescents' anime-inspired fanfictions: An exploration of multiliteracies. *Journal of Adolescent & Adult Literacy, 46*(7), 556–566.

Cope, B., & Kalantzis, M. (2000). *Multiliteracies: Literacy learning and the design of social futures.* London: Routledge.

Cope, B., & Kalantzis, M. (2003). *Text-made text.* Melbourne, Australia: Common Ground Publishing.

Fleishman, E. (2004). *Adolescent literacy: A national reading crisis.* New York: Scholastic.

Glencoe/McGraw-Hill. (2006). *Jamestown reading navigator* [curriculum program]. New York: McGraw-Hill.

Jenkins, H. (2004). Why Heather can write. *Technology Review,* Feb. 6. Retrieved December 27, 2005, from http://

www.technologyreview.com/articles/04/02/wo_jenkins020604.a
sp.

Kalantzis, M., & Cope, B. (2003). *Designs for learning.* Melbourne, Australia: Common Ground Publishing.

Lam, W. S. E. (2000). L2 literacy and the design of the self: A case study of a teenager writing on the Internet. *TESOL Quarterly, 34*(3), 457–482.

Lankshear, C., & Knobel, M. (2006). *New literacies: Everyday practices and classroom learning* (2 ed.). Maidenhead, UK: Open University Press.

Mackey, M. (2003). Researching new forms of literacy. *Reading Research Quarterly, 38*(3), 403–407.

National Association of Secondary School Principals. (2005). *Creating a culture of literacy: A guide for middle and high school principals.* Reston, VA: NASSP.

National Association of State Boards of Education. (2005). *Reading at risk: The state response to the crisis in adolescent literacy.* Alexandria, VA: NASBE.

New London Group. (1996). A pedagogy of multiliteracies: Designing social futures. *Harvard Educational Review, 66*(1), 60–92.

New London Group. (2000). A pedagogy of multiliteracies: Designing social futures. In B. Cope & M. Kalantzis (Eds.), *Multiliteracies: Literacy learning and the design of social futures* (pp. 9–37). London: Routledge.

PR Newswire. (2005). State leaders urge schoolwide reforms to improve reading skills and address national literacy crisis [syndicated news report]. October 13. PR Newswire US.

Steinkeuhler, C. (Forthcoming). Cognition and literacy in massively multiplayer online games. In D. Leu et al. (Eds.), *Handbook of new literacies research.* Mahwah, NJ: Lawrence Erlbaum

Stone, J. (Forthcoming). Popular websites in adolescents' out-of-school lives: Critical lessons on literacy. In M. Knobel & C. Lankshear (Eds.), *A new literacies sampler* (pp. 49-65). New York: Peter Lang.

Thomas, A. (Forthcoming). *e-selves | e-literacies | e-worlds: Children's identities and literacies in virtual communities.* New York: Peter Lang.

Response to Nichols

Rebekah Buchanan

The present dialogue around girls' literacy lives examines girls' participation in specific social groups (Blake, 1997; Bruce, 2003; Finders, 1997; Harper, 2000). Even though the makeup of each group differs, patterns of literacy practices emerge. Finders (1997) writes of how two different groups explore literacy in academic, social, and personal spaces. Blake (1997), Harper (2000), and Bruce (2003) approach literacy practices as they play out in the different classroom settings of which girls are a part. Each expresses how small writing groups helped to empower girls in academic settings. Nichols's chapter adds to this dialogue surrounding girls' involvement in literacy groups.

In her work, Nichols argues for examination into "hybrid spaces" where in-school literacy practices are performed in spaces outside formal classroom settings, yet still in school sites. To this end she focuses on *of*-school literacies, those literacies that both draw upon and extend school literacy practices. She breaches the dichotomy between in-school and out-of-school literacy practices in her examination into the literary / arts magazine she and her students created. This move away from either/or conceptualizations of literacies adds to the dialogue surrounding girls' identity construction through critical analysis of texts. It allows for identity construction through literacies using the discourses of school but not dictated by school to find its way into both girls studies and literacy scholarship.

I am also pleased that Nichols chooses to examine how young women use both written and visual texts. In the discussions around girls' literacy practices, especially as they participate in groups either *in*- or *of*-school, it is the written words that are privileged. However, as Nichols addresses, how girls do identity work through multimodal literacies, such as collage and visually enhanced texts, supports girls' engagement of cultural texts and artifacts to (re)create representations of their lives and experiences.

Nichols's work also makes me think about the girls' reading practices. She discusses a group of girls who are the staff of a school magazine. In reading her chapter, I see girls not only exploring their own literary / art interpretations of *Camouflage* and the section titles of "disguise / emerge / discover" through multimodal literacies but also interpreting how other authors' works represent the literacy world the girls are creating. Nichols accomplishes this through her discussion of the girls looking through poetry submissions and grading them on the basis of specific criteria. Thus, her work too becomes an exploration into girls' reading practices and how these girls explore identity through the hybridity—"fragmenting and mixing established con-structs to create new ones"—and intertextuality—"the presence within a text of elements of other texts"—of the literacy events of others. In this way, the girls form a discourse community around shared values of the interpretation of the written language of others.

Nichols begins her chapter by articulating her interest in the writ-ing lives of girls and the relationship between writing *"in-, out-,* and *of-*school." Like Nichols and Bruce (2003), whom she cites, I believe the writing lives of girls are underexplored. This chapter calls for even more exploration into these areas. The questions prompted by Nich-ols's work lead me to wonder how examining other areas of girls' writing lives might add to the discussion of girls' multimodal literacy practices. I am curious whether the work these girls did in interpreting the texts of their peers (other girls) influenced the writing lives of the girls who are part of the literacy/arts magazine staff. Did these girls redefine how they write as well as how they construct meaning outside of their work with *Camouflage*? Nichols stresses the risk taking of the girls' writing practices within the safe space created around the literary/arts magazine, but did it apply to work in-school or create out-of-school literacy practices? The next step in the analysis of these (and other) girls' multiliteracy pedagogies is to explore whether by moving in-school practices to of-school sites participants extend the practices to critical literacy work in other landscapes.

Nichols ends her chapter with both a critique of her work in a post–September 11 world and a call for youth workers to forge relationships with students that allow for sites created around respect. At a time when media texts are central to out-of-school meaning making, it is essential to find a way to bring interpretation and critical analysis of these texts into the classroom. For this to occur, creating learning spaces that value students' voices and allow students' agency in their learning process is vital. Nichols' work investigates one way to begin to make this possible.

References

Blake, B. E. (1997). *She say, he say: Urban girls write their lives*. Albany: State University of New York Press.

Bruce, H. E. (2003). *Literacies, lies and silences: Girls writing lives in the classroom*. New York: Peter Lang.

Finders, M. J. (1997). *Just girls: Hidden literacies and life in junior high*. New York: Teachers College Press.

Harper, H. J. (2000). *Wild words/dangerous desires: High school girls and feminist avant-garde writing*. New York: Peter Lang.

Chapter Six

Situating the Personal in Digital Media Production

Korina M. Jocson

Researchers in the field of education have argued that students learn best by situating what they are learning in what they know or are familiar with. Seeing students as agents, they emphasize the use of students' cultural knowledge as a resource in their learning process (Gutiérrez, Baquedano-López, & Turner, 1997; Ladson-Billings, 1994; McLaren, 1994; Nieto, 2002; Sleeter & Grant, 1991). In the field of literacy education, some have examined specific aspects of popular culture in learning (Dyson, 1997; Mahiri, 1998, 2004a; Morrell & Duncan-Andrade, 2002), while others incorporate broader uses of sociocultural approaches into theory and practice (Barton & Hamilton, 2000; Gutiérrez, Baquedano-López, & Alvarez, 2001; Lee, 2002; Street, 1984). Pedagogically, they draw on students' "funds of knowledge" to understand how tapping into local actors such as students themselves, parents, and other community members contributes to classroom learning (Moll & González, 1994). While these works inform us on how to see and actively engage students, they subtly suggest the pedagogical work involved for teachers. That is, what informs what teachers do? Or what is the learning process like through which teachers develop their own skills and knowledge in order to teach others about them? An understanding of this process is important particularly in instances that advance teachers' abilities to connect with students and offer possibilities for more relevant teaching in new media times.

In this chapter, I examine my own learning processes through digital media production and share an experience that demonstrates the value of a teacher/learner stance. I build upon the concept of an "agentive self" (Hull & Katz, 2002) and describe how it can be used as a resource to improve learning and teaching practices—both for teachers and for their students. For the purposes of this discussion, an agentive self is defined as both a *construct* and, in the case that follows, a *stance* that allowed me as a teacher, learner, and multimedia creator to act upon what I viewed as some transformative possibilities in digital media production. Methodologically, I draw from action research (Burnaford, Fischer, & Hobson, 2000; Cochran-Smith

& Lytle, 1993) and offer analyses based on my dual role as teacher/learner and researcher, a subjective position that allowed a particular perspective on the complexities of digital media production from a specific time and place.

In the summer of 2002, I participated in a free adult digital visual poetry workshop offered by the Digital Underground StoryTelling for Youth (DUSTY) program in Northern California (Hull, 2004; Hull & James, forthcoming). It was the first adult-centered class within the DUSTY program, a class that provided its participants with a space to construct poems laced with images and sounds. I happened upon this opportunity without knowing how it would lead to the enactment of an agentive self. In the process of planning, designing, and producing a digital poem, I learned about this agentive self and assembling it (so to speak) in meaningful ways. I discovered how to situate my life experiences through multiple texts (i.e., written, visual, oral, aural, and spatial)—and how to manipulate them—in ways that represented more than just a personal narrative. A melding of both personal and larger social struggles became a key guiding concept behind the production. Through this situated learning and experimentation with digital media, I was able to further ground my own teaching and approaches to writing, including my own digital visual poetry class for high school youth, at a later time. To clarify the complexity of this learning process, I describe in detail the creation of my digital poem, with emphasis on integrating my artistic visions with concrete life experiences. I also discuss how this process led to re-conceptualizing my teaching practices and further engaging digital media in both school and nonschool settings. I first turn to relevant literature on learning and literacy.

Conceptual Framework

Situated Learning

Lave and Wenger (1991) theorize that learning stems from social circumstances. They develop a perspective that differs from past theories and interpretations of situated learning, one that involves the whole person, the activity of that person in and with the world. This view avers that "agent, activity, and the world mutually constitute each other" (p. 33), thereby suggesting that all activities occurring in certain places and locations, such as in "novice-expert"-type relationships or "apprenticeships," are situated (see also Rogoff, 1990). Through what they call "legitimate peripheral participation," Lave and Wenger offer an analytic approach to examining how participants actually engage learning in and through social practice where power relationships and social structures are present.

> The form that the legitimacy of participation takes is a defining characteristic of ways of belonging, and is therefore not only a crucial condition for learning, but a constitutive element of its content. . . . Peripherality suggests that there are multiple, varied, more- or less-engaged and inclusive ways of being in the fields of participation defined by a community. Peripheral participation is about being located in the social world. (p. 36)

In moving across domains of practice (i.e., from partial to full participation), Lave and Wenger suggest, participants occupying certain "peripheral" locations within the larger social structure utilize legitimate peripheral participation as a way of engaging or acting in the world. Legitimate peripheral participation becomes a way of gaining access to and control over resources; in other words, participants position themselves in performing various roles within the very contexts they occupy in the world. This view builds upon Vygotsky's (1978) notion of zone proximal development, wherein legitimate peripheral participation enables "newcomers" to use "peripherality" as an opening to inherent social positions and structures. For the purposes of this chapter, it is important to consider this peripherality to understand the notion of teacher as learner. Teachers as social beings interact with others in particular sociocultural contexts, contexts that shape their everyday experiences and inform their classroom practice, including forms of media. Lave and Wenger provide a more detailed explanation for how learning occurs; here I focus largely on the conceptualization of legitimate peripheral participation as useful in developing new literacies in post-Fordist times (Cope & Kalantzis, 2000), a point to which I turn now.

New Literacies

A great deal of literature in the field of new literacy studies exists. Relevant studies have discussed the various cultural ways associated with reading and writing upon which people draw in their lives (Heath, 1983; Street, 1984, 1993, 1995). Others have focused on gaining access to other literacies that take place in new literate spaces (Gee, 2003; Hull & Katz, 2006; Lankshear & Knobel, 2003). For example, Street (1984) has long argued that literacy is ideological and that literacy practices are inextricably linked to cultural and power structures in society. He articulates how and why certain individuals carry out different literacy practices in different contexts by placing emphasis on the social, often complex, nature of literacy. Building on Street's ideological model of literacy theory, Barton and Hamilton (2000) conceptualize the link between the activities of reading and writing and the social structures in which they are embedded and which they shape. They suggest that literacy practices are *purposeful* and change as new ones are frequently *acquired* through processes of informal learning and sense making. In framing the coherence between practices (nonobservable), events (observable), and texts, they identify *written* texts as mediating tools in literacy activities and point out that different literacies involve different media or symbolic systems in different contexts. Key in their argument is the inclusion of *non(written)*text and text-based *images* present in film, television, and computers.

To clarify text framed within literacy as a social practice, Denzin (1997) asserts that performance text is a genre that dramatizes written texts—with motion and action—to create "multimedia tales" (p. 180). He recognizes that certain cultural texts such as poems and short stories can be read or performed before audiences, co-constructing new meanings and interpretations. In his examination of performing ethnography, Denzin argues that performance texts take many forms, ranging "from dramatic, natural, performance science, ethnodrama, to staged readings" (p. 185). He also claims that written texts can be performed or supplemented by other devices such as "pictures, slides, photographs, film, audio, music" (p. 207). Though his contentions are more specific to methodology, Denzin's work is relevant in illustrating key distinctions between texts, as well as in conceptualizing the social nature of texts as co-constructed in various contexts. For him, performance texts are messy and exist in spaces that integrate multiple genres. It is in these spaces where new experiences—or what I put forth as "agentive" new literacies—emerge.

Hull and Katz (2006) discuss a new literate space in DUSTY that combines narrative, identity, performance, and technology for crafting self. They describe and analyze how participants use multimedia literacy in digital storytelling to make sense of their past and present lives and to reflect on their life trajectories. Multimedia literacy in this case considers the various affordances in communication and representation through different modes or resources for meaning making such as writing, speech, image, sound, gesture, and movement (Kress, 2003). According to Hull and Katz, participants not only acquire new computer skills in the process but also speak about conceptions of self in forging new "agentive" identities. In other words, the stories participants tell simultaneously portray and shape who they are, how they see themselves, and what they plan to do in the future. Hull and Katz claim that, for individuals pushed into the margins of society, digital storytelling can serve as one medium for "second chances," *a way to change and direct self into new terrains*. Through au/oral, written, and visual text–based analyses of youth and adult participants' projects, they demonstrate how DUSTY as a new literate space offers possibilities for change either within an individual, in society, or both. Explicit in their work is how literacy is ideological and socially situated in nature; implicit are ways in which literacy learning is shaped by social factors and how it could lead to the transformative work of teachers.

For the purposes of this volume on media and learning, I extend the concept of "agentive self" by examining what it means for teachers to be active learners and agents in accessing, valuing, and utilizing digital stories and digital poems. This chapter focuses on the latter genre to illuminate the power of digital poems (often with stories embedded in them) as agentive tools that can serve purposes beyond personal "second chances." Highlighting one of these possibilities, Hull and Zacher (2004) posit the importance of digital visual poetry as an after-school program to assist youth in forging in-/out-of-school identities and fostering relationships across generations (e.g., between mother and daughter). Digital visual poetry as a new literate genre— and, as I will argue here, a performance text—gives regard to visual, and often musical, texts to provide authors "the space for concrete and symbolic images" that add "layers of meaning" to their written texts (Denzin, 1997, p. 27). Digital visual poetry participants interact and share some prior knowledge with one another through structured workshop sessions. As Hull and her colleagues have noted, what begins as a personal project for most participants turns into a highly social activity where language, race, class, gender, and experience merge, a place for imagining selves, constructing texts, acquiring new literacies, and evoking possibilities for social change. It is here where my story, my poetry, begins.

Situating My Learning and Teaching

Background

For years I have looked to prominent poets such as Langston Hughes, Maya Angelou, Adrienne Rich, Pablo Neruda, Jessica Hagedorn, and Sandra Cisneros for inspiration. Who knew that what began as an experimental outlet in my adolescent years would transform my whole perspective on poetry and, thus, outlook on life. My passion for poetry became a resource for the kinds of teaching acts I proceeded to engage in later years. Largely influenced by Paulo Freire's (1970) *concientizaçao* (loosely translated as consciousness or awareness of transformative and liberatory possibilities), my praxis focused on the needs of "the oppressed." I pushed myself to actively bring about change in my classroom through pedagogy and social action. Though the list was short of being comprehensive, I used multicultural works by various poets and other writers to form the basis of critical discussion and production of student work. I noticed that in these high school English classes students and I were able to tease apart themes that related to our histories, cultures, and experiences. And soon after my arrival at UC Berkeley as a graduate student, I was easily drawn to the Poetry for the People program and its mission to serve underprivileged and marginalized populations. Even though the poets mentioned above had already had effects on me, it was another poet who helped me to envision different possibilities of poetry in youth's lives. Her name was June Jordan.

For many, June Jordan was a walking political act, someone with an air of brilliance to whom Poetry for the People on the university campus is credited. She was a professor in the African American Studies department and a leading force in fighting for human rights. Jordan lived and breathed for the people. She imagined, demanded, and fought for equality like no other petite "slim lady" could.[1] She spoke against hate, censorship, and acts of counter-intelligence in renowned newspapers and journals such as *The New York Times, The Nation,* and *The Progressive.* Though at times censored herself, Jordan authored numerous books, from poetry to essays and others far too many to mention. And in 1999, I had the chance to meet her beyond text. I became first a student and later a student–teacher–poet, teaching and facilitating writing workshops at different locations with a cadre of other activists in the Poetry for the People program (Jocson, 2004, 2005).

Poetry for the People

June Jordan established Poetry for the People (P4P) at UC Berkeley in 1991. Its principal objective is to maintain a strong political stance in democratizing how "the people" are conceptualized in poetry. Through it programmatic efforts on the university and in the community, P4P uses poetry to shape the level of sociopolitical consciousness and actions of "the people," including the poor, homeless, prisoners, youth, and people of color. It also uses poetry to build a safe literary community to represent the works of and by historically marginalized populations.

The P4P program has been involved in various community projects and partnerships that primarily serve these populations outside the university campus. Its educational social justice agenda specifically draws on poetry as an empowering critical medium to move "the people" toward social transformation. This move, according to Jordan (1985), is an important one to advance poetry as a "consciousness"-raising tool, "comprehensible" and "not hidden away from the ordinary people" (p. 13). Hence, in the context of P4P, poetry is and has been treated as a tool for political and artistic empowerment. It is regarded as (1) a medium for telling the "truth" (lived experience), (2) reaching for maximal impact through the use of a minimal number of words (purpose), and (3) demanding utmost precision word by word (intensity) (Muller & the Poetry for the People Blueprint Collective, 1995, p. 36). According to these P4P-specific writing guidelines, the painstaking "precision" that delivers the intensity as well as density of language is what separates poetry from prose.

Over the course of three years through my involvement with P4P, I learned from Jordan herself what it meant to write, to use words as a form of action in changing the world. I also learned how to be a more conscious human being by giving back and investing in the fight for social justice. The irony in this story, however, is that never once did I imagine such a warrior would grace my life. In June 2002, Jordan passed away without my personally acknowledging the strength her presence had in my life. I was in Los Angeles visiting my family when I received the devastating phone call.

"June left us this morning . . . she died peacefully." My body felt numb as I contemplated the unimaginable.

"She's gone? She's really gone?"

For weeks I could not stop thinking about the times I let pass, of my not letting "June" know what and how much she meant in my life.

Through this grieving period, I realized that I had to do something. I wanted to have a chance to impress upon her symbolically the kind of woman, "soldier," revolutionary, and humanitarian she was. In a sense, I wanted to use this moment of vulnerability as a form of motivation to craft a "second chance" (Greene, 1990; Inbar, 1990). What came immediately to mind were June's infectious laughter and proverbial statements. Remembering the good times made me smile and enabled me to move on. I recalled one instance in 2000 when Jordan and her students, including myself, were discussing the topic of love poems in class. Pablo Neruda's work came up; so did hers, and eventually her stance on love, revealing that without love "change in the world" would not be possible. Students joined in the conversation and gave examples of selfless figures to build on her point. It was then that Jordan struck a chord in all of us. She noted the endless "fight"—the necessary fight and continued struggle alongside and for the people—to gain equal rights and justice. She said, "Love is about a revolution, and that revolution is about love."

"14 Reasons Why"

As a poetic homage to June Jordan's life, work, and legacy, I decided to embark on a five-minute video project entitled "14 Reasons," an original poem from 2001 (see the appendix to this chapter). The video begins with a pre-text echoing familiar words, "June Jordan always said, 'love is about a revolution, and that revolution is about love.'" As it fades in the next image appears, "A Tribute to June, Love, and Other Things." "Mermaid" by jazz and rhythm and blues artist Sade plays in the background to create a melancholy mood. This instrumental is enjoined by a series of photographs, depicting rainy and gloomy days. As noted in Denzin's (1997) notion of performance text, I used pictures and sounds to supplement the meaning of my words. The screen dissolves into black to show the title page, immediately followed by a voiceover starting with the title.

To fully explore the aesthetics behind the video, I first describe the poem's origins and thematic connections. The poem "14 Reasons Why" was written during a time in my life when poetry served as a refuge for self-building and contemplating hope. I tried to capture visions of horses running freely in the rain, galloping without pause or direction, to express solitude (and fortitude, for that matter) in more positive ways. What transpired were the beginnings of "14 Reasons Why," from jotted notes to fragments and eventually stanzas that enlisted modest, humanistic qualities often unnoticed in capitalist societies. At the very least, my vulnerabilities at that particular time set off the honesty that was to form the basis of the poem, the kind of honesty that I had learned from Jordan about poetry's "truth"-telling power. After the first line, "You enchant me," I soon realized the presence of P4P's guidelines in my writing, particularly the use of strong active verbs and imagery to create movement and to evoke emotion throughout the poem. Each of the fourteen lines represented what I deem as important to humanity and the connectedness between people; these were lines consisting of pronouns, "you" and "me," followed by real-life details that exemplify everyday revolutionary acts.

Indeed, the video poem's purpose was to trace these humanistic qualities while illustrating the contributions of past revolutionaries and connecting them to present-day struggles in various communities. The conditions I point out in the original poem became more than a script; in forging my "reasons why," I opted for a second chance and produced a video poem as a tribute to a revolutionary of *my* time. So weeks after Jordan's passing, I paid DUSTY a visit and formally met the director and his then-small staff. Though I had known about the program's existence from colleagues who had made digital stories, I did not show interest until an adult workshop specific to poetry was established in July 2002.

The Production and its Process

Seven adults of color participated in the two-weekend workshop, which covered various activities during the three phases of production (Table 1).[2] These included writing, storyboarding, scanning images, web image searching, voice capturing, selecting music, editing, and exporting. Four of the participants, including myself, had been involved with teaching and working in some capacity in California public schools. Several of us came prepared with previously written poems and expected that the entire production process would not take much time or effort. We were wrong. During "open" weeknights and weekends, the director and other digital story experts at the center offered the necessary assistance. For all of us, this situated learning context called for forging new relationships with other participants as well as with the center's staff. As Lave and Wenger (1991) suggested, novice and expert participants interact to facilitate learning; in this case, newcomers to digital visual poetry used the notion of "peripherality" to negotiate and position themselves as learners. Together we shared our prior knowledge and skills to create new ones. Each of us served as each other's apprentices, which then for me was significant as I realized the importance of knowledge exchange between participants and the kind of environment that facilitates it.

Table 1. Production stages and elements of digital visual poetry

	Preproduction stage	In-production stage	Postproduction stage
Poetry	Write Workshop		
Storyboarding	Brainstorm Sketch		
Voice capture		Practice/read poem Record poem Use Adobe Premiere* Save files	
Image scanning or searching		Scan photos Search Internet Save files	
Image (re)sizing		Use Adobe Photoshop Save files	
Music selection		Download song(s) Save files	
Editing		Use Adobe Premiere* Import files Create video/audio timeline Insert effects Insert titles and credits Save files	
Export			Print to video—

timeline to movie			transfer movie to VHS and DV tapes Save and transfer all files to CD and external hard drive
Wrap up and the "show"			Clear files from computer Make copies of video Invite friends and family, promote program Premiere of movie

* There are various editing programs, such as iMovie, Adobe Premiere, and Final Cut Pro, ranging from basic to professional use.

Unlike the other participants in the digital visual poetry course, I quickly grasped terminology used during hands-on demonstrations because of my previous experience with technology and video production in other contexts. Some of my own knowledge about how to operate the same editing software program (Adobe Premiere) transferred in the initial process. However, naïve about media production's many complex stages and activities, I tried to shortcut the initial process and later discovered that I was only shortcutting my own learning. It became more obvious, for example, that constructing a "project timeline" in Adobe Premiere first requires time to learn some basic technicalities and editing tools. I could not have used "transition" techniques such as motion or zoom effects on still photographs effectively without first learning simple functions such as fade in/out, cut, and dissolve.

To create a video poem, I manipulated seventy-three web-based images downloaded from the Internet using Google and other search engines (see Table 2 for specific names, locations, and events used as key words). I resized each of them to fit a 480 x 640 pixel format using Adobe Photoshop, and I conceived a timeline broken up into fourteen segments that set up the video's theme, setting, and narrative. The first eight segments were devoted to past figures or revolutionaries who left behind legacies for the world; the last six were focused on present-day conditions that affect "oppressed" populations—women, the poor, urban youth, and people of color, among others. Harking back to June Jordan and her life's work, I used what I know about certain literate skills (e.g., how to compose a narrative) to develop a sense of past and present history. For clarity, I categorized each segment and grouped images by theme (Table 2). The narrative that develops throughout the video poem was drawn from my personal, social, and historical experiences, using particular representations of people, places, and events that have had some influence on me. It was important to recognize the influences of these experiences because they served as a resource for my own literacy learning (Gutiérrez, Baquedano-López, & Turner, 1997). Each of them not only facilitated my own learning but also informed the nature of how I represented whom and what and how I saw myself in the video poem.

Table 2. Summary of "14 Reasons Why"
Segments, themes, and images

	Segments	Themes	Images (total number of images)
Pre-text		Hope, remembrance	Rain (4)
1	You enchant me …	Social justice, common struggles	June Jordan, José Rizal, Berkeley (4)
2	You inspire me …	Guerilla fighting	Rigoberta Menchú Tum, Pancho Villa, Leonard Peltier (5)
3	You galvanize me …	Education, literacy	Mother Theresa, Toni Morrison (6)
4	You paint me …	Racism, classism	Malcolm X, Martin Luther King Jr., Assata Shakur, The Black Panthers (5)
5	You embrace me …	Socialism	Che Guevara, Fidel Castro (7)
6	You balance me …	Leadership	Third World Liberation Front, Nelson Mandela, César Chávez, Mahatma Gandhi (7)
7	You ravish me …	Literature	Princess Diana, Maya Angelou, Angela Davis (3)

8	You bolster me . . .	Sisterhood	Prostitution (4)
9	You incapacitate me . . .	Terrorism	New York City, 9 / 11 (4)
10	You tickle me . . .	Violence	"Dream" and Oakland graffiti art (5)
11	You hypnotize me . . .	Poverty	San Francisco homeless patrons and war veterans (5)
12	You calibrate me . . .	Harassment, criminality	Police on patrol (4)
13	You fascinate me . . .	Writing, teaching	Children and youth in schools, Korina Jocson and her students (4)
14	You enthrall me . . .	Social justice, common struggles	Bay Area Rapid Transit, June Jordan, Corazón Aquino (6)
Post-text		Remembrance, in memory	Quote from June Jordan

The initial project timeline in the Adobe Premiere program did not take long to complete. I knew right away that I wanted to begin the video poem with Jordan's portrait and end with images that related to her legacy. What took the most time during in-production was the sequencing of other images in ways that not only reflected the words in the written poem but also flowed with the overall connection between love and revolution. I created a storyboard—one that was slightly different from the usual method of drawing. My storyboard was the result of color-coding the written poem by theme using Post-It notes in the margins, a method that served as a structural guide during the editing process. My storyboard also contained sketch notes (arrows and the like) to intertwine stories found in each stanza. I could have used a "real" storyboard (i.e., a visual text with lines for written text and boxes for illustration) but chose this peculiar way instead. This strategy allowed me to see the printed poem in its entirety and to visualize the connections between each stanza on one page. Later, I took this page to initiate the editing process (syncing words, images, and sound on the editing timeline). Table 2 summarizes the overall thematic structure of the video poem as well as the images represented in each segment.

Poetic Representations

As "Mermaid" plays in the background, a portrait of Jordan appears, followed by the cover of her second-to-last book, *Soldier*, published in 2001. It is accompanied by a distant shot of her on the microphone standing in front of UC Berkeley's infamous Sproul Hall. The words "actions have meaning, and meaning saves lives . . ." are heard amidst the tune, immediately followed by "like you save mine" and a portrait of Philippine revolutionary hero and poet José Rizal. This specific image leads to a series of others that, to me, represent the contributions of past and present "revolutionaries," including Rigoberta Menchú Tum, Pancho Villa, Leonard Peltier, Mother Theresa, Toni Morrison, Assata Shakur, Malcolm X, Martin Luther King Jr., Che Guevara, Fidel Castro, The Black Panthers, Third World Liberation Front, Nelson Mandela, César Chávez, Mahatma Gandhi, Princess Diana, Maya Angelou, and Angela Davis. In order to parallel the strengths of these individual figures, I synchronized each active verb—such as "inspire," "galvanize," "paint," "embrace," "balance," and "ravish"—with one of these faces. I purposely did this as a conscious effort to create emotion and movement in the visual poem. For each of the seven reasons in the first half of the poem, I used fade in/out to black to ensure that each figure received its due respect and emphasis. Within each one, I used either dissolve or cut to connect images and have a sense of temporal flow. I also added motion effects to give a sense of physical movement.

After the seventh reason, the focus turns away from figures and on to past or present events and situations. A cue for this shift in focus is visible in the written poem (italicized "phenomenal"). In the video, this subtle mark is followed by an image of Angela Davis before a series of "visions of a raceless and classless society," including prostitution, child abuse, hate, homicides, homelessness, police harassment, and schooling inequalities. For me, these images depict day-to-day struggles and, for greater effect in their representation, are purposefully juxtaposed with verbs in reasons 8 to 13: "bolster," "incapacitate," "tickle," "hypnotize," "calibrate," and "fascinate." Many are visual displays of the San Francisco Bay Area, particularly Oakland, that illustrate one community's challenges, needs, and hopes. Beyond merely adding aesthetic value, these images also establish a sense of location. As in the first half of the video, I used fade in/out as well as dissolve and cut effects to connect one struggle to the next. One dramatic effect occurs in reason 9, when my voice echoes indecipherably and the photographs also explode to portray the events of September 11 in New York City. To the quick eye, this echo effect may seem like a mistake. However, I actually used the effect to create confusion and chaos, a symbolic remembrance for the thousands of people killed in the attack on the Twin Towers.

Nearing the thirteenth reason, my voiceover remarks come together to connect previous images to who I am. The connections here become an articulation of identity, or what Holland, Lachicotte, Skinner, and Cain (1998) call identity in practice or "one way of naming the dense interconnections" of my personhood, not as "independent from but webbed within historical social worlds" (p. 270). I demonstrate through the connections I make this very notion of identity in practice as I too believe that people improvise certain responses because of or as constituted by their social landscapes. When I say, "You fascinate me/with every piece of advice you offer to every young person," a photograph illustrating a specific interaction I had with two former P4P students from a local high school appears. It is a photograph that was taken by their teacher during a group outing that culminated in an outdoor poetry reading one Saturday afternoon in the San Francisco Bay Area. In a momentary but pleasant surprise, this reading was concluded with an electric slide dance performed by four other students. Ironically, the photograph became and is still a part of their school website, not as an advertisement for one particular small learning community but as a product of a collaborative in-class project facilitated by students themselves in 2001. I had no prior knowledge that such an image existed on the Internet. Because I see myself as an ally to students and other young people, the selection of this particular photograph relates to some degree to Hull and Katz's (2002) assertion that conceptions of self in digital stories are telling of who we want to be as people and suggestive of our life trajectories.

Finally, the conclusion of the poem focuses on youth, depicting different age groups from different parts of the world. The last photograph before the fourteenth reason is of BART (Bay Area Rapid Transit) to give a closing sense of location and time. An unwavering sound similar to that of the train is heard in the background as a symbol of time passing. After a moment of silence, June Jordan's image once again appears on the screen. Her black-and-white portrait is then followed by two more during the *voiceover*, "You enthrall me/with every bit of gesture you make, every word you utter, every stride you take." Similar to the progression in the first reason, I drew upon an iconic Philippine figure to represent who I am, "Because without you/there is no me." I thought that it was appropriate to have an image here of Corazón Aquino, the first female president of the Philippines and widow of assassinated political leader Benigno Aquino. In the photograph, she has her arms up in the air, gesturing the "L" sign with each hand. Back in the EDSA Revolutions of the mid- to late 1980s, Aquino led a mass of Filipinos to oust then-president/dictator Ferdinand Marcos, which resulted, arguably, in the creation of a new democracy. The "L" sign that many of the Aquino followers held as a symbol for this struggle stood for *laban*, or "fight."

I closed out the last two lines of the poem with quick cuts to an image of June Jordan laughing. This is followed by a previously seen image of a group of women, including Angela Davis, before the image dissolves back into a portrait of June Jordan in a somber pose. After this last image, I use fade to black before "There is no chance we will fall apart / There is no chance / there are no parts," a quote from a book of love poems called *Haruko* (Jordan, 1994).[3] As in the beginning statement "Love is about a revolution/And revolution is about love," I made it a point to come full circle with Jordan's words to show her impact on me as a woman, teacher, and poet.

Symbolically and aesthetically, I intended for the concluding written-visual text to leave the audience in contemplation. The screen *fades to black* and provides viewers a moment to reflect and remember June Jordan. Soon, the credits roll, first with a dedication title, "In Memory of June Jordan (1936–2002)," followed by a series of production acknowledgments. The instrumental ballad that is still playing in the background begins to *fade out* as the screen gradually *fades to black*. At this point, "14 Reasons Why" is conceptually mastered and edited.

Postproduction

From the polished edited timeline, the next step was to export the entire project into a digital movie, which required just as much attention as editing. The transfer from one format (i.e., computer and software programs) to another (i.e., digital videotape and compact discs) was a not simple process and, as I experienced several times, could end in disaster (e.g., erasing or distorting the edited project). Finally, and most important, all folders containing various files on the computer needed to be saved, copied, and transferred onto at least two compact discs. These postproduction activities were essential for memory on the computers' hard drives to become available for future DUSTY participants. At the time of this production, there were approximately fifteen Macintosh desktop and laptop computers in the lab.

In December 2002, "14 Reasons Why" was one of several video poems featured during the DUSTY/ Digital visual Poetry public showing at the Black Box Theater in Oakland. Part of the preparation was to have all the digital stories and poems on a mini-DV tape for the best-quality playback on the big screen. The order in which the videos were shown followed the event's agenda, starting with youth in the early part and ending with adults. Several of my students, friends, and colleagues attended the showing. Afterward, to my surprise, a handful of audience members expressed their strong interest in learning how to create a video poem as one means to tell their own stories, a chance to reveal things that had been unsaid and unrecognized. Given what I had gained in this production process, it would have been remiss of me not to invite them to come and visit my class. It was the start of a conversation and a time to contemplate the need for more video poems, at the DUSTY lab and elsewhere.

Reflections of a Teacher/Learner

I am grateful for the time I spent on this project. Though image search-ing and editing were grueling, time-consuming steps, I gained invalu-able skills that I now use to do similar projects on my own and with others, including two experimental video poems entitled "Rest" and "Her Ways." Digital visual poetry and the processes involved in making a video poem are far from simple. The details I share in this chapter hopefully illustrate the kind of preparation and level of commitment necessary in digital media production. Goodman (2003), who chronicles his role as a facilitator in his work with youth and video production in New York, would agree. The three years I spent as one of the facilitators and instructors of the digital visual poetry class for middle to high school–aged youth in Oakland, California, shaped what I do today, and how, as a teacher educator and instruc-tional support to teachers who utilize media production in their classrooms.

Situating my own learning process as a digital media composer helped me to understand further what it means to be a teacher with more insight, depth, and innovative ideas. After Jordan's passing in 2002, I not only took the chance to create a personal project in a time of grief but also learned important lessons about self, identity, and reciprocity. Indeed, the project was a "second chance" opportunity to settle lost moments, yet, on a larger scale, it provided me with a vision that far extends into other moments. My use of present-day struggles to parallel past ones through word, image, and sound helped to enact an "agentive self" that reflects my personal experiences, social environment, and knowledge of history (Hull & Katz, 2006). Through the lacing of various texts, I was able to create "14 Reasons Why," which for me became an agentive tool to challenge existing social inequalities. This agentive tool is one that calls unto others the need for social action.

Moreover, in line with Rosenblatt's (1978) transactional theory between texts and readers, what I attempted to capture was the result of the transaction(s) between the various texts in my life and the ways in which I read, interpreted, and, thus, represented them in the video poem. This transaction with me as the artist and producer at the center had the potential to form the basis of other transactions. In this sense, multimedia products such as "14 Reasons Why" become what I call "transactions of transactions," which with their intertextual propensities could inform and guide the production of other video poems. This is similar to using a film in classroom contexts for the purpose of compelling audience members to think or act in agentive ways. In other words, it draws on the affordances of sound and visual communication to appeal to one's senses for meaning making (Kress, 2003), senses otherwise untapped by print-only texts. As I have learned in my own transaction, integrating various types of texts and constructing multiple meanings are important in new media times. Video poems and other multimedia products can be created for different purposes and different audiences, for personal reasons and beyond. Whether in school or nonschool settings, they allow for different interpretations and different genres to be explored.

Reflecting on the production of "14 Reasons Why" has impacted my self-perception as a learner and as a teacher. During my time in the DUSTY lab, I struggled to become a better teacher because I knew from firsthand experience what this kind of media production called for. Learning through this small-scale production demanded an understanding of the complexities of learning from the position of a learner. Today I am hopeful as a teacher and teacher educator in believing that, despite corporate media's commercial appeal, media systems and technologies can still offer endless possibilities for disrupting dominant discourses that often target young people and those who serve them. Digital visual poetry examined within a teacher/learner stance suggests the power of a new literate space for its participants to situate their visions, creativities, and experiences into a personal project while simultaneously tackling macro-level issues. Digital visual poetry reaffirms the power of poetry as a writing genre; it also takes advantage of new expressive forms and new processes of composing afforded by the logic of spatiality in speech, image, and sound. I now build on this experience to do similar work with teachers in other places.

Implications and Conclusion

Implicit in the process of creating video poems is the open invitation to teachers (and other adults) to take on a learning stance. This means engaging as a learner with technologies and texts that are otherwise readily accessed by students (and other young people). In some cases, it means to work together and create side by side with students. For teacher educators, it is an open invitation to embrace new media and to integrate digital technologies more fully into traditional methods courses in the preparation of preservice teachers. It is also an invitation to in-service teachers, instructors, and program coordinators for their continued professional development. At the heart of this investigation are the possibilities of digital media production for innovating pedagogical practices and addressing social inequities both inside and outside of classrooms, for students and teachers alike.

Digital visual poetry as a new literate genre illustrates the power of assembling texts by situating the personal in complex ways. It is, indeed, not an easy task. To produce a written poem, add voice, select music, search for images, edit a video, and export a movie requires much preparation. The process involves skills including storytelling, storyboarding, multitasking, and manipulating computer software. It also requires creativity, flexibility, patience, and, most of all, interactive exchanges with others in a participatory context that is attentive to both individual and social development. It is a process situated in a multilayered literacy activity, one that engages sophisticated skills for composing and manifests the personal in connective ways. In this light, digital media production serves as a pedagogical "third space" and allows for hybrid literacies to intertwine various types of texts, resources, and experiences (Gutiérrez, Baquedano-López, & Turner, 1997). The lacing of personal, social, and historical experiences illustrates part of a complex learning process involved in a digital writing genre such as digital visual poetry. It offers a way to craft, develop, and enact an "agentive self" (Hull & Katz, 2006) that can materialize as potential agentive tools for teaching and learning. My digital poem is far from exemplary. There are certainly many other ways of creating multimedia projects that center on or even build away from the personal. It is my hope, however, that the descriptions and analyses from this investigation demonstrate pedagogical possibilities of both personal *and* nonpersonal projects through the use of a particular medium to invigorate curriculum and innovate classroom practice.

Digital visual poetry is one approach that integrates technologies into teaching and learning that I now recommend to other classroom teachers, after-school program coordinators, and instructors. As I have argued throughout this chapter, digital visual poetry as one type of digital media production leaves plenty of room not only for experimentation to produce texts but also for participants to imagine selves and create meanings toward personal and social transformation. A salient feature in this complex process is for teachers and students to explore *together* their abilities to think, read, write, and create more critically.

From my own observations and experiences, digital media production is a demanding process as it requires multiple tasks and skills to create quality work. The process can be quite nuanced and jarring at particular stages. Even those who had prior knowledge of technology—whether to their liking or not—needed to become learners all over again. It was important, as in my case, to revisit software programs and refresh editing skills. As a former high school teacher, I believe that it is critical to share these complexities openly with students and impart to them that the making of video poems such as "14 Reasons Why" was made possible by collaborative influences and input from others, including students themselves. My story as a teacher/learner is part of my current pedagogy and has become one way to introduce digital media production in multiple settings. It is my hope that within this present story other teachers will see the value of their own participation in the learning and will create a classroom environment where teachers and students can build on each other's strengths and knowledge. It is also my hope that teachers will provide their students the resources necessary to access various literacies and the skills associated with them by tapping into youth media and other community-based organizations that are currently engaging young people in similar ways. As digital technologies continue to change, I cannot emphasize enough the importance of teachers also learning from students about new tools and new forms of production. This kind of active learning through collaboration is, after all, the quintessential "third space" that we as progressive educators maintain and often strive to create in our own classroom contexts.

In March 2003, "14 Reasons Why" was featured at the Eighth Annual Women of Color Film Festival in Berkeley, California. There I told the same story as I have told here and imparted a similar message about the power of digital media production for innovating pedagogical practice and moving toward achieving social justice. In April 2004, I found myself inside tenth-grade English language arts classes comprising mostly students of color in the San Francisco Bay Area. There, I used my written and video poem once again as an agentive tool to assist high school students in their writing process. Many of the students composed and entered their poems for competition in the inaugural June Jordan Poetry Prize Contest. The second-place winner announced in May that year was a student in one of those classes who wrote about everyday challenges in human relationships between families and communities. As Mahiri (2004b) put it, "talking the talk" in research on teaching is one thing, but "walking the walk" is another. Hands-on experience in digital media production exposed me to a variety of tasks and complexities in learning *and* teaching that otherwise would have been missed without reflection and action. I urge others to seek a similar experience.

Appendix—Original Poem

14 Reasons Why

You enchant me
> with simple words that form complex actions
> because actions have meaning and meaning saves lives
> like you save mine.

You inspire me
> with your fiery Leo passion
> to change the world as if you own it
> and have no intentions of selling out to the highest
> bidder.

You galvanize me
> to explore every thought of every child
> every time she asks a question, picks up a pen, or reads
> a book.

You paint me
> self-less visions of a raceless and classless society
> that Martin devoted his life for and never got to see.

You embrace me
> with your tattooed arms, so so tight, not ever wanting
> to let go
> like the two murdered boys and the memory of them
> you carry
> so they can live on.

You balance me
> with your sometimes endless days
> because you are always the first to arrive and the last to
> leave the battlefield.

You ravish me
> with silky whispers to my ear
> about the perfect Ralph Waldo Emerson quote
> or the perfect Maya Angelou poem
> > *phenomenal.*

You bolster me
>
> to straighten up, never slouch, and stand tall
> so fellow sisters understand that they are not alone in
> their struggle.

You incapacitate me
>
> with symphonic soundtracks like you incapacitate
> yourself
> at night when you lay almost sleepless, worrying
> always worrying about tomorrow's events.

You tickle me
>
> without the use of fingers or hands
> because you lent them to a young man so he forgets
> to clutch his own hands and accidentally squeeze a
> trigger.

You hypnotize me
>
> with hazelnut eyes that gaze at the homeless with hu-
> mility
> only to reach in your pocket, your wallet, pull out a $20
> bill
> and smile without hesitation.

You calibrate me
>
> with vicious overtones like pitbulls barking at strang-
ers
> just to illustrate how attacks and kills happen to stu-
> dents daily in schools.

You fascinate me
>
> with every piece of advice you offer to every young
> person
> because you know that if you don't no one will.

You enthrall me
>
> with every bit of gesture you make, every word you ut-
> ter
> because without you there is no me
> and without me there is no you
> and without us there is no love.

Notes

A version of this chapter first appeared online in *Current Issues in Education* in 2005. Many thanks to the editors of this volume for continuing the conversation and providing constructive feedback. Also, special thanks to Glynda Hull and DUSTY for supporting this work, and to Vivian Gadsden and Anne Burns Thomas for their critical responses.

[1] The phrase "slim lady" was born around the time rapper Eminem's "Slim Shady" album went gold in 2001.

[2] These phases of production refer to small-scale productions that may take place in classrooms or after-school programs. They are modeled after other types of documentary or film production. However, in this chapter, I define "production" to include editing and exporting the movie to a file, a phase that is typically considered a part of postproduction.

[3] In the video the date used for the quote is 1993 rather than 1994. I did not realize until after production that I had erred and chose not to make the change. It is one example (among many) of minor glitches that I would return to and polish had I more time. It is also an example of what I would call imperfections in the in-production process that denote the complexities of and demonstrate the need for more careful postproduction work. It is obvious that the finished product is not so finished; as an artist, I (re)visit this work and typically identify places for improvement—similar to (re)reading one's own writing and having the urge to change things as if one is still in the revision phase of the work.

References

Barton, D., & Hamilton, M. (2000). Literacy practices. In D. Barton, M. Hamilton, & R. Ivanič (Eds.), *Situated literacies: Reading and writing in context* (pp. 7–15). London: Routledge.

Burnaford, G., Fischer, G., & Hobson, D. (Eds.). (2000). *Teachers doing research: The power of action through inquiry*. Mahwah, NJ: Lawrence Erlbaum.

Cochran-Smith, M., & Lytle, S. (Eds.). (1993). *Inside/outside: Teacher research and knowledge*. New York: Teachers College Press.

Cope, B., & Kalantzis, M. (2000). Introduction: The beginnings of an idea. In B. Cope & M. Kalantzis (Eds.), *Multiliteracies: Literacy learning and the design of social futures* (pp. 3–8). New York: Routledge.

Denzin, N. (1997). Performance texts. In W. Tierney & Y. Lincoln (Eds.), *Representation and the text: Re-framing the narrative voice* (pp. 179–217). Albany: State University of New York Press.

Dyson, A. H. (1997). *Writing superheroes: Contemporary childhood, popular culture, and classroom literacy.* New York: Teachers College Press.

Freire, P. (1970). *The pedagogy of the oppressed.* New York: Seabury.

Gee, J. (2003). *What video games have to teach us about learning and literacy.* New York: Palgrave.

Goodman, S. (2003). *Teaching youth media: A critical guide to literacy, video production, and social change.* New York: Teachers College Press.

Greene, M. (1990). Revision and interpretation: Opening spaces for the second chance. In D. Inbar (Ed.), *Second chance in education* (pp. 37–48). London: Falmer.

Gutiérrez, K., Baquedano-López, P., & Alvarez, H. (2001). Literacy as hybridity: Moving beyond bilingualism in urban classrooms. In M. de la Luz Reyes & J. Halcón (Eds.), *The best of our children: Critical perspectives on literacy for Latino students* (pp. 122–141). New York: Teachers College Press.

Gutiérrez, K., Baquedano-López, P., & Turner, M. (1997). Putting the language back into language arts: When the radical middle meets the third space. *Language Arts, 74*(5), 368–378.

Heath, S. (1983). *Ways with words: Language, life, and work in communities and classrooms.* Cambridge, UK: Cambridge University Press.

Holland, D., Lachicotte, W., Skinner, D., & Cain, C. (1998). *Identity and agency in cultural worlds.* Cambridge, MA: Harvard University Press.

Hull, G. (2004). Youth culture and digital media: New literacies for new times. *Research in the Teaching of English, 38*(2), 229–233.

Hull, G., & James, M. (Forthcoming). Geographies of hope: A study of urban landscapes, digital media, and children's representations of place. In P. O'Neill (Ed.), *Blurring boundaries: Research and teaching beyond a discipline.* Cresskill, NJ: Hampton.

Hull , G., & Katz, M. (November, 2002). Learning to tell a digital story: New literate spaces for crafting self. Paper presented at the meeting of the American Anthropological Association.

Hull, G., & Katz, M. (2006). Crafting an agentive self: Case studies of digital storytelling. *Research in the Teaching of English*, 41(1), 43–81.

Hull, G., & Zacher, J. (2004). What is an after-school worth? Developing literacy and identity in school. *Voices in Urban Education, 3*. Retrieved July 1, 2007, from http://www.annenberginstitute.org/VUE/spring04/Hull.html.

Inbar, D. (1990). *Second chance in education*. London: Falmer.

Jocson, K. M. (2004). Beyond borders: Poetry slicing through steel gates and barbed wires. *English Journal, 93*(3), 15–16.

Jocson, K. M. (2005). "Taking it to the mic": Pedagogy of June Jordan's Poetry for the People and partnership with an urban high school. *English Education, 37*(2), 44–60.

Jordan, J. (1985). *On call: Political essays*. Boston: South End.

Jordan, J. (1994). *Haruko/love poems*. New York: High Risk.

Jordan, J. (2001). *Soldier: A poet's childhood*. New York: Basic Civitas.

Kress, G. (2003). Literacy in the new media age. New York: Routledge.

Ladson-Billings, G. (1994). *The dreamkeepers: Successful teachers of African American children*. San Francisco: Jossey-Bass.

Lankshear, C., & Knobel, M. (2003). *New literacies: Changing knowledge and classroom learning*. Buckingham, UK: Open University Press.

Lave, J., & Wenger, E. (1991). *Situated learning: Legitimate peripheral participation*. Cambridge, UK: Cambridge University Press.

Lee, C. (2002, April). *Cultural historical activity theory as analytical frame and methodology*. Paper presented at the Center for Urban Education Forum, University of California, Berkeley.

Mahiri, J. (1998). *Shooting for excellence: African American and youth culture in new century schools*. New York: National Council of Teachers of English & Teachers College Press.

Mahiri, J. (2004a). Street scripts: African American youth writing about crime and violence. In J. Mahiri (Ed.), *What they don't learn in school: Literacy in the lives of urban youth* (pp. 19–42). New York: Peter Lang.

Mahiri, J. (2004b). Researching teaching practices: "Talking the talk" versus "walking the walk." *Research in the Teaching of English, 38*(4), 467–471.

McLaren, P. (1994). *Life in schools: An introduction to critical pedagogy in the foundations of education* (2nd ed.). New York: Longman.

Moll, L., & González, N. (1994). Lessons from research with language-minority children. *Journal of Reading Behavior, 26*(4), 439–456.

Morrell, E., & Duncan-Andrade, J. (2002). Promoting academic literacy with urban youth through engaging hip-hop culture. *English Journal, 91*(6), 88–92.

Muller, L., & the Poetry for the People Blueprint Collective (Eds.). (1995). *June Jordan's Poetry for the People: A revolutionary blueprint.* New York: Routledge.

Nieto, S. (2002). *Language, culture, and teaching: Critical perspectives for a new century.* Mahwah, NJ: Lawrence Erlbaum.

Rogoff, B. (1990). *Apprenticeship in thinking: Cognitive development in social context.* New York: Oxford University Press.

Rosenblatt, L. M. (1978). *The reader the text the poem: The transactional theory of the literary work.* Carbondale: Southern Illinois University Press.

Sleeter, C., & Grant, C. (1991). Mapping terrains of power: Student cultural knowledge versus classroom knowledge. In C. Sleeter (Ed.), *Empowerment through multicultural education* (pp. 49–67). Albany: State University of New York Press.

Street, B. (1984). *Literacy in theory and practice.* Cambridge, UK: Cambridge University Press.

Street, B. (1993). Introduction: The new literacy studies. In B. Street (Ed.), *Cross-cultural approaches to literacy.* Cambridge, UK: Cambridge University Press.

Street, B. (1995). *Social literacies: Critical approaches to literacy in development, ethnography and education.* London: Longman.

Vygotsky, L. (1978). *Mind and society: The development of higher psychological processes.* Cambridge, MA: Harvard University Press.

Response to Jocson

Anne Burns Thomas

In the current educational context marked by the de-professionalization of teaching, those engaged in the process of learning to teach—students, teachers, and teacher educators—must strive to make their learning transparent. As a former urban middle school teacher and a new teacher educator, I have seen and been saddened by the marginalization of teacher autonomy and intellect through mandated, scripted curricula that ask teachers to be little more than tools for delivery of someone else's knowledge. Far removed from the interconnectedness and complexity required by today's technological society, teachers are being asked to set aside their personal, social, and intellectual histories in the quest to produce ever more homogeneous, sterile classroom environments. These conceptions of "teacher" leave little room for an understanding of the importance of relationships, those between students and teachers, teachers and their colleagues, and teachers and knowledge. One of the central questions that this volume addresses is the ways that putting media texts at the center of the teaching and learning processes can change traditional educational dynamics. Rich, detailed accounts of teachers and students engaged in meaningful learning with media at its center can serve to challenge these prevailing trends. One of the least understood aspects of teaching—the ways in which teachers come to know what they know and will teach—is explored through Korina Jocson's thoughtful description of her own learning as she engaged in a digital media project.

In her chapter, Jocson describes her socially situated learning process, which moved between a highly personal place of grief over the loss of a friend and mentor and a place of political transformation through the creation of a digital poetry project. As she describes her efforts to honor June Jordan's amazing legacy through digital poetry, the author points to the ways in which the use of technology can make explicit the choices teachers and students make when they tell stories. The identity of the teacher, the poet, is central here as she selects words and images to bring a tribute to life. The author did what we ask students to do every day: she took an experience that was meaningful to her and crafted a story that allowed for multiple interpretations, multiple ways in, and new insights. Work of this nature creates the possibilities for different relationships with students as the students and teachers learn an unfamiliar process using technology with which the students might be more comfortable. By taking this risk, Jocson was able to see new possibilities for herself as a teacher. She could learn with her students, not privileging her power or authority but becoming vulnerable as a learner through this new technology. In traditional professional development, teachers are not often asked to be learners in the respectful manner described in this chapter—as adults with identities who are making choices and have the potential to contribute something beautiful at the same time they are learning new skills. By opening up her learning process, Jocson encourages us to consider the educational, social, and political benefits of making media texts central to teaching and learning.

This kind of digital media work, work that engages multiple interpretations of texts and multiple understandings of literacy through media, has the potential to engage teachers in the learning process in new and different ways. Through the creation of digital video and poetry projects, teachers are placed in a different relationship to knowledge, which points to the socially situated nature of many literacy acts. In stark contrast to the teacher-as-technician model endorsed by many school and curricular reform movements, Jocson's chapter makes visible the ways that teachers make decisions grounded in layered and nuanced identities. The teacher in this portrait is interacting with a body of knowledge with deep roots: in her personal relationship with the subject of the poem, in her political and activist work, in her appreciation of poetry and images, and in her work with other teachers and students. For teacher educators, placing the identities of our students and ourselves at the center of our work can challenge shallow conceptions of the profession. Through digital media projects, stories of teachers can begin to emerge who, as Jocson says, "simultaneously portray as well as shape who they are, how they see themselves, and what they plan to do in the future."

Jocson connects the work of digital video poetry to the development of an agentive identity. Embedded within this understanding is the idea that the stories that teachers tell through the process can change and shape their commitment to political action. The author's journey through the digital poetry project is compelling for the questions that it poses about continuing this kind of political work with students and colleagues. What does it look like when a group of teachers engages in this kind of work together? How are relationships with students changed when technology is placed at the center? What kind of political transformation is possible through digital poetry projects such as the one that Jocson describes? As she honored June Jordan with the creation of a digital poem, so too does she honor the message grounding Jordan's work with Poetry for the People. We see the power of digital poetry to challenge the current understandings of teachers, their relationships with students, and their relationships with knowledge. By making the process of her learning visible, and not "hidden away from the ordinary people," she urges us to engage in a similar project of political transformation.

Response to Jocson

Vivian L. Gadsden

A fundamental question guiding the conceptualization of this volume and the writing of chapters in it asks: What is at stake when media texts play a central role in teaching and learning processes? This question could be posed for a range of new ideas, concepts, and practices in education, particularly those related to students' literacy engagement. However, for media, as a long-standing literary and performance genre, this question takes on and takes up a special poignancy because of the relatively limited ways media have been used in classrooms and by teachers and because of the (dis)comforts that they create. Such (dis)comforts are as likely as not to result from the new knowledge required of teachers to understand the multiple possibilities of media and media use in classrooms and media's situatedness in new technologies and modalities—whether accessing the evening news through MSNBC, peering into the hip-hop generation, or producing digital media—about which Korina Jocson provides a rich and textured analysis.

Media and the uses of media as scripted, performative, and personalized text have been at the heart of cutting-edge work in the field of literacy and education more broadly, particularly in the study of inner-city African American and Latino youth. The focus on media in the 1980s and 1990s was simply not the same as it is today, as scholars of media, communications, education, and the social sciences find themselves uniquely linked to each other in the ideation, development, and implementation of different media forms and as teachers and students use these media as modes of self-expression, identity formation and revision, and personal and academic representation.

Jocson's work suggests that media images are at one and the same time narrowly defined and multifaceted, depending on the observer, and that by expanding historically accepted genres in literacy and learning, they invite students to develop and reconfigure literacy practices and behaviors and to create "media texts." In particular, the focus of the work by newer scholars such as Jocson on middle and high school students recognizes the significance of adolescence as a particularly complex developmental period of youth, during which students utilize a range of intellectual abilities, negotiate emerging personal identities, and seek intellectual guidance and support to grasp and grapple with difficult issues.

Youth draw upon and revise existing language and linguistic genres to construct their own language(s) and linguistic codes and to make choices about whether and how they enter or remove themselves from the familiar and the strange, irrespective of whether these sit in local or larger spaces. Media, the messages of media, and the stories from media are critical to the engagement of youth in the acts, events, and processes of learning. Thus, questions about how and why students access different forms of media, how they read media and the academic and personal texts that result, and how students' interactions with different forms of media in settings outside of school are translated into school experiences persist as complex terrains of study and interpretation.

Jocson offers a compelling and well-grounded argument for examining digital production within the context of situated learning, the agentive self, and methodological frameworks that acknowledge the performance of media, the space it creates for learners to explore meaning and symbolic images, and the layering of meaning that results (Denzin, 1997; Gutiérrez, Baquedano-López, & Alvarez, 2001; Hull, 2004; Hull & Katz, 2006; Lave & Wenger, 1991; Mahiri, 2004; Rogoff, 1990). Readers of her work will immediately recognize these frameworks and ways of thinking about the questions, approaches to studying them, and interpretive lenses used to understand them as familiar and appropriate. Research in arts and education (Eisner, 2002; Greene, 1995), arts and literacy, and media and literacy (Gee, 2003; Morrell, 2002; Staples, 2005) has taken on the intersections of the cultural, social, and cognitive dimensions of learning and the ways in which youth form, inform, and revise traditional genres of thought on literacy while engaging and being engaged by newer forms created and defined by youth themselves.

As Jocson leads us through the theoretical frameworks that inform her work, she urges us to examine and offer critiques on the multidimensionality of her own conceptualization and practice. In sharing the personal, she presents a provocative analysis of her own evolution as learner and teacher and the opportunities afforded to her when she allowed these two complementary positions, roles, and the stances attached to them to intersect and enhance her pedagogy, her daily practice, and her research about teaching. In situating her professional learning within a personal and agentive self, Jocson reminds us that youth are rarely engaged in classroom discourse that examines the intersections of complex social issues or that allows them to develop, articulate, and refine their stances.

Moreover, in revealing herself, Jocson also responds to a second question raised by the editors of this volume: What possibilities exist for engaging school learning differently when media and media texts are part of the learning fabric? Jocson skillfully connects traditional ways of engaging students in poetry with state-of-the-art media approaches to expressing self. Hence, she complicates the idea of learning in isolation and the practices associated with teaching by positioning teachers' own learning and ways of seeing the world as a contested and public space for teachers and others to question. In my own pedagogy and work with teachers, I have found the processes of uncovering our own experiences as learners and intentions as teachers to be among the most challenging and enriching activities if we hope to make learning more transparent and the structures in which learning takes place less daunting for students.

Jocson's work demonstrates the ways in which media push the boundaries of teacher knowledge to highlight transformations in teachers' learning and the strengths of using digital media to transform. The meticulous nature of her inquiry and the process of using digital media require teachers to wrestle with a range of complex issues in teaching—e.g., race, class, gender, culture, sexuality, and difference in general—and difficult social problems—e.g., crime, child abuse, policy harassment, homelessness, poverty; to map these against other real-world problems facing students, families, and communities; and to use them as forays into discourses about and action to promote social transformation.

Finally, the editors raise questions about the types of relationships that are enabled and constrained as a consequence of the recognized presence of media and media texts. The salient issue in this question is not simply media and media texts but the inextricability of the current focus on media as learning and teaching contexts, texts, and tools to support youth. This requires a focus on youth themselves. Jocson's chapter takes us through her journey from youth to professional, allowing us to co-examine her situated learning, her transition into an agentive self, and her critique and revisioning of existing epistemologies and pedagogies. Although Jocson does not belabor the issue of youth, choosing appropriately to embed youth in her analysis of media rather than foregrounding it, I think it is useful to discuss it briefly here. It is no surprise that even now research and pedagogical activities on media take place primarily outside of regular school hours, as an addendum to sanctioned teaching activities, in after-school or alternative programs.

A significant part of the intrigue and discomfort of focusing on media and youth is connected to society's views of youth— how youth are perceived by adults and how they come to see themselves and build and revise identities. Consider some of the references to youth—perpetrators (criminals), hedonists (e.g., drug users, addicts, promiscuous), victims (unemployed, abused, neglected, etc.), or prodigies (Delgado, 2002; Griffin, 1997; Males, 1996; Rook, 1998). In such representations, youth are seen either as a drain on national resources, as a group to be feared, or as having qualities that "ordinary people" can never emulate. In every case, references to youth are associated with a deficit perspective. Then, there is the more positivist perspective on youth—as asset, contributor, and real and potential purveyor of change. In this perspective, youth are positioned to effect change—to support and to transform—rather than to receive of the transformation (Barton, Watkins, & Jarjoura, 1997; Checkoway, 1999; Heath & McLaughlin, 1991; McLaughlin et al., 2001; Way, 1998).

Jocson's work asks us to take seriously the discourses and resulting pedagogies around media that can be used not simply to engage youth in classroom but to contribute to their roles in effecting change—both in exploring the self and the ways in which our learning and teaching are situated and in contributing to new constructions of literacy, learning, and teaching themselves.

References

Barton, W. H., Watkins, M., & Jarjoura, R. (1997). Youths and communities: Toward comprehensive strategies for youth development. *Social Work, 42*(5), 483–493.

Checkoway, B. (1999). Involving young people in neighborhood development. *Children and Youth Services Review, 20*(9–10), 765–795.

Delgado, M. (2002). *New frontiers for youth development in the twenty-first century: Revitalizing and broadening youth development.* New York: Columbia University Press.

Denzin, N. (1997). Performance texts. In W. Tierney & Y. Lincoln (Eds.), *Representation and the text: Re-framing the narrative voice* (pp. 179–217). Albany: State University of New York Press.

Eisner, E. (2002). *The arts and the creation of mind.* New Haven, CT: Yale University Press.

Gee, J. (2003). *What video games have to teach us about learning and literacy.* New York: Palgrave.

Greene, M. (1995). *Releasing the Imagination.* San Francisco: Jossey-Bass.

Griffin, C. (1997). *Representations of youth. The study of youth and adolescence in Britain and America.* Cambridge, MA: Polity Press.

Gutiérrez, K., Baquedano-López, P., & Alvarez, H. (2001). Literacy as hybridity: Moving beyond bilingualism in urban classrooms. In M. de la Luz Reyes & J. Halcón (Eds.), *The best of our children: Critical perspectives on literacy for Latino students* (pp. 122–141). New York: Teachers College Press.

Heath, S. B., & McLaughlin, M. W. (1991). Community organizations as family. *Phi Delta Kappan, 72*(8), 623–627.

Hull, G. (2004). Youth culture and digital media: New literacies for new times. *Research in the Teaching of English, 38*(2), 229–233.

Hull, G., & Katz, M. (2006). Crafting an agentive self: Case studies of digital storytelling. *Research in the Teaching of English, 41*(1), 43–81.

Lave, J., & Wenger, E. (1991). *Situated learning: Legitimate peripheral participation.* Cambridge, UK: Cambridge University Press.

Mahiri, J. (2004). Writing for their lives. In J. Mahiri (Ed.), *What they don't learn in school: Literacy in the lives of urban youth.* New York: Peter Lang.{AQ: Page numbers?}

Males, M. A. (1996). *The scapegoat generation: America's war on adolescents.* Monroe, ME: Common Courage.

McLaughlin, M.; Irby, M.A. and Langman, J. (2001). *Urban Sanctuaries: Neighborhood Organizations in the Lives and Futures of Inner-City Youth.* San Francisco: Jossey-Bass.

Morrell, E. (2002). Toward a critical pedagogy of popular culture: Literacy development among urban youth. *Journal of Adolescent & Adult Literacy, 46*(1), 72–77.

Rogoff, B. (1990). *Apprenticeship in thinking: Cognitive development in social context.* New York: Oxford University Press.

Rook, A. (1998). At-risk youth art programs come up tall. *Youth Today, 7,* 14–17.

Staples, J. (2005). Reading the world and the word after school: African American urban adolescents' reading experiences and literacy practices in relationship to media texts. Unpublished doctoral dissertation, University of Pennsylvania.

Way, N. (1998). *Everyday Courage: The Lives and Stories of Urban Teenagers*. New York: NYU Press.

Chapter Seven

Negotiating Identity Projects: Exploring the Digital Storytelling Experiences of Three African American Girls

Heather M. Pleasants

Sitting in the computer room, waiting for this funky Pentium II computer to boot up. Tonisha and I begin talking about the pictures she's taken to go along with this story about her cat, Todd. She has grown so much over the past year; her pants are a couple inches too short and she is all elbows and knees. She spins the old office chair around a couple of times and out of the blue, exclaims with a grin that "technology is MY LIFE!" Not quite sure where that came from . . . (Field notes, November 2004)

Monique and ReShonda, narrating together: "This is Momma Kim, she's at work. She is great guidance to us. We love her very much, she's special to the both of us. … Even though we may act up at the wrong times, and she has to correct us. Kim we are very sorry." ("Big Sitters" Script, Fall 2004)

Introduction

The opportunity to explore identity as an ongoing discursive negotiation is facilitated by digital storytelling, in which authors talk about texts, pictures, and music that combine to make a digital story (Davis, 2005; Hayes & Matusov, 2005; Hull & Katz, 2006). This chapter explores the digital storytelling of Tonisha, Monique, and ReShonda, three African American girls who participated in the Carrolton House Digital Storytelling Project over the span of two years. Within the context of their digital stories and their interactions in a community center, examples are presented that illustrate how their identities were negotiated through and by language. These identity negotiations, enacted at micro- and macro-analytic levels, encompassed and transcended the day-to-day relationships of the girls and those with whom they interacted.

From the beginning of the Carrolton House Digital Storytelling Project, Tonisha was an enthusiastic participant, suggesting topics for her second and third story before the first was finished, encouraging me to let her take the digital camera home so that she could do some "homework" for her storytelling ideas, and repeatedly asking to use the printer to make copies of images of the rapper Lil' Bow Wow and the boy band B2K to put in her project folder. Monique and ReShonda, on the other hand, were initially reluctant to join the project, but they maintained a high level of engagement throughout their extended involvement in storytelling work. Each of the girls moved between a variety of social borders within their local and school communities, and each represented ideas about who she was and who she was becoming relative to friends, peers, families, and the larger world. Their storymaking, and their interactions with others and me in the project, revealed an agentive engagement in developing, refining, and negotiating identities across multiple contexts (Hull & Katz, 2006).

In this chapter, in addition to exploring identity as a discursive negotiation, I consider the possibilities and challenges inherent in directing digital storytelling projects that are often situated within a variety of discourses concerning who African American kids are and who they have the potential to become. Below I describe the community context and my role as the director of the Carrolton House Digital Storytelling Project, through which I came to know Tonisha, Monique, and ReShonda.

Context

The Carrolton House Community Center is located in Carrolton Heights, a small community on the outskirts of Waterford, a small metropolitan city on the East Coast. Of the 2,200 residents in Carrolton Heights, 85 percent are African American. Manufacturing and commercial plants and scrap yards border the housing projects and row homes of Carrolton Heights residents. During the time of the project, community members documented more than "brownfields"—land demonstrated or believed to be contaminated by hazardous substances or pollutants (Environmental Protection Agency, 2006) within and surrounding Carrolton Heights. Early on in the digital storytelling project, several kids used their digital cameras to take pictures of these brownfields and other areas in the community in need of attention, such as crumbling curbs and sidewalks, and abandoned cars in overgrown lots.

Around 40 percent of the homes in Carrolton Heights are headed by single mothers, and more than half of the households in the community earn less than half the median income. Most Carrolton Heights adults are at an educational disadvantage: only 9 percent of adults over twenty-five years of age have a college degree; only 65 percent have a high school diploma (Carter & Love, 2006). High unemployment and murder rates have been recurring themes in the news for several years, and, according to residents of the city, the most serious neighborhood problems are the lack of recreational programs for juveniles, groups of people hanging around on the streets, and drugs being sold on the streets (Barnekov,

1998). This fact is not lost on the kids attending after-school programs at the Carrolton House Community Center, as shown in this rap/digital story written by two of the boys in the project:

> Feens on the block stay scopin it out
> Dam, Money selling smack when it's late in
> the night no coke in the hood
> Cops raiding it out many niggas getting money
> Some chilling it out Kee
> That's me dog I'm just running
> The route no coke no dap cause cops
> Run in your house can't afford no D
> Charge cause they six to nine'n it out
> My boy Tone pull up in the whip then we out

This depiction of addicts hoping to score a hit, drug dealers, and police involved in curtailing drug activity may be influenced by the continued glamorization of life in "the hood" in popular media. Yet, Kee's and Tone's consciousness about the consequences of getting caught up in the drug trade is representative of the struggle of young people in Carrolton Heights to break through the cycle of poverty in a community that is isolated geographically and socially from the rest of the city.

There were two main entrances to the Carrolton Heights community: a bridge that connected the west side of Waterford with Carrolton Heights, and a highway exit to the south, the main purpose of which was to act as a entry/exit point for semi-trucks carrying cars and other cargo from the docks. Most often, I entered Carrolton Heights from this southern exit. From this direction, the unofficial marker of the neighborhood was a pedestrian bridge that had once connected the housing projects to a park across the street. The bridge's walkway had long been removed and the street-level gate padlocked shut. All that remained was a rusted metal arch that spanned the four-lane street, and I came to view it as both an urban monument and a reminder of my shifting insider/outsider status within the project and the community center.

Despite the many indicators of urban blight in statistics about Carrolton Heights, signs of vibrancy and life were clear. For example, many of the row homes displayed potted plants and flowers on neatly swept stoops and wreaths on brightly painted doors. Mature oak and maple trees provided a canopy of shade over many of the city streets, and kids and adults could often be seen out walking or having conversations in front of homes, bars, churches, schools, and basketball courts. Though there was only one small gas station in Carrolton Heights and an overpriced convenience store was the only option for groceries, there were also small barbecue spots around the community, and a Jamaican restaurant had recently opened up around the corner from the community center. Home ownership was a major thrust of the Carrolton Heights Civic Association, and, with help from the community center and local businesses, several new two- and three-bedroom townhouses had been built a block away from the community center and had been quickly sold.

The Carrolton House Community Center itself was a modern, three-story brick building situated squarely in the middle of Carrolton Heights—two blocks from a community medical center, four blocks from the housing projects, and a few blocks away from Martin Luther King Jr. Elementary and Middle School. Sidewalks surrounding the center were neatly maintained, with carefully tethered and mulched young trees around the periphery of the building. Activity around the front of the community center was gauged mainly by the coming and going of kids being dropped off in the morning and after school, and being picked up in the evenings by caregivers.

The first floor of the center comprised a large meeting area, a small chapel, a reception area, a glass-enclosed receptionist's desk, and a child care center. The child care center housed six classrooms for kids aged 2–5 and the meeting area was used as a space for exercise classes, for meetings for staff and community members, as an overflow area for kids enrolled in summer camp activities, and as a venue for teenagers to hold dances. The second floor of the building was divided into two main areas. In the first area were offices, cubicles, meeting and storage rooms, and a lunch/break area. In the other part of the space, classrooms and a recreational area that had once existed as part of an experimental alternative education program for kids now housed after-school tutoring and family programs. The third floor of the building had been newly renovated in 2002 to house a Family Technology Center funded through the efforts of the executive director of the community center, the governor, the mayor, and local businesses. In the technology center, two classrooms outfitted with Pentium III computers, projection systems, and dry erase boards were used for adult technology classes and as a space for kids to access the Internet under supervision of adults. With its emphasis on education and social services, the Carrolton Heights Community Center was a focal point for residents and visitors to the community.

Role of the researcher and origins of the Carrolton House Digital Storytelling Project

A set of circumstances that bridged aspects of my personal and professional life culminated in the creation of the Carrolton House Digital Storytelling Project. Shortly after the birth of my daughter, I began experimenting with a web page on which I combined autobiographical and poetic writing with pictures and video. This website was primarily a means for me to make sense of what it meant to be an African American assistant professor on the tenure track who was also a wife, mother, writer, and community literacy advocate. At the same time, I was supervising a multicultural education practicum for preservice teachers that took place in local communities. As my undergraduate students began to work with kids in community centers on multimodal literacy projects (videos, websites, photoessays, etc.), I began conceptualizing a participatory action research project through which digital storytelling could provide a space for kids to explore issues of identity through oral, written, and visual literacies. With the assistance of a small grant, this project came to be located at the Carrolton House Community Center.

Within the project, I was situated firmly on the participant side of the participant/observer ethnographic continuum. I was often torn between hiding out in the center's computer lab to type field notes and spending just a little more time preparing for the day's work with the kids or assisting them in working after the project was officially over for the evening. The role I developed in relation to the kids was relatively informal and was dissimilar to that of other African American women in the center, women who had worked together for years, who lived in Carrolton Heights, and whose relationship with the kids was often predicated on their role as elders who occupied prominent positions within local churches. In contrast to the prefix of "Mama" by which most other women working in the community center were known, kids coming to the project alternatively referred to me as "Miss Heather," "Dr. Heather," and "Heather Boom Boom."[1]

Over time, I gained provisional membership in the Carrolton House community. My daughter attended the Carrolton House Preschool while I was working at the center, so I was able to get to know the parents and teachers there through frequent pick-up/drop-off conversations and my participation as a chaperone on field trips to zoos and amusement parks. In addition, I volunteered my services as a grant writer for the center, served on parent committees, and gradually got to know the people who worked in the center through informal conversations in the morning, at lunch time, and in the evening as kids were dismissed from after-school programs and as parents came to pick up their kids from the child care center. After the daycare closed, I would sometimes bring my daughter upstairs to the second-floor computer room, and teenagers working on stories would take turns coloring and drawing with her while we wrapped up our work for the day. This in turn led to Monique and ReShonda occasionally bringing their baby nephews and cousins to the project to fulfill child care responsibilities while still getting the opportunity to work on their stories and "hang out." The blurring of lines between personal lives and the roles normally enacted by adults and kids in more formal institutional settings was typical in the community center and it was an important foundation on which subsequent interactions within the project between me and the kids were based.

Theoretical Frame

I conceptualize the digital storytelling of Tonisha, Monique, ReShonda, and the other participants in the Carrolton House Digital Storytelling Project as enacted identity negotiations. These negotiations are always ongoing and discursive in nature and are defined through the lens of what Bakhtin describes as the centrifugal and centripetal forces of language (1981, pp. 271–273). These forces serve an important role within a discursive conception of self, with the centripetal forces allowing us to be "seen" by others as enacting recognizable identities (through discourse) and the centrifugal forces giving us a liberatory reprieve from centripetal constraints. These centrifugal forces therefore also provide opportunities for innovative interpretations of existing language and discourse in the service of making each of our identities a uniquely fashioned construction rather than an essentialized and static caricature. Seen in this way, our stories about ourselves and our world become representations of embodied struggles between the unifying characteristics of language (as represented in social groups of varying levels) and the new meanings and understandings of ourselves and our world that discursive interactions with diverse others make available to us. If identity is indeed, as Bakhtin and others assert, relational and viewable through discourse, then the multimodal stories and discourse of Tonisha, Monique, and ReShonda can be explored as an artistic rendering of the way that centrifugal and centripetal forces of language reveal identity negotiation in action.

However, their digital stories also point out that there can be important points within all of our lives when we stop to reflect, figure out, and reevaluate who we are, why we are here, and what it is we think we are doing anyway. In a sense, these moments lift us momentarily out of the maypole of centripetal/centrifugal language activity. In this way, identity is not embodied solely in discursive activity but is also a kind of ongoing, identifiable project that each of us as an individual takes up, considers, and moves forward. Holquist, in synthesizing Bakhtin's work, writes that the projects of "selfhood" are "dominated by a 'drive to meaning,' where meaning is understood as something still in the process of creation, something still bending toward the future as opposed to that which is already completed" (1990, p. 24). These instances of reflective work on our identities are like projections of shadows on a wall—simultaneously within and beyond our reach. But these shadows are malleable—through their temporal nature and through the discourse that we have with ourselves and others about our future selves.

This conceptualization of identity as both discourse based and as an ongoing project builds on and extends the idea of "figured worlds" articulated by Holland and Eisenhart (1990) and Holland, Lachicotte, Skinner, and Cain (1998), who define figured worlds as "socially and culturally constructed realms of interpretation in which particular characters and actors are recognized, significance is assigned to certain acts, and particular outcomes are valued over others." The idea of identity as an ongoing project situated within figured worlds privileges the idea that people exhibit agency in the selves that they create, even while these selves must be negotiated with others. For Tonisha, Monique, and ReShonda—and for myself—the process of being involved in a digital storytelling project helped to reveal our figuring of worlds and the negotiation of our respective identity projects.

Methods

The data presented in this chapter are a part of a larger ethnographic project on digital media and literacy learning in urban contexts (Pleasants, 2004) that spanned two-and-a-half years. The project's trajectory comprised an initial "pilot" stage during the first summer of meetings, with seven kids who met to take pictures and begin composing digital stories, and a larger segment that took place over two years and involved a larger group of ten to fifteen kids and their work to complete digital stories.

As individuals joined the project, I began by simply showing them a few examples of digital stories created by other kids and asking each participant to think about what they wanted to express in their own story. Further into the project, when I was asked, I provided a general idea for how a story might be constructed, on the basis of a basic narrative structure (beginning/introduction, middle/point of conflict, and end/resolution) and story arc. I told the kids that generally a good story

> gets someone interested right in the beginning, then talks about something interesting, or weird or exciting that happens to the main character in your story—which can be you—and then it finishes by talking about the way that the person in the story reacts to what happens to them. (Field notes, December 2004)

Despite this direction, I also wanted to create a space in which kids had the freedom to construct stories that might not conform to this general narrative structure. As the project director, I vacillated between wanting to provide feedback that would assist them in developing conventional literacy skills (the centripetal aspect of literacy) and creating a space for innovative (the centrifugal aspect) use of the genre of digital storytelling. In many ways, my acknowledgment of those goals mirrored an attention to centripetal and centrifugal discursive activity that was an increasing focus in my research.

Because of the multiple roles I occupied as project director, researcher, grant writer, and preschooler parent, it was necessary for me to develop a flexible structure for collecting data about the project. The main body of data that was collected was composed of digital audio recordings of conversations, videotapes of kids working at computers together and taking walks around the neighborhood, several hundred digital pictures, drafts of scripts, audio files of narrated stories, and field notes taken by myself and an undergraduate student from the university who assisted me during the first year of the project.

The data analyzed for this chapter detail the experiences, conversations, photographs, and written and/or spoken digital stories of three girls who participated in the project—Tonisha, Monique, and ReShonda. Tonisha completed two individual stories and was working on a third at the conclusion of the project, while Monique and ReShonda collaborated to produce one digital story, and Monique continued to work on a second digital story on her own after the first had been finished. Although there were many other participants in the project (including boys of varying ages), these three girls maintained a consistent level of involvement. Furthermore, the positions that Tonisha, Monique, and ReShonda occupied relative to each other, others in the project, and adults in the community center and schools provided a variability that was helpful in revealing the micro- and macro-analytic metaphors of centripetal and centrifugal forces of language at work in identity negotiations. These three girls were also representative of the range of attitudes toward writing held by the larger group of participants in the project, with Tonisha being more open to expressing herself through writing and Monique and ReShonda being much more self-conscious about their writing. Below I detail the work of these three girls, highlighting how their digital storytelling provided glimpses into the intertwined centripetal and centrifugal discursive forces inherent in their identity work.

Tonisha

I first met Tonisha after distributing a recruitment flyer for the digital storytelling pilot program and visiting with several groups of kids attending after-school activities at the community center. Ten years old, a bit gawky, and still learning how to manage her newly acquired height, Tonisha lived in Carrolton Heights with her grandmother and her cousin Robby, who was also a participant in the digital storytelling project. Although she had been identified as qualifying for special education services, most adults in the community center thought of Tonisha as "a very smart young lady" and a "good student."

Despite her enthusiasm and interest, Tonisha struggled a bit at first when deciding on the topic of her story. She decided to take pictures first and then look at the pictures to better formulate the story she had in mind. For Tonisha and other participants in the project, these images formed the beginnings of first stories. Tonisha's first try at narrating her story from a quickly drafted text based on a group of family photos she had assembled was a bit choppy:

1 Hi—My name is Tonisha Walker. This title of this story is called Happiest Moments::
2 But first, when my sister Tonya got her four awards and one trophy, she was very
3 excited and my grandma was very proud of her. Second picture . . . is w—was when my
4 grandma met::someone special, his name is Mr. Big.
5 Se—next—third is my baby cousin, Candace Demita DeLondra Walker when she
6 first ate her birth:day cake, boy was it a mess. The happiest moment that happened to
7 me is when I went to my second banquet. Boy was I proud.::My cousin Robby's

8 happiest moment was when h:e became an uncle for the first time. The ha-last two,

9 well, fir—the last two, the happiest moment in my cousin Michelle's life is when she

10 became a mother. It was like a dream come true for her.

11 ::Last but not least, the happiest moment in cou—in my cousin Eric's life is when he

12 first got his car. He was ex<u>cited</u>.

Pride, accomplishment, and fulfillment dominated Tonisha's narration, though the pictures she used as markers for the narration did not necessarily correspond to the "happiest moments" she described. After Tonisha listened to this first attempt at narrating her story, it was clear that she was not happy with it. For this reason, I encouraged her to write a more fully developed script to help eliminate the stops, starts, and pauses that characterized the narration.

Tonisha's desire to produce a better narration provided one of the first among many opportunities for making decisions regarding the direction of the project. Ultimately, I wanted to create a social space that creatively addressed issues of identity and individual participants' literacy development through digital media. However, because of students' differing levels of engagement with writing (either in or out of school) and with talking about themselves, actualizing a project that focused on identity through literacy was difficult. Although I was interested in seeing and being a part of how kids chose to represent themselves through their stories, at least half of the kids were reluctant to write their stories during the project time. Consequently, my first goal was simply to encourage kids to compose a text in whatever space and style was comfortable for them. Starting stories without scripts was an important first step for many of the kids. After hearing and being dissatisfied with their initial, unscripted narrations, kids would then either write out a script at home and bring it in or literally memorize a narrative that they would recite into the microphone. This process helped to emphasize the significance of editing (whether written or mental) as an organic part of developing a good story. Later, owing to increased interest and the continued hesitance of other kids to write stories/scripts while in the computer room, we would require that new kids to the project bring in a completed text before they could begin taking pictures and working on the computer. This proved to be a good strategy for determining level of interest and involvement and was also a helpful beginning point for kids as they started to work on putting together elements of their digital stories.

In Tonisha's case, the "Happiest Moments" story went through several iterations as she added more pictures of her mother, her niece, her grandmother's dog, and herself. She later titled it "The Story of Pain" because "there were happy moments and sad moments" that were captured in the photographs depicting her family. Rather than narrating who individuals in each picture were and what moment the picture represented, Tonisha worked with an undergraduate student to place her pictures against the backdrop of a plaintive ballad by the late R & B singer Aaliyah, who was one of Tonisha's favorite recording artists. In perfect time to the beat of the song, a succession of pictures quickly faded in and out.

After completing "Happiest Moments"/"The Story of Pain," Tonisha struggled for several weeks to develop an idea for her next story, finally deciding that the second story should be about her kitten, Todd. Unlike her previous story, Tonisha wrote a narrative for "Todd Story" that demonstrated all of the elements of a typical written (and mainstream oral) narrative—it had an identifiable beginning: "my heart was jumping like a jelly bean when I first got my kitten," and a point of conflict toward the middle of the story:

> As the kitten started to get use to the house he was becoming a lot to handle. He peed on the floor ewwwwwwwwwwwwwwwwwwww. It stinks. Now I have to clean all of this mess up . . . The next thing I know Todd was on the kitchen counter eating the left over tunafish. ("Todd Story," Spring 2004)

At the end of Tonisha's story about Todd, there was also a "moral" to be learned—"that having a kitten is a lot of hard work"—and she offered advice to the viewer not to "let it go into the kitchen because it might eat some of the dinner that your parents made."

Perhaps because of the way that it represented a recognizable narrative with traditional story structure, the Todd story was popular among the adults and undergraduates, who often stopped by to see how the storymaking was progressing. But again, my direction and definition of what constituted a good story raised significant questions for me regarding my role in establishing a balance between creativity and helpful structure. On one hand, Tonisha's composition demonstrated her understanding of important elements of traditional narratives, and conceptually the Todd story could be seen as a textual representation of the centripetal discourse about the idea of story. Thinking of Tonisha's story in this way was also a helpful reminder for me, as the director of the project, to be constantly aware of the ways that centripetality and centrifugality evidenced themselves in the different discourses about identity exploration and literacy development within the project. For Tonisha, these discursive forces materialized through an increasing connection between school work and her work in the digital storytelling project. For example, after the "Todd Story" script had been completed, Tonisha expressed interest in writing a story about Dr. Martin Luther King Jr., and another about interesting animals (snakes, lizards, chinchillas) to have as pets. Each of these topics corresponded to activities she was working on in school. However, these story ideas remained unrealized projects, as her time became increasingly limited owing to her preparation for the state assessment test and also owing to limited access to the computers used for editing stories. In the final months of the project, most of her time was devoted to campaigning for a position as a student representative on the Waterford City Council. She shared with me her speech, excerpted below:

> Good morning my name is Tonisha Walker. To be a good city councilperson I think you should act like your neighborhood is your home. I live in Waterford and there are some things I don't like. There are problems I wouldn't like around my home such as fighting. In the summer there is a lot of fighting about money, drugs or just someone's crew trying to show another crew how tough they are. Adults with the help of city council need to find a common ground to solve our problems. Maybe you think I watch too much Oprah but that is the truth. In the words of Martin Luther King Jr.: "We must combine the toughness of the serpent and the softness of the dove, a tough mind and a tender heart." My grandmother is that kind of a person. Where I live she is known as: "The Momma of the block." They call my Grandmother that because she is not afraid to get involved in neighborhood problems. If you elect me to the city council I will try to live up to the role model my grandmother has been for me. I will earn your trust and respect . . . (Tonisha's speech, Spring 2005)

In the weeks and days leading up to giving this speech, Tonisha talked often about being both excited and nervous. The day before she was to recite the speech, she asked if I would listen to it, which I did. This speech seemed to mark an important point for Tonisha in her thinking about the kind of student—and the kind of person—she wanted to be and the goals associated with this role she was beginning to occupy. Over the span of time she was active in the project, it appeared that Tonisha increasingly internalized the view of adults (most notably her grandmother) that she was an academically talented student and a leader, and this vision of herself was supported, to some extent, by her work in the digital storytelling project. Eventually, however, it was not possible for Tonisha to maintain involvement in the digital storytelling project and pursue a variety of school-related activities, and Tonisha spent the majority of her after-school time working with adults in the homework help program or doing other academic enrichment activities.

Monique and ReShonda

> A favorite pastime for Monique and ReShonda— cracking on people. They have it BAD. Today they started talking about one of the younger girls that was here for homework help—when they noticed the gaping holes at the knees of her stockings, they started laughing uncontrollably, and began to sing a song to the tune of a church hymn: "Hole-y, Hole-y, Hole-y, your stockings are HOLE-YYY!" I said that I wouldn't want them to be talking about me if I were the girl, and that for all we know, she could go home and be really upset. Their reactions were that she shouldn't have worn holey stockings if she didn't want anyone to talk about her. Monique, in particular, said that the girl needed to toughen up, and that people talk about her all the time and she didn't care . . . (Field notes, November 2004)

Monique and ReShonda were merciless in their "cracks"[2] on other people and each other, and their playful yet stinging critiques were usually tolerated. At other times, their comments and teasing were catalysts for fights with other kids or suspensions from their church, school, or the community center. In their interactions with people at the Carrolton House, Mo and Shonda constantly walked the line between mischievous disruption and a nonchalant disregard for how anyone else might need or prefer the social environment to be defined.

Both of the girls thrived on the attention that their behavior brought to them, and despite their gift for creating pockets of chaos, there was an unspoken understanding that Monique and ReShonda needed to be able to come to the center. This understanding was rooted in adults' belief that Monique and ReShonda could benefit individually and the belief that their presence had broad significance to the work of the center. In several instances, the executive director of the center, Mr. Webber, conveyed his belief that if adults at the center could not assist Monique and ReShonda in actualizing positive futures, then perhaps their approach to supporting kids needed revision.

Mr. Webber and other adults in the community center saw Monique and ReShonda as being at a critical juncture in their development as young women. Although Monique had struggled academically in the past, she had recently shown "great progress" in Mr. Webber's eyes. This was evidenced by better grades at the end of her seventh-grade year as well as through a speech that she had given to the student body at the conclusion of the year. Monique was also being unofficially mentored by Miss Rina, the person who directed the youth outreach programs at the center. Monique was a talented athlete in flag football and basketball, and there was an expectation that she would have opportunities for higher education through athletic scholarships if she could continue to do reasonably well academically. Monique was highly attuned to the idea of equity and fairness, and if she believed she was not being treated fairly she did not hesitate to let others know. In combination with her talent for insults, Monique's forthrightness was not always well received; during the span of the project, she was suspended from school several times for being disrespectful to her teachers and was periodically suspended from attending after-school programs at the community center as well.

ReShonda was older than Monique by about two-and-a-half years but had been retained such that she was in eighth grade at the start of the project. She assisted in the child care center after school and talked often of wanting to be a pediatrician some day. As a tall, physically developed teenager, ReShonda received a good bit of attention from boys who frequented the center, and her reaction to this attention was alternately awkward and flirtatious. As with Monique, for ReShonda the center had a special significance in her daily life. She came to the center to be social, to be helpful, and to talk with adults about school-related issues. In the past, she had used the center as a place to hide when she did not want to go to school, but for the most part, ReShonda came to the center to be engaged in positive activities.

In the absence of the other, ReShonda and Monique were respectful, courteous, and generally well behaved. However, when they were together their demeanor changed radically. It was not uncommon for their work in the project to devolve into yelling matches with other kids in the project, or into very physical wrestling matches with each other that would result in chairs and other furniture being knocked over. During the span of the project, ReShonda and Monique were involved in a repetitive cycle of being "in trouble" with different members of the Carrolton House staff (myself included), being banned from the center for a period of days or weeks, and then gradually patching up relationships, only to undo this with more bouts of behavior deemed unacceptable by adults. Toward the end of the project, they were not permitted inside the building unless I escorted them to the computer room.

At Mr. Webber's request, I asked Monique if she wanted to be involved in the project in the fall of 2004. Her first response was that she could not participate because she was working for Miss Victoria, doing filing, copying, and other clerical tasks. When Mr. Webber told her that she could "take a break" from that work to do a digital story, Monique said, hesitantly, that she wouldn't mind giving it a try. After my initial conversation with Monique, I saw her several times and we began to play a game in which I would ask when she was going to "come through" and see us, and she would duck around a corner or into a restroom when she saw me coming. Eventually, she and ReShonda came in to see me and told me that they wanted to do a story together, about their friendship. Monique and ReShonda completed this digital story during the span of the project and entitled it "Big Sitters," a play on the word sisters and on the fact that when they came to the community center, they would often sit in two chairs opposite the second floor elevator doors. On purpose or accidentally, these chairs would often end up overturned, with ReShonda and Monique on the floor convulsed in laughter about something they had done or said to each other or to other kids and adults at the center.

After their initial meeting with me, we immediately started taking pictures for the project—these early pictures included photographs of Monique and ReShonda outside the center, at the church they both attended, and at various places in the center posing with adults. Two weeks after we started taking pictures, Monique and ReShonda arrived at the computer room with a meticulously handwritten script for "Big Sitters." Whereas most of the kids' digital stories were approximately one to three minutes in length, the "Big Sitters" script was nine pages long and included a cast list and a dedication. The final "Big Sitters" story was approximately twelve minutes in length and included several video clips. Their story began with an explanation for why they were doing the project:

(Mo & Shonda) We decided to get together and make a movie on ourselves to let people know about the sitter relationship we have. Our story is gonna be called Big Sitters!!!!! . . .

(Mo) We thought we should get together and make a video about ourselves because we want people to know more about us. Also, this is a great chance to use the talent that God has given us. We also, wanted people to know what we do, who we love spending time with. Some of our favorite people. Places we enjoy being and places we hang out. ("Big Sitters" script, Fall 2004)

After this introduction, the "Big Sitters" story proceeds similarly to Tonisha's initial story, with a narration of pictures of themselves and what they are doing in the pictures ("Here we are sitting in our favorite chairs. Don't we look weird?"). As pictures of themselves with adults begin to dominate the story, Monique and ReShonda took turns discussing who is pictured and what they think about them:

> (Mo) This is Momma Tory and I together in her office. Having such a good time and talking. Momma Tory is so supportive to me. She's very special, helping and much, much more. I love Momma Tory. She's such a wonderful role model . . .

> (Shonda) Now here is Ms. Tory and I. We're just chill, talking about our day. Ms. Tory is such a wonderful person. Momma Tory is always happy whenever I see her. If she's ever mad or down in the blues u could never tell. She always let God's light shine on the world. ("Big Sitters" script, Fall 2004)

Abruptly, in the middle of their description of adults they talked to regularly, Mo and Shonda performed a choreographed dance routine to the tune of what was then a current R & B song by the artist Usher. In this routine, Mo and Shonda together did the "A Town Stomp," "the muscle," and "the rockaway" and each dance move was called out as a part of the script. Toward the end of this thirty-second routine, their dance transformed into a free-form creative physical expression, and, as I recorded them, Mo began to advance toward the camera doing slow-motion Karate movements with her hands and lifting her leg as if to prepare to fight. While Mo did this, Shonda continued in an animated, bouncy dance, colliding with Mo. This collision became part of the dance as they bounced together and then around the room, until Shonda began slapping her butt with her hand to the beat of the music. Then, as abruptly as it started, the clip ends and the story continues with descriptions of adults in the community center given in deadpan, presentation-like voices. Later, at the conclusion to "Big Sitters," this video clip is played a second time. In context of the rest of the story, this repeated clip bursts into the viewers' presence with the frenetic and raucous energy that most closely approximates the day-to-day enacted friendship of Monique and ReShonda. Juxtaposed against the (re)presentation of their relationships with significant others at the community center, ReShonda and Monique's dance clips underscore both the playfully centrifugal quality of the majority of their interactions with adults *and* their acknowledgment of the benefits of engaging in the adult-defined discourse of the center.

A more micro-analytic perspective on this identity work in progress was represented in the naming of photographs to go into the "Big Sitters" story. Monique, who did the majority of the work of importing photographs into the timeline, often named the photographs not just by nominal description but in terms of relationship. For example, a group of adults that she and ReShonda came into contact with most often were named "not us" and "them and not us" while other pictures taken of friends and significant others were named "just like me," "us girls," "half ma crue," and "my peoples and me." When the "not us" group of adults was pictured individually, Monique's global label transformed, and pictures were named "go heather," "uncle web," "Momma Victoria / Kim / Rina," and "we love u Tory."

Ironically, as the "Big Sitters" project neared completion, Mo and Shonda were no longer close friends—they recorded the last aspects of the story separately, with Monique doing the last video editing alone. In talking with the director and other adults at the center, I discovered it was the clear opinion of most that Monique and ReShonda were better off not being in each other's presence. Certainly, when they were participating in activities at the community center apart from each other, Monique and ReShonda fit more easily into the adult-defined social rhythm of the center, with ReShonda often volunteering in the child care center and Monique playing basketball or continuing to work on the "Big Sitters" story.

Monique, in particular, began to take a more active role in after-school activities, probably as a result of Momma Rina's mentorship. After the "Big Sitters" story was completed, she began to work on a story tentatively called "Basketball Is My Past, Present, and Future." In this story, Monique writes:

> My academics are good, and I'm smart on the court as well as off the court also. Now of course I can't do this alone. I have someone who cares so much about me. I bet she didn't know she inspires me in basketball as well as others. She has helped me make it to where I am now. Her name is Momma Rina. She is my role model, friend, helper, mentor, coach, and more. Sometimes I feel down when I'm on the court but she lifts me in the time of need. If I can't depend on anyone else to be there, I can count on her. . . . Everyone has a right hand man. Well, Momma Rina is my right hand man. She helps me with basketball, school, and everyday problems. Thank you Momma Rina. ("Basketball Is My Past, Present, and Future," Spring 2005)

Monique's basketball story was seven pages long, and though it remained unfinished at the conclusion of the project, it was an important written and visual documentation of her development as a young woman. Even as she continued to define herself against the "adult" discourse of the center, Monique continued to be supported and grounded by her relationship with Momma Rina. In addition to acknowledging the significance of Momma Rina in her life, Monique's coaching of an eight and-under basketball team mirrored the kind of relationship they had. In her basketball story, she wrote:

> Out of all of my years being involved in basketball this has been the best. My eight & under team has inspired me so much. They were like my little brothers and sisters. I took care of each and every one of them. . . . They all did respect me and their team mates as well as themselves. They played a darn good season. I am so proud of them. I had fun making them food, playing with them, taking them places, keeping them over my house for hours. Sometimes overnight. I really enjoy coaching them this season. . . . I look forward to next year. They have helped me notice how much people care about me like I cared about them.

Through this emerging story the identity work that Monique was doing outside of the project found a space for written, verbal, and visual expression. This was perhaps most apparent in the final weeks of the project, when she and Marquisha (an eight-year-old whom she had coached and who had also been a part of the storytelling project) went out together with me to take pictures for Monique's basketball story. Marquisha, even at eight, had demonstrated a fantastic eye for taking photographs, but at the beginning of the project, Monique and Marquisha had an ambivalent relationship—competing for time with adults in the project and for time on the computer. On this particular day, Monique consented to having Marquisha take pictures of her for the basketball story. Eventually, Marquisha handed me the camera and I took pictures and short video clips of Monique helping Marquisha to shoot a basketball correctly. It was the first time I had seen Monique express care in this way for another child at the center, and in this interaction I saw a "different" Monique from the one I had previously gotten to know, a Monique who was patient, caring, and supportive, a Monique who was actively appropriating the kinds of relationships that Momma Rina had with her in her interactions with other kids at the center (Figure 6).

Figure 6. Marquisha in flight, shooting the basketball with Monique (outside the frame)

Life and Language in the Carrolton House Digital Storytelling Project

Bakhtin (1981)writes that:

> every concrete utterance of a speaking subject serves as a point where centrifugal as well as centripetal forces are brought to bear. . . Such is the fleeting language of a day, of an epoch, a social group, a genre, a school. . . . . It is possible to give a concrete and detailed analysis of any utterance, once having exposed it as a contradiction-ridden, tension-filled unity of two embattled tendencies in the life of a language. (p. 272)

Conceptualizing digital storytelling activities as opportunities fo adolescents to negotiate their own identity project with others require constructing understandings of the way that centripetal and centrifuga forces of language play themselves out at different levels and in differen ways within our lives and the lives of others. Considered from a comprehensive perspective, the unitary, centripetal forces of discourse ar easily recognizable in presentations of adults' power and ability to defin social spaces and activities—as expressed, for example, in my action and questions regarding my role as project director of the Carrolton House Digital Storytelling Project. But these centripetal tendencies ar also apparent in kid-defined and -enacted discourses. It is the centrifuga utterances/performances that are more difficult for individuals to recognize and make room for, especially given our tendency to defin ourselves by and through the unitary qualities of the discourses in whicl we participate. We are inextricably bound to the centripetal forces o discourse as a means to understand who we are, and the playfulnes inherent in centrifugality can easily become a threat rather than a opportunity given our general orientation about our own "identit projects." However, within these identity projects, it is just as importan to acknowledge moments of centrifugality, since these points o divergence and conflict within discursive interaction often create a contrast necessary for further clarification and negotiation of identities Through the use of digital storytelling as a medium for the analysis o these centripetal and centrifugal moments, aspects of kids' and adults discourse are given a privileged space for examination and reflection With this in mind, I focus in on three elements of the Carrolton Hous Digital Storytelling Project that informed my understanding of th operationalization and intertwining of centripetal and centrifuga language forces, referencing the work of Tonisha, Monique, ReShonda and other participants in the project where applicable.

Ghosts of School Discourse

The first element of the digital storytelling project that clearly represented centripetal and centrifugal discursive moments (at both a macro- and a micro-level) was the overarching presence of the institutior of school in the life of the community center. Though the digita storytelling project took place after school, and in the context of a community center, the "ghosts" of school discourse were always a presence lingering in the background of our minds and our work. The specter of school-based ways of talking about literacy learning was present even in the initial stages of the project. During this time, I had several discussions with Mr. Webber and with other adults who worked in after-school programs about the ways that the digital storytelling work that kids would be doing was connected—and disconnected—from the work they were doing in school. The broad question of the connection of the project to school-based literacy learning was not an esoteric one, given the extent to which many of the kids in the project were struggling to meet basic levels of literacy for their age/grade.

In addition to the institutional presence of school, the relationship of day-to-day school life to kids' work in the project was evident. All the kids attended "homework help" before coming to work on their stories, and often kids would stop briefly in the project room to show me a book they had been able to take home or the work they had done in school that day. Several students, Monique included, also shared report cards indicating that they had gotten good grades for a particular marking period. Whether in Monique's conversations about unfair treatment and/or suspensions initiated by teachers, Tonisha's ideas for stories based on school topics, or ReShonda's characterization of how school seemed irrelevant to her daily life, how their teachers "saw" them, and how individual kids accepted or disputed others' vision of themselves, was an important and ever-present theme in the stories they created. The positioning of kids in school was also clear in the negative views that some participants had of their abilities. One ten-year-old boy, Oliver, who was receiving special education services during the time of the project, often articulated his belief that "he can never keep up with everyone else" and that his ideas for stories were "stupid." Given these linkages between in-school and after-school, an implicit goal of the project was to support each participant's literacy work in such a way that he or she would have positive experiences that might carry over into school activities.

The clearest connection between approaches to in-school literacy and the literacy work required for completing a digital story was evidenced in kids' production of story scripts. Although I was interested in spending time facilitating the creation of stories that were vivid, imaginative, and thoughtful, over time I became less concerned with witnessing participants' creative writing process and more concerned with whether kids produced a script/story at all. Though this flexibility was helpful for the kids, it also highlighted the need for me to think carefully about how the activity of composing a text is highly individualized—and, initially, often very private. Admittedly, it was still difficult for me to extricate myself from a teacher-like role—echoing in my head were the tenets of what the Center for Digital Storytelling (CDS) characterized as elements of an effective story: point of view, consideration of a "dramatic question," emotional content, economy, and pacing. As kids produced their stories, I found myself attempting to develop ways to encourage creative critique. In hindsight, I realized that often I had simply substituted the (centripetal) discourse of the school curriculum for the discourse of the curriculum offered by CDS. Though my intent was to create a safe space for experimentation, and though I tried to be cognizant of what each participant wanted and needed that safe space to be, it was often difficult to rein in my urges to direct individual participants' work. I found that keeping regular field notes of our daily activities assisted me in deemphasizing the use traditional narratives when it made sense to do so and stressing these narratives when appropriate. In addition, my extended time with the regular participants created a social space when they felt comfortable asserting their creative vision. With field notes and honest kids as guides, the texts that participants developed ranged from CSI-type crime stories, to recounting of important events through photographs, to tributes to parents and caregivers, to short documentaries of friendships and activities that kids participated in while at the community center.[3]

Social and Physical Spaces

The physical space and the social space of the Carrolton House Digital Storytelling Project were important in defining the kinds of discourse that took place between kids and adults. Although we were fortunate to have a room for project use, the space that housed the digital storytelling project was small, with other after-school personnel using it to store academic enrichment materials and miscellaneous supplies. In addition, most of the computers in the room were only marginally functional, with just three or four computers being consistently ready for digital media work.

Either because of or despite the physical characteristics of the space, in addition to being a room for doing digital storytelling work, the social space that we created seemed to be an aberrant growth attached to the preexisting social space of the community center. While most of the other areas in the center had clearly defined functions and participants, the digital storytelling room's boundaries were amorphous. Kids who were and were not actively working on the project often came into the room to talk, to view or work on stories in progress, to research school projects on the Internet, and to just hang out. Project work and participants would often migrate to nearby empty rooms when the room became crowded or when quiet spaces were required to record narrations.

When I could, I made brownies and cupcakes for participants' birthdays and planned other relatively informal activities to encourage our sense of community. Because of this character, the project space existed for the kids as a kind of neutral ground and a place for testing the boundaries of what constituted acceptable behavior. As issues came up, we attempted to address them—was it okay to play hip-hop or R & B music with expletives or sexually explicit lyrics? What were appropriate activities for the space? What ways existed to manage our limited resources? Were the conversations that took place in the project space supposed to stay in the project space? Although I attempted to raise these questions when situations arose, I did not exhibit authority in the answers that were produced, as frequent interactions between myself and the kids in the project demonstrated. Within these moments, there was ample opportunity for witnessing the centrifugal "spinning out" as our discourse about the space diverged. However, this discursive flexibility also facilitated the creation of centripetal understandings between myself and other participants regarding the purposes and roles of the space.

In addition to these interactions, the project space provided extended opportunities for all of us to experiment with the equipment—cameras, computers, digital audio recorders, mics and audio mixers, computers, and printers. This experimentation engendered opportunities to depart further from adult-governed spaces with highly specified routines and purposes and often provided a catalyst for the examination of issues and ideas that remain invisible to adults—as Kee and Tone's rap poem, cited earlier in the chapter—illustrated.

Relationships

From a Bakhtinian perspective, identity negotiations are never ending, never fixed, and always contingent on and constituted through discourse. This perspective was helpful in thinking through how the identity negotiations of participants in the project revealed both histories and possible future realities. In addition to the interactions that took place between myself and the kids that have been explored throughout the chapter, the relationships that existed among kids and the relationship I had with other adults in the community center revealed the way that our digital storytelling work was situated within a variety of different discourses.

Limited computer resources and the tight space of the computer room necessitated sharing. The kids working on stories would often have to take turns with the computers, and, while not working on the computer, remained in the computer room. Some kids worked on homework during this time, others surfed the Internet, some played around with word-processing and drawing programs that were available on computers not connected to the Internet. Because the first group of kids to do work in the project were younger than the next, larger group of kids, I hoped that this would help to set up a dynamic in which the younger kids could demonstrate and teach the older kids. However, the teenagers actively resisted the idea of younger kids showing or teaching them how to do any of the work. This resulted in the creation of simultaneously occurring spheres of interaction that were gender, age, and family specific. These spheres often bumped up against one another and connected, but not in a way that altered the overall pattern of discourse. Representations of this were apparent in Tonisha and Robby's talk with each other, the talk of Monique and ReShonda, and the (separate) conversations of a group of older teenage boys and a group of girls who were seven to nine years old. When these groups conversations did connect, it was fleetingly, and the connection often served to reinforce the boundaries between the groups. On one occasion, Tonisha sat drawing while Monique and ReShonda worked on the computer together. After a while Tonisha had to leave to attend another after-school program, but before she did, she handed me a picture (Figure 7). She had addressed it to ReShonda. Taking it from my hand, ReShonda asked me who drew it. "Tonisha," I replied. Quickly, she added, "You mean Scratch Face?" (referencing a long scratch on Tonisha's face that her cat, Todd, had made). Later, when I asked Tonisha why she had decided to give ReShonda the picture, she simply shrugged. This exchange, typical of the kind of conversation that took place across social groups, was the closest Tonisha came to developing a relationship with either Monique or ReShonda and ultimately it did not change the dynamics between them.

In addition to the kinds of relationships that existed between kids, another significant set of relationships that impacted the work of the project were between myself and the other adults in the community center. An ethos existed in the center that was largely guided by the sensibilities of African American women who staffed the front desk, managed the child care center, ran the technology center, directed various outreach programs related to basic needs of adults in the community, and were "other mothers" (Collins, 1991) of many of the kids at the center through their work at the center and involvement in local churches.

Figure 7. Drawing created for ReShonda by Tonisha

Although most of the women had informal mentoring relationships with many of the kids that transcended the formal boundaries of culture and institution, this informality did not extend to their interactions with kids at the center as a whole. In addition, because many of these professional women's jobs involved interacting with other adults outside of the Carrolton Heights Community Center, it was important that activities involving the kids not disrupt their work and business. This tension was delicately managed by the women, and not so delicately managed by the kids, particularly those involved in the digital storytelling project, as my excerpted field note below conveys:

As she stands at the copy machine in the community center break room, Kim asks me "So, when is the last day for your kids?" Pausing, I ask, "Do you mean for everyone—or for Monique and ReShonda?" Smiling, she replies "Of course I'm talking about them." I tell Kim that Monique and ReShonda are on the homestretch in completing their first digital story, but after that, I really don't know. I tell her that although I hope they will continue with the project, "Mo" and "Shonda" have to decide whether they would like to do another story. Kim turns, looks me in the eyes, and says, contemplatively, "We give our kids too many choices, don't we?"

Through this exchange, Kim verbalized an undercurrent of sentiment that most of the African American women working in the community center had expressed. The idea that the project was "too open," that the kids had too many choices, was a common refrain and was heard most often when young women such as Mo and Shonda succeeded in disrupting the work of others in the center through their raucous behavior. Admittedly, though I remained committed to creating a space that was largely directed by kids' interests and activities, at times I too shared their questions about the degree of flexibility and blurred boundaries within the program. However, these characteristics of the project were instrumental in creating opportunities to witness the centripetal and centrifugal forces at work in kids' identity negotiations.

Conclusion

The ability to tell stories in their own voices, and render these stories visually, was a powerful experience for participants. Within the first summer of the project, most of the participating kids had completed their first story, and during the school year they continued to come to the project space to complete work on other stories, despite changes in their schedules and mine. The power of this work also existed in the ability of the kids' stories actively to challenge the notion that African American kids living in impoverished urban communities are "at risk."

However, my work with the kids who participated in the Carrolton House Digital Storytelling Project also demonstrated that engaging adolescents in multimodal[5] literacy activities within after-school contexts is always more complex than providing kids with opportunities to tell their stories through computers and digital media. This is particularly important within the current edupolitical climate, in which funding for after-school programs is explicitly tied to the federal agenda for education. Examples of this can be found in the federal 21st Century Community Learning Center grant program, which aims centrally to "provide expanded enrichment opportunities for kids attending low performing schools" through "*tutoring services* and academic enrichment activities designed to *help students meet local and state academic standards* in subjects such as reading and math" (www.ed.gov/programs/21stcclc/index.html, my emphasis).

These levels of accountability are layered over issues of access, entry to, and involvement in communities that have specific cultural, social, and historical characters. This layering of political, social, cultural, and historical is an aspect of digital storytelling work that individuals involved in after-school work with adolescents must also be aware of and must take an active and reflective stance toward.

Our identities are built—however shakily—on the day-to-day discursive activity that is itself a "give and take" between what Bakhtin describes as the centripetal and centrifugal forces of language. Identity, as actualized through discourse, is predicated on relationships between self and other. As Holquist (2002) writes, "[T]here is an intimate connection between the project of language and the project of selfhood: they both exist in order to mean" (p. 23). Negotiation is therefore a central aspect of Bakhtinian conceptions of identity, as it involves disagreement, cooperation, concession, and "give and take." In this view, identity and self-as-subject are products of ongoing discursive activity. However, while contractual or mediational negotiations may revolve around reaching a mutual agreement between two parties, the negotiation of identities is always necessarily a partial and contingent agreement, hinged on the constantly evolving and shifting practice inherent in the social relations between others and self.

Within these identity negotiations, the centrifugal and centripetal forces of language can be seen in operation at macro- and micro-levels of social activity and relationship. They are apparent in the language and discourse of adolescents interacting with peers and adults in their everyday life, in the digital stories that they create, and in the way that they negotiate their identities with others who may have productive and/or destructive ideas about who each of these young people is and is becoming.

Notes

[1] Though I attempted many times, I was never able to convince Monique and ReShonda, the girls who gave me this nickname, to reveal what this name meant.

[2] "Cracks" are one among several terms, which also include "signifyin,"
"jankin," and "snapping," used to refer to a practice of verbal
sparring and insults originating from West African oral traditions
(Saloy, 2001).

[3] In hindsight, I wish that we had had more opportunity for kids to talk
with each other about their story ideas—for more and better
articulation of why they made the kinds of stylistic choices that they
did. In addition, I do not think we have thought enough, perhaps,
about ways to step aside and let kids and their peers develop critical
conversations about the texts they create.

References

Bakhtin, M. M. (1981). *The dialogic imagination.* Austin: University of
Texas Press.

Barnekov, T. (1998). *Attitudes of Wilmington residents toward crime, public
safety & police service: Attitudes of Wilmington residents.* Available from
College of Human Resources, Education and Public Policy, University
of Delaware, Newark, Delaware 19716.

Carter, D., & Love, S. (2006). *South Wilmington special area management
plan.* Retrieved July 1, 2007, from
http://coastalmanagement.noaa.gov/pmm/cmm2006.pdf.

Collins, P. H. (1991). *Black feminist thought: Knowledge, consciousness and
the politics of empowerment.* New York: Routledge.

Davis, A. (2005). Co-authoring identity: Digital storytelling in an urban
middle school. *THEN: Technology, Humanities, Education & Narrative,
1*(1). Retrieved on June 6, 2005 from: http://thenjournal.org/
feature/61/.

Environmental Protection Agency (2006). Brownfields Cleanup and
Redevelopment. Retrieved December 10, 2006 from:
http://www.epa.gov/swerosps/bf/about.htm

Hayes, R., & Matusov, E. (2005). From "ownership" to dialogic
addressivity: Defining successful digital storytelling projects. *THEN:
Technology, Humanities, Education & Narrative, 1*(1). Retrieved on June
6, 2005 from: http://thenjournal.org/feature/75/.

Holland, D. C., & Eisenhart, M. A. (1990). *Educated in romance: Women,
achievement, and college culture.* Chicago: University of Chicago Press.

Holland, D. C., Lachicotte, W., Skinner, D., & Cain, C. (1998). *Identity
and agency in cultural worlds.* Cambridge, MA: Harvard University
Press.

Holquist, M. (1990). *Dialogism: Bakhtin and his world*. New York: Routledge.

Holquist, M. (2002). *Dialogism*. New York: Routledge.

Hull, G. A., & Katz, M. (2006). Crafting an agentive self: Case studies of digital storytelling. *Research in the Teaching of English, 41*(1), 43–81.

Pleasants, H. M. (2004, November). Identity negotiations in writing and relationships: Digital storytelling with African American adolescent girls in an urban community center. Paper presented at the 103rd Annual Meeting of the American Anthropological Association, San Francisco.

Saloy, M. L. (2001). Still laughing to keep from crying: Black humor. Louisiana Folklife Festival booklet. Retrieved November 15, 2005, from http://www.louisianafolklife.org/LT/Articles_Essays/still_laugh.html.

Response to Pleasants

Glynda Hull

Faith Ringgold, the renowned multimodal artist and author who uses cloth, image, and word to portray African American life in vivid and joyful detail, created a famous quilted portrait of children with the Mona Lisa (Cameron et al., 1998). It is called "Dancing at the Louvre" and shows three young girls, dressed in Sunday best, pigtails flying, arms akimbo, faces bright with glee, kicking up their heels in a most un-museum-like manner in front of da Vinci's most famous portrait, while the famous face remotely, sedately, silently smiles on. I have long loved Ringgold's rendering—for its irreverence and boldness, for the in-your-face way it jars the repose of expected response, for the way in which it puts forward unabashedly a different aesthetic, for how it dares anyone to be so foolish as to condescendingly say, "Girls, let's behave."

I think of Ringgold's painting, and I think of one of the digital portraits offered in Heather Pleasants's research, as capturing the spirit of Bakhtin's notion of "carnival." Placing a premium on freedom, on at least a momentary liberation from norms of expected behavior, and on collective, sensuous, subversive delight, carnivalesque language and ways of being can loosen the strictures of dominant discourses and their centripetal force. According to Bakhtin's analysis, such language was "frank and free, permitting no distance between those who came in contact with each other and liberating [them] from norms of etiquette and decency imposed at other times" (1984, p. 10). Bakhtin took as his point of departure ancient and medieval times, exploring the systems of meaning created through popular cultural forms such as feasts and carnivals, as well as comic vernacular literature that privileged parodic language and humor. His project traced the lineage of these cultural artifacts in the novel, especially in the comedy of Rabelais. It was Bakhtin's belief that these popular cultural, unofficial forms accumulated liberatory potential, contributing to the questioning of official orders of church and state, and constituting what he called a parallel "second life." "Carnival is the people's second life," Bakhtin wrote, "organized on the basis of laughter" (Moss, 1994, p. 198).

It is indeed interesting and apropos to use Bakhtin's metaphors of centripetal, or socially unifying, and centrifugal, or heteroglossic and socially differentiating language forces, as Pleasants has so helpfully done, to theorize new media and youth culture. Joining these ideas to his notions of carnival further reminds us of Bakhtin's fascination with the power of the transgressive and the hope it can engender. He was optimistic, and some would say overly so, about the possibility that sustained systems of oppositional meaning could contribute to the liberation of human consciousness (cf. Morris, 1994). Is there a way, we might ask along with Pleasants, to view youth's use of digital media out of school similarly? Might we have a moment now, a window in which popular cultural forms can dance at the Louvre, challenging old orders of literacy, schooling, and privilege?

In Pleasants's chapter we are introduced to Monique and ReShonda, the "Big Sitters," as they humorously punned, and their provocative, mostly jointly constructed digital story. The story includes a conventional set of photos of friends and family paired with voiceover tributes ("Mamma Tory is so supportive to me") and labels of relationships ("my peoples and me"). But these photos are interrupted by a video featuring the music of R & B artist Usher and, more important, a choreographed dance routine featuring Monique and ReShonda. Their self-identified dances—"the rockaway," "the muscle"—quickly morph into free-form movement and increasingly energized bodily expression. Pleasants writes that this clip, repeated in the story's conclusion, "bursts into the viewers' presence with the frenetic and raucous energy that most closely approximates the day-to-day enacted friendship of Monique and ReShonda." Like the girls' behavior at the community center, which ranged from mildly cooperative to merely mischievous to more seriously disruptive, their digital story seems to evidence, as Pleasants argues, centripetal and centrifugal forces in juxtaposition, as one might expect particularly in the identity projects of adolescents. Of the digital stories and other texts discussed in the chapter, all of which follow a more familiar narrative line, "Big Sitters" fascinates me most with its unconventionality, with its refusal to completely conform in terms of genre, style, and ideology. Pleasants suggests, and I believe quite rightly so, that we would do well to pay attention to such moments of centrifugality in daily interactions, creative products, and other instances of intense realizations of self, what Urciuoli (1995) calls "performative moments" (p. 202; cf. Hull & Zacher, forthcoming). And Pleasants's research also amply reminds us that such instances of the carnivalesque are now ripe for picking in young people's uses of digital media.

Pleasants's research took place out of school at a community center, where young people had considerable license, under Pleasants's wing, to experiment with textual and extra-textual forms of self-representation. Here too, of course, as she wisely observes, institutional and community norms, expectations, and resources came into play, setting limits on the girls' freedom and influencing their activities, interactions, and the shape of their digital products. It would, of course, be mistaken to assume that the learning that kids do in out-of-school programs is exempt from its own special set of constraints. Yet, most innovation in the use of digital media—the blending of genres and modes, the merging of media types, the rampant rise of participation in social networking sites, and in general the use of digital forms as the means and materials for "symbolic creativity" (Willis, 1990)—now takes place beyond the schoolhouse door. Ironically, those who think about the skills, dispositions, and knowledge believed to be needed in the new century place a premium on the ability to innovate, to flourish in the face of the new, and, of course, to incorporate information and communication technologies into everyday decision making, expression, and interaction (cf. Partnership for 21st Century Learning Skills, http://www.21stcenturyskills.org). It is no doubt time, as we think about taking digital media to school, and as we confront the daunting vista of a globalized world where all feel increasingly at risk (Kirsch, Braun, Yamamoto, & Sum, 2007), to think also about the role of the carnivalesque in learning—of energetic play, of raucous laughter, of imagination, emotion, and the subversive. This is what Pleasants has powerfully done.

Do new media offer an especially potent outlet for centrifugality, and if so, how, and why is this the case? How do young people benefit from opportunities to express and experience the carnivalesque, and where does its danger lie? What are the relationships between these uses and the press to master more conventional language forms and social conventions? How do space, place, institution, and their participant structures intersect with opportunities to embody the carnivalesque, as well as to appropriate language that simultaneously pays homage to the centripetal? These important questions remain, inspired by Pleasants's work.

Notes

Many thanks to Mark Nelson and Lalitha Vasudevan for their helpful comments on this response.

References

Bakhtin, M. M. (1984). *Rabelais and his world*. Trans. H. Iswolsky. Bloomington: Indiana University Press.

Cameron, D., Powell, R. J., Wallace, M., Hill, P., Gouma-Peterson, T., Roth, M., & Gibson, A. (1998). *Dancing at the Louvre: Faith Ringgold's French Collection and other story quilts*. Berkeley: University of California Press.

Hull, G., & Zacher, J. (Forthcoming). Enacting identities: An ethnography of a job training program. *Identity: An International Journal of Theory and Research*.

Kirsch, I., Braun, H., Yamamoto, K., & Sum, A. (2007). *America's perfect storm: Three forces changing our nation's future*. Princeton, NJ: Educational Testing Service.

Morris, P. (Ed.). (1994). *The Bakhtin reader: Selected writings of Bakhtin, Medvedev, Voloshinov*. London: Edward Arnold.

Moss, G. (1994). The influence of popular fiction: An oppositional text. In D. Graddol and O. Boyd-Barrett (Eds.), *Media Texts: Authors and Readers* (pp. 180–199). Clevedon, UK: Multilingual Matters.

Urciuoli, B. (1995). The indexical structure of visibility. In B. Farnell (Ed.), *Human action signs in cultural context: The visible and the invisible in movement and dance* (pp. 189–215). Metuchen, NJ, & London: Scarecrow Press.

Willis, Paul (with Simon Jones, Joyce Canaan, and Geoff Hurd). (1990). *Common culture: Symbolic work at play in the everyday cultures of the young*. Boulder, CO: Westview Press.

Response to Pleasants

Iris Dixon Taylor

In her chapter Heather Pleasants presents a thought-provoking study that allows us to witness and grapple with the possibilities, tensions, and politics at play when engaging African American girls in multimodal literacy practices through digital storytelling. Using Bakhtin's construct of the centripetal and centrifugal forces of language, Pleasants frames digital storytelling and the multimodal literacy practices it engenders as sites for ongoing negotiations of identities and relationships. Pleasants draws our attention to youth agency. She explicates the ways her participants position themselves within dominant or centripetal discursive forces and draw upon centrifugal forces to position themselves in unique and inventive ways.

Pleasants reveals how the space of the Digital Storytelling Center (DSC) allowed students to explore identities negotiated through relationships with family, peers, and members of the community center. Although Pleasants examines the negotiations of social identities such as how participants positioned themselves within and sometimes in contradistinction to dominant discourses of student, friend, community member, and youth, I wondered how cultural identities as well as social identities were being negotiated within these spaces? In what ways did these *African American girls from an under-resourced urban community* negotiate intersecting gendered, racialized, classed, sexualized, spiritual, and aged positionings, for example, within these digital stories and storytelling spaces? In what ways were these positionings of difference impacting and impacted by their digital storytelling?

Throughout the chapter Pleasants engages readers with rich examples that illustrate the potential of digital storytelling to facilitate multimodal literate identities and to interrupt dominant notions of literacy and what it means to be literate. Storytelling in Pleasants's DSC involves more equitable literacy pedagogies where youth have many choices and many chances to construct and engage with multimodal texts. These texts include the audio texts of music, the gestural texts of dance and movement captured through video, the visual texts of pictures, and the oral and print texts of written and recorded scripts. Children and youth enter into the storytelling through any of these modalities. The written texts, which many of the participants struggle to produce, are not privileged in the DSC.

Printed texts become a possible, but not a mandatory, tool used in conjunction with visual, oral, aural, and gestural sign systems. Stories can be constructed differently through the diverse forms of technology used. Entrée into the world of digital storytelling does not presuppose, or hold as a prerequisite, a facility with written language.

I was particularly struck by the use of multimodal literacies in ReShonda and Monique's "Big Sitters" story. In this digital story, where the girls used video, music, pictures, and oral language, I began to see how digital storytelling is an embodied literacy practice, a notion that I explore in my work examining the interplay of critical literacies and identities of African American youth (Taylor, 2006). In my study the use of the body as texts was prevalent as youth participants scripted their bodies through critical literacy practices such as hair grooming, dancing, getting "loud," adorning the body through dress, and physically positioning their bodies in contested spaces. Similarly, embodied literacies, or the ways meaning is communicated and interpreted on and through the physicality of the body, are evidenced in ReShonda and Monique's multimodal literacy practices. In their digital stories, these youth scripted their bodies as texts to be read and drew upon centrifugal discourses that sat in opposition to the discourses of conformity espoused by adults. In these instances the body became a medium through which youth not only communicated and interpreted meanings but asserted and affirmed identities.

Acutely aware of the politics of literacy, Pleasants calls attention to the tensions and negotiations that must occur in using media and media texts when these resources and access to them are limited. These conditions can lead to a reversion back to privileging the tools that are more readily available (paper and pen) and the print-based literacies they engender. This negotiation was evident as Pleasants resorted to requiring students to bring in a full script (either written or recorded) before being able to engage with the media. Pleasants works within these limitations, and her students are able to produce a diverse range of digital stories. Her struggles, however, remind us that, as social justice educators, we must wage our battles against the persistence and perniciousness of both dominant discourses that position African American youth as lacking and institutional structures that limit their access to media resources. This dual approach is imperative if educators are to affect the lived realities and future possibilities of African American youth living in under-resourced communities.

Pleasants also shares with us the negotiations she must make in her desire to trouble the notion of what count as stories and storytelling. She reveals pedagogical dilemmas of teachers who want to push on the boundaries of dominant academic or centripetal discourses while recognizing the importance of these discourses and how they impact the academic success and life trajectories of their students. This dilemma has been discussed extensively in the work of scholars such as Delpit (1995) and Fecho (2002). Pleasants shows that these tensions do not go away when we engage students in working with media and media texts.

I would argue that these tensions need to be negotiated by educators for youth, but also with youth. Youth are aware that knowledge is not neutral. They understand that some knowledge is valued over other knowledge and that certain ways of exhibiting knowledge carry more cachet than others (e.g., the privileging of printed texts over visual texts in school contexts). This was made evident to me in my own work with African American youth (Taylor, 2006) when a male participant, challenging the privileging of written discourse in schools and of standardized tests, explained that he would be considered a genius if he could draw instead of write his answers on the high-stakes high school exit exam.

How might a digital storytelling classroom be transformed if youth, alongside their teachers, were engaged in critically examining this political reality as they compose their digital stories? In their framework for a pedagogy of multiliteracies, Kalantzis and Cope (2000) describe "critical framing." By employing critical framing as a pedagogical move, educators engage students in stepping back and critically examining the construct of storytelling and whose interests are served in what count as stories. Students can then investigate what storytelling means and has meant within their local contexts and within different historical, sociocultural, and political contexts. Students can analyze how these varied ways of storytelling clash and coincide. Through critical framing students examine the social construction of knowledge and make deliberate and informed choices about the stories and ways of storytelling they engage in. The structures of these stories are then not arbitrarily determined but based on the purpose and audience they are designed to address.

Pleasants's work is both timely and essential, as African American girls daily are negotiating a plethora of multimodal texts (including discourses and structures) and identities as they traverse the contexts of their multiple worlds. These texts often construct them as deficient and lacking. Pleasants offers us digital storytelling as a possible site where these youths' negotiations of texts and identities can be worked on and carried out in supportive yet challenging spaces. Youths' critical engagements within these spaces are essential if educators and youth are to impact their life opportunities and abilities to engage in acts of social justice to transform their worlds.

References

Delpit, L. (1995). *Other people's children: Cultural conflict in the classroom*. New York: New Press.

Fecho, B. (2002). Madaz publications. *Harvard Educational Review, 72*(1), 93–119.

Kalantzis, M., & Cope, B.(2000). A multiliteracies pedagogy. In B. Cope & M. Kalantzis (Eds.), *Multiliteracies: Literacy, learning, and the design of social futures* (pp. 239–248). London: Routledge

Taylor, I. (2006). Dangerous literacies: Contextualizing the interplay of critical literacies and identities of African American youth. Unpublished doctoral dissertation, Teachers College, Columbia University, New York.

Contributors

Rebekah Buchanan is Assistant Director of The Writing Center and a doctoral candidate in Urban Education at Temple University.

Greg Dimitriadis is an Associate Professor of Sociology of Education at the University at Buffalo, SUNY.

Vivian L. Gadsden is the William T. Carter Professor in Child Development and Education at the University of Pennsylvania, Graduate School of Education.

Leif Gustavson is an Assistant Professor of Education and Coordinator of English Education Programs at Arcadia University.

Renee Hobbs is an Associate Professor of Communication at Temple University.

Glynda Hull is a Professor Education in the Language and Literacy, Society and Culture Program at the University of California, Berkeley Graduate School of Education.

Katie Hyde is the Director of the Literacy Through Photography program at Duke University's Center for Documentary Studies.

Decoteau J. Irby is a community educator, hip-hop enthusiast, and doctoral student in Urban Education at Temple University.

Korina M. Jocson is a Postdoctoral Fellow & Visiting Scholar at Stanford University School of Education.

Valerie Kinloch is an Assistant Professor of Literacy and English Education in the College of Education and Human Ecology at the Ohio State University.

Michele Knobel is a Professor of Education in the Department of Early Childhood, Elementary and Literacy Education at Montclair State University.

Marc Lamont Hill is an Assistant Professor of Urban Education at Temple University.

Rachel E. Nichols is a teacher of secondary English and Gifted Education in the Lower Merion School District, Pennsylvania.

Heather M. Pleasants is an Assistant Professor in Qualitative Research Methodology at the University of Alabama.

Audra Price is an Assistant Professor of Art Education at Lander University.

Katherine Schultz is an Associate Professor of Education and the Director of the Center for Collaborative Research and Practice in Teacher Education at the University of Pennsylvania, Graduate School of Education.

Jeanine M. Staples is an Assistant Professor in the Special Education Department of the University of Maryland College Park.

Iris Dixon Taylor works as a program associate in the Center for Literacy at Learning Point Associates in Naperville, Illinois.

Anne Burns Thomas is an Assistant Professor in the Foundations and Social Advocacy Department in the School of Education at SUNY College at Cortland.

Lalitha Vasudevan is an Assistant Professor of Technology and Education at Teachers College, Columbia University.

Kelly K. Wissman is an Assistant Professor in the Department of Reading at the University at Albany, State University of New York.

Index

Y

Colin Lankshear, Michele Knobel,
& Michael Peters
*General Editor*s

New literacies and new knowledges are being invented "in
the streets" as people from all walks of life wrestle with
new technologies, shifting values, changing institutions,
and new structures of personality and temperament emerging
in a global informational age. These new literacies and
ways of knowing remain absent from classrooms. Many education administrators, teachers, teacher educators, and academics seem largely unaware of them. Others actively
oppose them. Yet, they increasingly shape the engagements
and worlds of young people in societies like our own. The
New Literacies and Digital Epistemologies series will explore this terrain with a view to informing educational
theory and practice in constructively critical ways.

   For further information about the series and submitting
manuscripts, please contact:

          Michele Knobel & Colin Lankshear
          Montclair State University
          Dept. of Education and Human Services
          3173 University Hall
          Montclair, NJ 07043
          michele@coatepec.net

   To order other books in this series, please contact our
Customer Service Department at:

          (800) 770-LANG (within the U.S.)
          (212) 647-7706 (outside the U.S.)
          (212) 647-7707 FAX

Or browse online by series at:

          www.peterlang.com